The Fatigue of the Shari'a

Palgrave Series in Islamic Theology, Law, and History

This groundbreaking series, edited by one of the most influential scholars of Islamic law, presents a cumulative and progressive set of original studies that substantially raise the bar for rigorous scholarship in the field of Islamic studies. By relying on original sources and challenging common scholarly stereotypes and inherited wisdoms, the volumes of the series attest to the exacting and demanding methodological and pedagogical standards necessary for contemporary studies of Islam. These volumes are chosen not only for their disciplined methodology, exhaustive research, or academic authoritativeness, but also for their ability to make critical interventions in the process of understanding the world of Islam as it was, is, and is likely to become. They make central and even pivotal contributions to understanding the experience of the lived and living Islam and the ways that this rich and creative Islamic tradition has been created and uncreated, or constructed, deconstructed, and reconstructed. In short, the volumes of this series are chosen for their great relevance to the many realities that have shaped the ways Muslims understand, represent, and practice their religion, and ultimately, to understanding the worlds that Muslims have helped to shape, and in turn, the worlds that have helped shape Muslims.

Series Editor:
Khaled Abou El Fadl is the Omar and Azmeralda Alfi Distinguished Professor in Islamic Law at the UCLA School of Law, and chair of the Islamic Studies Program at UCLA. Dr. Abou El Fadl received the University of Oslo Human Rights Award, the Leo and Lisl Eitinger Prize in 2007, and was named a Carnegie Scholar in Islamic Law in 2005. He is one of the world's leading authorities on Islamic law and Islam, and a prominent scholar in the field of human rights.

Titles:

Custom in Islamic Law and Legal Theory: The Development of the Concepts of 'Urf and 'Adah in the Islamic Legal Tradition
Ayman Shabana

The Islamic Law of War: Justifications and Regulations
Ahmed Al-Dawoody

Shi'i Jurisprudence and Constitution: Revolution in Iran
Amirhassan Boozari

Constructing a Religiously Ideal "Believer" and "Woman" in Islam: Neo-traditional Salafi and Progressive Muslims' Methods of Interpretation
Adis Duderija

The Fatigue of the Shari'a
Ahmad Atif Ahmad

The Fatigue of the Shariʿa

Ahmad Atif Ahmad

palgrave
macmillan

THE FATIGUE OF THE SHARI'A

First published in 2012 by
PALGRAVE MACMILLAN®
in the United States—a division of St. Martin's Press LLC,
175 Fifth Avenue, New York, NY 10010.

Where this book is distributed in the UK, Europe and the rest of the world, this is by Palgrave Macmillan, a division of Macmillan Publishers Limited, registered in England, company number 785998, of Houndmills, Basingstoke, Hampshire RG21 6XS.

Palgrave Macmillan is the global academic imprint of the above companies and has companies and representatives throughout the world.

ISBN: 978–0–230–34036–7

Library of Congress Cataloging-in-Publication Data

Ahmad, Ahmad Atif.
The fatigue of the shari'a / by Ahmad Atif Ahmad.
p. cm.
ISBN 978–0–230–34036–7
1. Islamic law—Interpretation and construction. 2. Ijtihad (Islamic law) I. Title.

KBP453.A445 2012
340.5′9—dc23 2011038852

A catalogue record of the book is available from the British Library.

Design by Newgen Imaging Systems (P) Ltd., Chennai, India.

First edition: April 2012

To Dima, Iyad, and Kindah

الذين أعادني حبّهم إلى نفسي التي كنت غادرتها زمناً

..... ثم عاد حبهم فغيّرني إلى غير رجعة

Ahmad

عن عبد الله بن عمرو بن العاص قال سمعت رسول الله صلى الله عليه وسلم يقول "إن الله لا يقبض العلم انتزاعاً ينتزعه من العباد ولكن يقبض العلم بقبض العلماء حتى إذا لم يُبق عالماً اتخذ الناس رؤساء جهالاً فسئلوا فأفتوا بغير علم فضلوا وأضلوا."

—Bukhari's Sahih, #100 (Chapter 3, On Knowledge = Kitab al-'Ilm)

حدثنا ابن حميد قال حدثنا سلمة قال حدثني محمد بن إسحاق عن نافع عن ابن عمر قال سمعت النبي صلى الله عليه وسلم يقول "ألا إنما أَجَلكم في أجل مَن خلا من الأمم كما بين صلاة العصر إلى مغرب الشمس."

حدثنا أبو كريب قال حدثنا عثّام بن علي عن الأعمش عن أبي خالد الوالبي عن جابر بن سمرة قال كأني أنظر إلى أصبعيْ رسول الله صلى الله عليه وسلم –وأشار بالمسبحة والتي تليها- وهو يقول "بعثت أنا والساعة كهذه من هذه."

—Tabari's History of Prophets and Kings (Cairo: Dar al-Ma'arif, 1971), vol. 1, pp. 11, 12.

عن أنس بن مالك عن النبي صلى الله عليه وسلم قال "إن قامت الساعة وفي يد أحدكم فسيلة فإن استطاع أن لا تقوم حتى يغرسها فليغرسها.

Contents

Series Editor's Preface

When I was invited to become the editor of the Palgrave Series in Islamic Theology, Law, and History, I sought to find works that are not just interesting but compelling—works that can be described as publishing events. I sought to find works that leave an indelible mark on the field that neither the conscientious scholar nor student can rightly ignore. The present book by Ahmad Atif Ahmad, an already accomplished scholar in his own right, is without a doubt an event in the history of Islamic Studies. Ahmad's *The Fatigue of the Shari'a* is highly original, addictively readable, and awe-inspiringly brave; it is the kind of book that justifies the very existence and continuation of this series. Reading Ahmad's book has been a full-fledged event in my own intellectual life to the point that I feel genuinely fortunate to be given the privilege of introducing it to specialists and nonspecialists alike.

In this meticulous and singularly unique book, Ahmad takes his readers on a thrilling and thought-provoking journey through Islamic law, theology, and history. He deals with a little-known, practically forgotten, debate that has thoroughly profound implications for contemporary Muslims. Ahmad asks the notoriously incendiary question: What if, due to the change in times and people, the divine law or the norms ordained to human beings through Revelation cease to be relevant? In Ahmad's language, the fatigue of divine norms means a condition in which, for whatever reason, God's laws or prescriptions are no longer compelling or fitting for the believers. The issue he deals with is the very existence of divine guidance for every age and time, and whether it is conceivable that God's law would become unavailable, or, for whatever the circumstance, absent from the lives of the faithful.

What makes this study invaluable is that Ahmad offers a very accessible and comprehensive review of the Islamic classical theological and jurisprudential debates on these issues. The discourses found in the classical tradition are rich, nuanced, and very often surprising, and they are also extremely relevant to contemporary Muslims and non-Muslims alike. Ahmad does not shy away from investigating the implications of the classical debates on contemporary understandings of the nature and role of Shari'a. Beyond this, in what must become compulsory reading for all students of the Shari'a, he analyzes the ways that the discourses on what he calls "the fatigue of divine norms" ought to affect the analytical assumptions and methodologies of any serious scholarly study of Shari'a.

Having said all of this, I have hardly done justice to Ahmad's masterful work. The classical debate on the fatigue of divine norms raises critical foundational questions on the relationship of divine revelation to Shari'a; the eternality and changeability of Shari'a; the status of pre-Islamic revelation, including Jewish and Christian divine norms; and the role of pluralism, tolerance, and orthodoxy. Of equal importance to this topic are the debates on *ijtihad* and the *mujtahid* as the instrumentalities of avoiding the fatigue of the Shari'a, the confrontation between Shari'a and modernity and postmodernity, and the various reform movements in contemporary Islam that sought to avoid the atrophy of Shari'a values in Muslim societies.

I described this book as an event because if it gets the attention it deserves, it will force the rethinking of much of the inherited platitudes about Shari'a, and it will also challenge the often tiresome banality that plagues the field of Islamic Studies. Without a doubt, it will raise the standard for scholarship in the field. But well beyond this, I hope that Ahmad's book will eventually be translated to Arabic, Persian, and Turkish, among other languages. Although many Muslim scholars will be familiar with the historical materials that Ahmad relies on, they will not have seen or conceived of the problem in quite the same way. I do strongly suspect that if this book reaches the Muslim world, it will spark a debate, controversy, and new fields of investigation that will become a part of this book's enduring legacy.

KHALED ABOU EL FADL
Los Angeles, California
November 2011

Preface: Speaking of History in a Time of Change

As I delivered ten lectures on "the fatigue of divine norms" in a graduate seminar on Islamic political philosophy (RGST 281) at the University of California in Santa Barbara during the winter quarter of 2011, the Egyptian revolution of January/February 2011 was raging. The significance of this revolution will certainly be debated for a long time, most likely beyond and after our lifetime. I could not offer a real-time interpretation of this revolution, but I could reflect on some of its potential consequences for the subject.

As I tend to focus on the long view in reading the life and transformations of Muslim societies, I am fairly unconcerned about the immediate aftermath of this revolution, compared with its potential long-term effect. I am also skeptical about the suggestion that an immediate change in the customs and practices of the Egyptian society (and other Muslim societies) will result from this revolution, although I would not be surprised if a slightly faster change (faster, i.e., measuring by the pace of the past three centuries) occurs after this revolution. I do not see this revolution as a "revival-of-the-Shari'a" moment, based on political action. Perhaps on the social level, and again looking through a long-term lens, a breakdown in the social structures that supported certain versions of the Shari'a may be foreseen. But no government could be charged with the task of bringing the Shari'a to life, if this Shari'a had already lost its life (something I contest here).

The 2011 Egyptian Revolution took place, many will remember, after a new Tunisian revolution (December 2010 and January 2011), two decades after an Algerian 'revolution' was aborted (1989–1991), and three decades after the Islamic revolution of Iran (1979). The resonance of the Egyptian revolution, with steps forward and backward in the days to come, will probably go in an overall direction of reconsideration of many aspects of social, moral, and political life, now a reconsideration from within Muslim societies, which is bound to lead to conclusions different from the "reform" movements of the twelfth/eighteenth–fourteenth/twentieth centuries. No prophet could have foreseen this revolution; hence, no prophecies should speak to its future with authority. As always, we only have the lessons of history, which remain inconclusive and sometimes even deceptive, but that is all we have. (Note that the history that has been taught for a long time in European and North American universities will be asked questions it could not answer, compared to, say, the way things were about half a century ago. Stable times allow the thriving of dogmas. I feel privileged not to live in these times.)

In the lectures I delivered before my students at the University of California in the winter of 2011, I attempted to draw on the medieval debate on the fatigue of the Shari'a, stating that insights from those who participated in it, notably Mu'tazili, Ash'ari, and Hanbali theologians and jurists, help us to see how the status of the Shari'a could be seen from within, from the perspective of those who have a commitment to it, full or partial. We could learn from the Mu'tazilis not to exaggerate the importance of specific readings of divine norms at any given generation, whether those given by the early followers of the Prophet Muhammad or the schools that were subsequently established. We could learn from the Ash'aris a religious version of the idea that change is a factor in history just as powerful as continuity—hence even divine norms might simply cease to be available through the usual "means" of scholars or *mujtahids*. We could learn from the Hanbalis that individual responsibility could not be forgotten, during and after the times of the strength of institutions such as the *madhhabs*.

I also argued, knowing that this is an easy target for critique, that reconciling the three positions is not impossible, if we do not insist on the rigid faith that old positions mean virtually nothing in new contexts (because ideas mean something only in their context), and after that, they could only "pose to be pictured" (as if this were possible), rather than studied for insights.

In my lectures, I also discussed the changes the medieval debate underwent, throughout the times of the confidence and critiques of modernity. The present moment seems to be a new point of departure, which invites us to a wait-and-see posture.

Acknowledgments

In 2008 Khaled Abou El Fadl provoked me, with theses and questions, to revisit the question of *futur al-Shari'a*, which I had first encountered in a reading of Zarkashi's (d. 794/1392) *Bahr* in the early 1990s. In the ensuing three years, I went back to this and related questions repeatedly, and in the process, what was a minor interest in old and new debates about the life and destiny of the Shari'a crystalized into the thoughts I put into the following chapters. It is now Khaled Abou El Fadl who deserves to be acknowledged before anyone else at the outset of this publication.

I also acknowledge the contribution of my graduate students who attended my lectures on "the fatigue of divine norms" at the University of California in Santa Barbara during the winter term of 2011. I thank Nathan French, Ahmet Temel, Sohaira Siddiqui, Burhan 'Ali, Samaneh Oldi Ghadikolaei, and Munther al-Sabbagh for their input and questions. Thanks also to Nasser Rabbat of MIT, who continued to hear me talk about this topic and offered critique until he got tired of it; to Charles Butterworth and Barbara Stowasser, who offered questions and comments after a lecture I gave under the title "Debating the Fatigue of the Shari'a" at Georgetown University in 2010; a Palgrave anonymous reviewer of an earlier draft who drew my attention to an important Achilles' heel; and Suni Ann Sebastian of Newgen Knowledge Works for editorial suggestions that improved my prose.

Introduction

Could God's guidance, available to previous generations as religious histories tell us, simply cease to be accessible at some point? Has this already happened; is it about to happen? Assuming these questions are clear enough, at least the following potential answers can be given to them: (1) Yes, this has already happened—the revelations of "prophets" such as Abraham, Moses, and Muhammad are already irrelevant to modern life; (2) no, knowledge and adherence to divine revelations has not faded away, but this might happen soon, in the near future, that is—or some may want to put it this way—we will soon be unable to access or make sense of any of these "divine revelations"; (3) no, this will never happen, because God will never abandon humanity. I deliberately ignore (for now) answers that make distinctions among the different revelations, saying that some will survive because they are the true revelations while the false ones will wither away. I ignore this family of answers for several reasons; for one, I am not writing about all the religions for which the aforementioned prophets or other sources of God's guidance are relevant. Nor do I plan to mediate amid different claims to the truth.

One (likely) way to answer the aforementioned questions is to raise another set of questions about the terminology employed and the criteria one is allowed to use to answer them. I will discuss several strategies of answering the *question* of the "fatigue" of divine norms with *questions*, since this is at the heart of this project. Bur before proceeding any further, I must state that what follows is a commentary on the debate on the destiny of religious teachings from the point of view of Muslim jurist-theologians and those who engaged the intellectual production of these jurists and theologians.

There are multiple forms of the debate (or multiple debates) on the destiny of "God's guidance" that could be invoked in this context. Many readers will assume that the perspectives employed in these debates must neatly fall into two categories, the theological and the nontheological (perhaps societal, political, or epistemological, among other possibilities). The assumption is reasonable, since there must be two different perspectives from which to look at this issue, one attached to the divine revelations in question and another detached. This separation, however, is easier to make in theory than to apply in practice. The theological dimension, at least in the context of this debate, could not be separated from nontheological, empirical or theoretical, assessments of social and political life, inasmuch as it relates to the question at hand. Moreover, the theological dimension could not easily be disentangled from a priori epistemological assertions that could be argued without any reference to God, divinity and the divine, or anything of this type.

My focus on how Muslim theologians and jurists debated the destiny and the status of God's guidance does not preclude discussions of pre-Muhammadan revealed laws. Non-Muslim followers of pre-Muhammadan laws would probably not concede the points Muslim theologians and jurists made about the destiny and status of previous revelations. But it is important to note that the issue for my purposes does not come down to true and false revelations. (Muslims, incidentally, say that they believe all the revelations given to all these prophets are true.) The question is more about the degree to which several of God's revelations have remained available over time. The relationship among different "revelations" or "religions," at any rate, is not the central issue here. The central question I am considering is the destiny and current status of God's guidance, taken from a Muslim perspective. The inquiries concern whether humans could live in a world without guidance from God. If yes, what should the believers do then? How could one learn or ascertain that God's guidance is no longer available? Do we already inhabit that world of the fatigue of guidance, the fatigue of divine norms, the fatigue of the Shari'a?

* * *

Once upon a time, the question of "whether the Shari'a was going to survive until the end of time" was debated by jurists and theologians who, in a sense, participated in the making of this Shari'a. These jurists first asked some basic questions about what the survival of the Shari'a should mean. When a majority of them defined the survival of the Shari'a as the availability of "knowledge" of it through scholars, they set out to discuss the nature of this knowledge and how it may be deemed available or unavailable. Some of the participants in this debate were theologians who looked at it as logically contingent on the question of God's justice (and the perfection of God's world) and whether this justice and perfection allowed such a condition as the inaccessibility of God's norms. Some participants used "empirical" data: their observations made these think, for example, that knowledge of the Shari'a was both abundant and on the rise and hence could not easily be subjected to dissipation before the end of the world. And many saw the issue of "unavailability" of God's norms as multifaceted and connected with other inquiries.

Come modern "change" in Muslim societies, the Shari'a was asked to justify itself, and a debate about modern laws and their relationship to the Shari'a started. The parameters of the discussion were different, and the question moved from the "future" to the "present" tense. Is this (behavior that took place or suggested normative behavior) compatible with the Shari'a? Is this the Shari'a? What is the Shari'a? But the old debate offered many lessons that could not be ignored. The medieval jurists offered insights about the Shari'a that we could still use in studying the modern debate on the Shari'a.

The tense moved once more from the "present" to the "past." Some now discuss the demise of the Shari'a as a fact of the past. The medieval debate with its insights and the modern history of the Shari'a (being an essential background to the postmodern "death-of-the-Shari'a" thesis) remain relevant to this most recent debate. There is a risk in discussing all of these in one long essay, but believe it or not, ignoring any part of the story carries a higher risk. I will take the first risk (which consists of conceptual and analytical difficulties), and if I have failed to make my views clear in this essay, I could revisit the issue to clarify and explain in the future. The other risk, that is, losing old insights and eclectically considering a complex issue as if from a simple privileged standpoint, is one for which there is no remedy. The medieval debate continues to give us a challenge that I think is insurmountable. It insists that empirical research (while useful) will continue to fail to provide a satisfying answer. The difficulties inherent in the concepts of knowledge and "Shari'a" itself will survive any assertion of the death of the Shari'a.

Foundations: Chapters One–Three

Chapters one and two attempt to show that, to be fully understood, the debate on the destiny or the current status of God's norms must be split into several more manageable inquiries and (perhaps perplexingly for some) connected to other inquiries. Chapter one addresses the splitting and chapter two the connecting.

Chapter one suggests that a debate on the fatigue of the Shari'a may be seen as having occurred in three overlapping phases, as I indicated earlier. The first has jurists at the center and includes the medieval Mu'tazili, Ash'ari, and Hanbali positions. This debate by itself suggests splitting the question of the fatigue of the Shari'a into several questions. The conceptual complexities of the issue arise, almost fully, in this phase. One learns that defining the Shari'a is a challenge, that defining fatigue is another, and that even when the fatigue of the Shari'a is defined as the death of a certain type of scholarship, the debate does not end.

The second phase of the debate has society and government at its center and draws on old themes from medieval Islamic political philosophy but is also affected by political developments that attended colonialism and the modern nation-state. The historical moment was characterized by a diffusion of the teaching of Islamic law among several institutions, many of which stood at the juncture of the remaking of this law. In this phase, the nature and role of the Shari'a in society and government were argued, and so was the influence of these two elements (in their modern version) on all functioning laws. This phase of the debate also witnessed an emphasis on the prophetic tradition, the *hadith* of the Prophet Muhammad, placing *hadith* at the center of the sources of norms, as opposed to the *madhhab* or schools of law that dominated medieval legal thinking.

The third phase of the debate has epistemology and power at its center. In this phase, one could draw as much as one likes on the past but the judgment is finally rendered based on an empirical observation, which also assigns different values to what one could observe today. The chief analytical tool here, however, is foreign to the whole system under consideration. It is ultimately a judgment about what "knowledge" is, about the conditions of the possibility of certain types of knowledge, and about knowledge's connection with power. The Shari'a, in this post-Foucaultian world, must be dead, not because jurists who participate in it think that. In fact, it is because those who claim to be qualified to participate in the production of the Shari'a are unaware of the impossibility of their endeavor that they must be seen as unqualified to speak to the question of the life of the Shari'a. The real Shari'a is dead, so notes the neutral observer.

This division (of the phases) appeals to concepts and analytical tools more than it does to history, given the overlap among its phases. Chapter one explains the limits to which this project may be considered a work in Islamic legal history, arguing, in effect, that more is gained by considering the debate on the fatigue of the Shari'a a continuous one, which employed several tools and attended to different conditions. If our moment is privileged, it is because it could draw on the insights gained from each one of these "phases" rather than subject their concepts to criticism or subvert one of them to the benefit of another.

Chapter two demonstrates that the question of the fatigue of the Shari'a is connected to other inquiries, notably (a) the unaided intellect's ability to arrive at binding norms, and (b) the possibility and meaning of lacunae in fully functioning Shari'a models. The chapter shows the importance of these issues especially in understanding the phase of the debate that has jurists at the center. Chapter two also points to the relationship between legal and theological reflections on the fatigue of the Shari'a and medieval Islamic political reflections on society and government (to which I go back in some detail in chapter eight). This latter connection is significant in analyzing the fatigue debate with society and government at the center.

Chapter three tackles the basic term whose elusiveness causes the issue to be complicated further, namely *ijtihad*, the effort required to reach God's guidance. Understanding this term is essential in understanding the debate in all its forms, but arriving at a simple convention is not the aim here. Even jurists who shared the same context had differing concepts of *ijtihad* as they debated its availability; and the polemics of Sakhawi (d. 902/1497) and Suyuti (d. *ca.* 911/1505) about whether the latter possessed the qualities of *ijtihad* illustrate this point.[1] Chapter three discusses *ijtihad* theory, arguing that the elasticity of the term conditions our inquiry but does not make it impossible.

Jurists and Nonjurists: Chapters Four–Six

Chapters four–six delineate the positions taken in this debate where, at least from the perspective of those who argued about it in the most detailed manner (the Ash'aris), jurists were firmly at its center. While acknowledging the limitations of this exercise, I must resort to characterizing positions by schools of thought. The Mu'tazili position drawing on reason's capacity for independent judgment, the Ash'ari position that God's control and possession of the world makes Him unanswerable to humans' sense of justice, and the Hanbali position relying on the popularization of *ijtihad* and its insistence on the foundational sources (Qur'an, Sunna) as the basis of the Shari'a—all lead to one of two basic conclusions on the fatigue of the Shari'a: *Yes* it could happen, so said the Ash'aris, and *no* it could not happen, so asserted the rest. All participants in this debate, once again, understood the question to be one of the survival of access to God's norms through some form of *ijtihad* or human effort. I see each one of these positions as offering different insights, and I am prepared to try to reconcile them in different ways before putting my energy into rejecting any one of them.

Chapter four focuses on loosely connected stances, notably the Mu'tazili position that rejected the possibility of the fatigue of God's norms, which provoked Juwayni (419/1028–478/1085) to refute it. This position, that of Ka'bi (d. 319/931), is not only consistent with the Baghdadi Mu'tazili school with which Ka'bi is associated, but also does indeed explain many basic Mu'tazili doctrines that predated Ka'bi and were later engrained in Mu'tazili *usul al-fiqh* through Abul-Husayn al-Basri's (d. 436/1044) *Mu'tamad.* (Though

I am told by Aron Zysow that I should think of Ka'bi as a revolutionary figure whose view may not be consistent with any one, Zysow acknowledges that the thinness of the evidence of Ka'bi's detailed ideas makes one resort to secondary sources in any case, and one needs a good argument to grant a general privilege to non-Ash'ari over Ash'ari sources in the exercise of recovering the lost nuances of Ka'bi's ideas.) This chapter also explains other positions from the same family of ideas that emphasize the role of reason in arriving at conclusions one may attribute to God. Ibn Rushd comes up with an interjection of a different flavor, and his view of the ultimate harmony of reason and revelation is discussed in this chapter.

Chapter five focuses on the Ash'ari position that continued for close to a millennium from Juwayni to 'Attar (d. 1250/1835) [a major figure in between is Taj al-Din al-Subki (d. 771/1369)]. The Ash'aris leveled their argument against Mu'tazili and Hanbali opposition (against the Mu'tazili in the earlier centuries and against the Hanbali position more pronouncedly in the later centuries). Some Ash'aris came close to holding aspects of the positions their school opposed. This aside, the Ash'aris stood against both Mu'tazilis and Hanbalis, accepting that it was possible for the fatigue of the Shari'a to occur, with many of them going as far as saying that it would likely occur.

Chapter six focuses on the Hanbali position that introduced the roots of a limited "*ijtihad* for all" doctrine and emphasized the access to the Prophet's tradition (*hadith*) as the basis of God's guidance. The arguments are made by the likes of Abu Ya'la al-Farra' (d. 458/1066) and Abu al-Khattab al-Kalwadhani (d. 511/1116). Ibn Taymiyya (d. 728/1326) lays the groundwork for some of these arguments to develop further and acquire a different texture in later centuries. This position will partly influence Shah Waliyyullah al-Dihlawi (d. 1176/1762) but will be appropriated most cleverly and effectively by Shawkani (d. 1250/1834) as an "ultrafoundationalist" position in a different version of the debate in the early modern phase—the position that even after the *madhhabs* die, the Shari'a lives on.

Maturidi (Hanafi) jurists and theologians had more or less forged their positions as hybrids out of the other positions and, hence, will not receive separate treatment.

Modernity and Its Questions: Chapters Seven–Eight

Chapters seven–eight address the conceptualization of the Shari'a without a strong emphasis on the *madhhab* and how adding the elements of government and society to the mix affects the equation of the vigor or infirmity of the Shari'a.

Chapter seven tackles a shift in Sunni jurists' status in their societies that weakened the debate about the fatigue of the Shari'a with jurists at the center. Some would probably argue that, by then, the old debate and the Shari'a itself could be spoken of only with a tinge of metaphor. The buzzwords for discussions on the Shari'a have become "*tajdid*" or renewal, "*taqnin*" or codification, and *islah* or "reform" rather than *ijtihad*. The accessibility of the Prophet's tradition was seen to play a role in the debate roughly paralleling the position previously occupied by the *madhhab*. Even those who opposed the newly formed and confidant *ultrafoundationalist* view, such as Bakhit al-Muti'i (d. 1354/1935), acknowledged its strength. This chapter addresses the position of Shawkani (d. 1250/1834), who practically trivializes the medieval debate, as another sign of these shifts that affected the Muslim world and prepared for new perspectives on the Shari'a.

Chapter eight discusses the relevance of government to the question of the functionality of the Shari'a. The chapter addresses an aspect of the test of the life of the Shari'a not captured by the Mu'tazili/Ash'ari/Hanbali discussion addressed in chapters four–six. I will not repeat my detailed discussion, in a previous work, of the impact of social and market standards ('urf) on Sunni legal provisions. Instead, I will focus my discussion on the role of government in a Muslim society and its affinity with the Shari'a. Juwayni's classic on government (the *Ghiyathi*) guides my discussion of this multifaceted issue, which remains confined to the theoretical realm. (The prospects of a poststate world in our time makes me look forward to a new negotiation of the relationship between "government" (broadly conceived) and the Shari'a.)

These two chapters will focus on the aforementioned basic themes of the debate, rather than retell the full story of colonialism, modern developments in adjudication, education, and public knowledge in the Muslim world and in the world as a whole (nor do I plan to dispute much of the accepted narratives of these developments here).

Beyond Modernity: Chapters Nine–Ten

Chapters nine–ten discuss recent views that the Shari'a may have already become a case of lost knowledge or lost tradition. This discussion, while capable of reminding us of aspects of the medieval debate, came out of a different context and employed novel conceptualizations. I point to the pitfalls involved in the task of assessing the strength of this claim, where competing descriptions of "what the status of the Shari'a is" are inevitable and difficult to mediate. Chapters nine and ten tackle the implications of an astute treatment of the issue by Wael Hallaq, pointing some disagreement with his thesis. Much less systematic and frankly unworthy discussions of the issue (clinging to some of Hallaq's generalizations) will be indicated but not treated in any detail.

Part I

Foundations

An exposition of the nature of the debates on the fatigue of the Shariʿa, and a treatment of the concepts of lacunae or absence of norms, *ijtihad* as the generator of norms, among other conceptual themes of relevance to the fatigue question.

Chapter 1

Truth and Fatigue

The Fatigue of the Shari‘a: A Modern Commentary

During the past two decades I lived in environments very different in their relationship to Shari‘a norms. I have, one could say, inhabited different worlds of relating to these norms, all sharing the same historical moment (i.e., our present time) while being virtually separate worlds, and in these worlds, observers who engaged in an assessment of the role of the Shari‘a in society saw the matter very differently as a result. And the situation is fluid; a couple of decades may not be a short period of time any more. I myself saw the issue differently at different stages in my life (change being capable of affecting both subject and observer). In this project, I try to capture the difficulties emanating from how these considerations affect an inquiry into the status of the Shari‘a in the world.

This project is a commentary on debates that address the fatigue of divine norms (from an Islamic viewpoint) rather than a "historical account" of these debates. One of my main aims is to clarify the relationships between the concept of the fatigue of the Shari‘a and other concepts and institutions, such as reason (*‘aql*), independent systematic reasoning (*ijtihad*), school of law (*madhhab*), the Prophet's tradition (*hadith*), and government (*sultan, siyasa*), and introduce some conclusions based on these relationships.

This commentary could be read as a long conversation with Abu al-Ma‘ali al-Juwayni (d. 478/1085), whose treatments of the subject in his *Burhan* (in legal theory) and *Ghiyathi* (in political theory) influenced, if not created, the debate for the subsequent centuries. Juwayni put his hands on the two most significant philosophical questions that could be raised in connection with the issue of the fatigue of the Shari'a. *First* is the question of whether we live in a perfect world with a plan whose perfection and "plan" could be discerned by the mere human reason unaided by divine revelation. Juwayni's answer is a "no"; not to be confused with any postmodern despair that might sound like it, just as (I think) his opponent's optimistic "yes" should not be confused with a hegemonic modern "yes we know the world." The *second* of the two questions concerns the extent to which government could be seen as a prerequisite to ordered and meaningful life. Juwayni's work suggests that government's value could be inflated, and no mature community should make the mistake of entitling government with any existential role (if you will).

As odd as this might sound, and as I already indicated in the acknowledgments section at the start of this book, I needed to be provoked to undertake this project, and I saw it at first as a long essay that continues the old argument on the fatigue of the Shari'a rather than as part of any modern discussion about the Shari'a. As the reader will note, I ended up with more-than-implicit comments on the value of current scholarship on the status of the Shari'a. The ensuing chapters will make this clear.

I do not want to question the value of a historical narrative of the debates and ideas on which I draw; I will only defend my choice. There is a lot one need to do to deeply understand the basic positions and arguments in all debates, major and minor, on the status and future prospects of the Shari'a, and I came to believe that a commentary on these positions and arguments is worthier of my effort than chasing every probable or improbable historical connection, or establishing an interpretation for an event (political, social, intellectual, or otherwise), or explaining away the relevance of an argument by insisting that it makes sense only in a given context.

Some history is clearly inevitable. The positions of the Mu'tazili, Ash'ari, and Hanbali legal theorists and theologians I present in chapters four–six must be explained in terms meaningful in their authors' worldviews, rather than simply imported and modified for a modern context. The same will apply to the position of Shawkani (d. 1250/1834), who I label (only on functional grounds and without any attachment to labels) as an *ultrafoundationalist*—a position that searches for the Shari'a in the Prophet's tradition rather than the *madhhabs*—and that of Muti'i (d. 1354/1935), who may be seen as a neo-*madhhabist* or a neo-*madhhab* adherent by accepting some modifications to medieval *madhhabs* while insisting on the value of their systematic frameworks.

My presentation will still have a partly chronological character, and this is defensible in several ways. Concepts live and die (or at least their currency and immediacy dwindles) in time. Take the concept of *ijtihad*. I am skeptical about assertions that *ijtihad* makes sense only in the medieval world, but I accept the idea that its prominence and immediacy weakened, that it may have started to be more confusing in ways that are beyond simple repair. Therefore, I can't force all aspects of a debate that understands *ijtihad* in a more disciplined and less confused sense to obey the modern conventions of how the term is used. In this commentary, there are chapters that are mostly governed by medieval terminology, and others that are not. I do not attempt to assign equal weight to the different historical debates on the position of the Shari'a in the world. This is one of the features that make this a commentary, rather than a historical account.

There will be objections about placing all discussions of the status of the Shari'a and its future prospects in the same basket. Good objections will again insist on distinguishing stances and sets of terminology. Some will say that the medieval debate has been interrupted, reaching a full stop, perhaps after 'Attar (d. 1250/1835), and is, moreover, irrelevant today. Some will think that my interest in Hallaq's version of the death-of-the-Shari'a discourse does not justify its inclusion after a discussion of the medieval debates on the fatigue of the Shari'a, which enjoys a different quality and vibe.

One thing that must be noted is that a debate about whether *ijtihad*, the tool to generate Shari'a norms, had disappeared is not a modern idea. (This puts the end of the Shari'a in the past tense by implication, though not in the same way a modern debate addresses the issue.) The question of the fatigue of the Shari'a (defined as the absence of jurists, *khuluww al-zaman min al-mujtahid*) was indeed discussed alongside and sometimes conflated with the question of the closure of the gate of *ijtihad* (*insidad bab al-ijtihad*), which addressed whether an end of ijtihad had already taken place. In chapter three, I will present the difficulties embedded in using the terms *ijtihad* and *mujtahid* (which could denote a founder of a *madhhab*, school of law, or a skillful contributor to an existing school). Suffice it here to tell the reader that the religious and philosophical implications of these debates allow them to be poured into one pot.

Again, I do not want to overstate my case or trivialize contextual, historical research of this topic, but there is no reason to turn our interest in history into a stance that makes historical and contextual research about the Shari'a the only meaningful form of thinking about it. In any event, I do not belong among those who think the Shari'a can only be seen as history. I was taught by scholars who assimilated medieval Mu'tazili and Ash'ari views and made them their own. I am certainly not one of them, but I have some understanding of their positions and worldviews. I also do not think that we could exclude the components of these views from being proper materials for discussion for the benefit of our world of today, even if these views were simply history.

There are different assumptions and tools embedded in the different debates I discuss. I will attempt to clarify these, and through the clarification, I hope the reader can learn something, rather than be left with an empty feeling of a pleasure attained through the act of reading but then come to ask "so what"? I do have a few positions I would like to advocate—one of them is that we should split the question of where the Shari'a stands today into several questions and address each separately. I promise the reader not to hide behind the postmodern license to say nothing and only suggest questions. This work may also open doors for the reader that can be exploited in discussions of political philosophy, for example, which is one of my interests that comes here only as a side.

Phases of a Debate, or Multiple Debates?

At least since the third/ninth century, the destiny and the status of God's guidance in the world were the subjects of debates by Muslim theologians and legal theorists. God's guidance, according to Sunni legal theorists, lies in the availability of norms to be applied in the practical affairs of life from prayers to sale, and from marriage to war, while presupposing faith and knowledge of God. Though broadly unified by subject (the availability of knowledge of God's norms), this debate shifted with time, with original arguments, with political circumstances, with social and educational transformations, and with other variables. The concern with the health and frailty of the Shari'a, whether ascribed to the present or projected to the future, also existed outside of this systematic debate on the fatigue of the Shari'a.

Let us speak, as we already indicated, of a traditional or medieval version of the debate that is attested roughly between the third/ninth and the twelfth/eighteenth centuries. In this debate, Ash'ari legal theorists and theologians defined the *fatigue* of the Shari'a as the extinction of qualified jurists (*mujtahid*s of all types). This fatigue, they argued, could take place in the future. The Ash'aris then disagreed on how this condition must be addressed. Mu'tazili and Hanbali legal theorists and theologians argued (from diametrically opposed theological positions) that the fatigue of the Shari'a was impossible, again diverging in their characterization of what this should mean. In this debate, the *madhhab* (school of law, for lack of a better translation) plays a major role in giving the term *mujtahid* (qualified jurist) its texture.

> ***The Phases of the Fatigue Debate***
>
> ***First Traditional Phase: Third/ninth–eighth/fourteenth cents.***
>
> *Mu'tazilis: No fatigue; God's guidance at least through reason persists*
>
> *Ash'aris: Fatigue conceded*
>
> *Hanbalis:* Ijtihad *a collective duty; no fatigue*
>
> ***Second Traditional Phase: Eighth/fourteenth–twelfth/eighteenth cents.***
>
> *Hanbali emphasis on foundations picks steam*
>
> ***Early Modern Phase: Eighth/fourteenth cents.***
>
> *Ultrafoundationalists: Sunna is the basis of the Shari'a/*
>
> *Hybridists: Madhhabs needed*
>
> ———
>
> *Government support decisive/ Government only one player*
>
> ***Current Phase: Post Fourteenth/twentieth cent.***
>
> *A Question of Knowledge and Power*

Recent debates about the Shari'a moved the focus from the future prospects to the present state of the Shari'a. In addition, one can find a shift of emphasis on the criteria to be discussed to gauge the health or frailty of the Shari'a. *First*, the medieval Mu'tazili, Ash'ari, and Hanbali positions and arguments metamorphosed into the position of those who may be called *neo*-madhhab *adherents*, who don't do away with the medieval *madhhab*s while accepting some modifications of these. This position may be set against *ultrafoundationalists*, who emphasize the Prophet's Sunna rather than the *madhhab* as a yardstick for God's norms. *Second*, an array of views surfaced considering the influence of popular opinion and government in assessing the normal life and old age of the Shari'a. In this development, jurists were assigned a status lower than they have been accorded in medieval times, although this would assume that all participants in the medieval debate consented to jurists' centrality in assessing the vigor of the Shari'a, which would unreasonably give the Ash'ari description of the issue a disproportionate weight (this will be clarified in chapter seven). *Third*, and most recently, the language of an epistemic shift was introduced, seeing the issue to be an issue of lost knowledge and its chances of being recovered.

Inquiring about the fatigue of divine norms, thus conceived, is connected with many inquiries about the nature of God's guidance and the theoretical meaning of the availability of this guidance and then how to "descriptively" assess this availability. The tools on which the arguments stood were also varied; they ranged from a priori (logical and theological) to empirical, and under each one of these rubrics, many subcategories of argument are found. I attempt to engage rather than simply restate these arguments and connect them to other basic arguments and positions that make them more intelligible.

A historian could speak of a debate on the fatigue of the Shari'a in the tradition of Islamic theology and legal theory that equates these two terms *futur al-Shari'a* (the fatigue of the Shari'a) and *khuluww al-zaman min al-mujtahid* (the absence in a given era of a qualified jurist). This historical discussion could speak of how adherents of the positions taken in this debate disagreed among themselves within the same school. The historian might also note that the position of the main protagonists of this phase, the Mu'tazilis, Ash'aris, and Hanbalis, are not fully irreconcilable. (In other words, there are disagreements within the same school and ways to reconcile the positions of different schools.) To be sure, each one of these positions promoted different views on the meaning of guidance and the nature of human *exertion of effort* seeking God's guidance (*ijtihad*), consistent to a great extent with their views on other subjects.

Ash'ari theologians and legal theorists who debated the question of the loss of divine norms as these present themselves in medieval Islamic legal theory identified it thus: "What happens when the Shari'a experiences fatigue, that is, when its qualified jurists disappear?" Medieval Muslim legal theorists, who debated this question, disagreed, not only on how to answer it, but even on how to characterize it. Some of them thought of the question as a pure hypothetical, while others considered it a significant inquiry with important applications. As we shall see in the next chapter, debating the fatigue of the Shari'a was surrounded by other inquiries of legal and political philosophy, creating a cluster of debates about the sources of God's laws before and after the revelations of the Prophet Muhammad, the mutations of laws over time, the survival and extinction of the memory of the past, and the role of government in the establishment of law and custom, among others.

Let us continue with the historian for a moment. This medieval or "traditional" phase of the debate may be further divided, not without reason, into two subphases or stages. This will separate the millennium (almost the entire period) that witnessed this debate into two eras, with a dividing line around the eighth/fourteenth century. The second subphase would then go from the eighth/fourteenth through the twelfth/eighteenth centuries. This subphase is characterized by a new separation of the fatigue of the Shari'a from the authority of the *madhhab*s, the so-called schools of law, such as the Hanafi, Maliki, Shafi'i, and Hanbali *madhhab*s. It would be a mistake to let this leave the impression that an abandonment of the *madhhab*s could be associated with this separating line, or that a totally new argument came about in the second stage of this traditional phase.

But it would not be unfair to say that this separating line signifies a minor shift in the tone of the debate, accounting for a sense that a return to pre-*madhhab* versions of the Shari'a was not fully inconceivable. This trend would lead the debate out of its medieval or "traditional" phase in the twelfth/eighteenth century to the beginning of a new phase.

The historian may elect to stop here or move to the early modern era's new ways of thinking about and debating the issue—from the twelfth/eighteenth until the end of the fourteenth/twentieth century. The turning point at the start of this period would be an accumulation of support for the Hanbali position in the old phase of the debate, most strongly supported by Ibn Taymiyya (d. 728/1328) and Shatibi (d. 790/1388) during the second stage or subphase of the traditional phase, coupled with an increase in the interest in *hadith*. This early modern phase also witnessed the rise of colonialism and the rise of new elites in Muslim societies, who were concerned with reforming their societies under *Western* guidance. The resulting early modern debate gives us Shawkani's argument against the possibility of the fatigue of the Shari'a. The Shawkani argument could reasonably claim the lineage of an Ibn Taymiyya/Shatibi position, already inherited from the traditional phase, but could also be read as, and to many it will sound like, a break with the parameters of the early debate. This phase of the debate was about the survival of the foundations of the Shari'a, not the survival of traditional (*madhhab*) legal reasoning itself, and the opposition was between those who saw the foundation as sufficient for a new mutation of the Shari'a and those who insisted that these were not sufficient. In this phase, Shawkani would turn the Hanbali view of the traditional phase into an argument against *madhhab*ic legal reasoning, while the Hanafis Bakhit al-Muti'i and Muhammad Zahid al-Kawthari (1296–1371/1878–1951) would disagree with what amounted to a popularization of *ijtihad* or did away completely with the Ash'ari-Maturidi understanding of it.

The temporal and subject overlaps among the different aspects of the debate, broadly conceived, will challenge our attempts at clarifying where one argument begins and another ends. It is not impossible, however, to distinguish between a debate whose protagonists are the Mu'tazila, Asha'ira, and Hanabila of old times—on the one hand—and one in which ultrafoundationalists appear to play a major role with less than full reverence for the *madhhab* as an intellectual umbrella for debates on the Shari'a. The difference between the two debates, as I said, may be seen as both (a) historical, as the first debate mostly occupies medieval times and the second begins around the time the first ends, and (b) conceptual: the first one still presupposes the *madhhab*, as elusive as it may be, as a reference point for juristic agreement and disagreement. The first debate will introduce us to names such as Abu al-Husayn al-Basri (d. 436/1044), Abu al-Khattab al-Kalwadhani (d. 511/1116), Taj al-Din al-Subki (d. 771/1369), and Ibn Taymiyya. The second moves from the time of Shawkani and Bakhit al-Muti'i to encompass scholars of Islamic law who studied it in schools such as al-Azhar, the several law schools (*Kulliyyat al-Huquq*), and *Dar al-'Ulum* (founded 1871) in the Arab world.

Then building on the shift from the medieval world of the Mu'tazilis/Ash'aris/Hanbalis into the world of *Sunna-or-madhhab?*, another tone appeared. Influenced by politico-epistemological analysis at the end of the fourteenth/twentieth century, recent discussions of the status of the Shari'a spoke of an epistemic shift that ended the Shari'a as we once knew it. The thought itself can be gathered from writings outside of this topic, but it is most directly argued by Wael Hallaq. To attend to this discussion, one must relinquish many of the arguments of the medieval and early modern debate, but whether we like it or not, a position arguing that the Shari'a is alive still reasonably draws on medieval tools and connects them to contemporary institutions and practices. (In this, I disagree with Hallaq that all there is in these positions is living in denial.)

The most interesting aspect of this third debate is that it takes place among scholars of Islamic studies who are not themselves participants in either producing or consuming Shari'a norms. That is, they are neither authoritative jurists nor necessarily practicing Muslims. The debate is now about loss of knowledge, about an epistemic shift.

A question remains about whether the medieval debate may have descended from ancestors in early debates in the pre-*madhhab* era. This seems to invite the old, tired quarrels about what may be known about the first two Islamic centuries, with ready dogmas that are attested in the literature capable of branching into arguments in this area. Hints of early debates about the destiny of the Shari'a could be found in several Arabic sources, but the question is what one should do with sporadic arguments of a different tone, especially under the threat of the boring and unusually simple charge of anachronism many seem to fear (those who amuse me when they note the anachronistic usage of modern words of well-known histories to speak about premodern contexts but decline to discuss the fact that most of the words we use to speak of medieval Islamic history are three hundred years old or younger and, if some did not notice, are words from a language fully foreign to the ideas expressed in the medieval Arabic that once conveyed these ideas). The historian might assert the right to remain silent about a pretraditional, pre-*madhhab*, or a companions' phase for this debate, since aside from scattered evidence here and there, it will be more or less based on an intuition that the three positions of the traditional phase may be projected (albeit with different nuances) to earlier times—that is, to a time before the third/ninth century—against a rejection of this exercise as simply unuseful.

Once again, even in a historical project, the word "phases" need not be taken in an absolutely strict temporal sense. The phases of which one may speak have rough edges, and the impact of earlier phases on the later ones is palpable. Moreover, and a bit surprisingly, the early modern phase of the debate, clearly preceded by the medieval literature on government, does not simply draw on the most recent concepts of society and government in the Muslim world to assert the impact of these elements on the life of the Shari'a. In fact, both the political realities of the medieval Muslim world and their theoretical treatments, which have survived against the odds, find themselves involved in a modern debate on the Shari'a. Medieval debates on the fatigue of the Shari'a did not emphasize the role of the government on the Shari'a in the same way, and an insight from this medieval world could again change the debate in the future. Hence, in any event, the best sense of "phase" here is thematic and conceptual rather than strictly temporal.

This, as I said in the introduction, is a commentary and not a historical narrative. There is sufficient room for debate about my theoretical treatment of the topic, which is the essence of my contribution. My employment of historical themes and arguments should not take away from the theoretical nature of the discussion or invite the same arguments about the inevitable connection between ideas and contexts—leading, when shoved into the discussion, to an alienation of ideas from all contexts, except perhaps an esoteric context that is of use to the author alone. (My worry about how the insights of studying "ideas in context" applied in Islamic studies is less about the validity of the exercise than about the problematic habits of its consumers; an irony here is that those most qualified to produce these histories do not care to put any energy into that, because they have better things to do with these ideas than to claim they could represent them in ways most irrelevant to our modern context.)

A Note on the Term *Futur Al-Shari'a*

The "fatigue of the Shari'a" (Arabic: *futur al-Shari'a*) is a term of art medieval Sunni legal theorists, as I said, define as the absence of qualified jurists (Arabic: *mujtahids*) in the whole world. For these legal theorists, the fatigue of the Shari'a is the same as "the absence in an age of a jurist" (*khuluww al-zaman min al-mujtahid*). This should be distinguished from the absence in a given place, not the whole world in a given age, of *mujtahids*.

For this Muslim jurists could have invented a different term—the absence in a territory of a jurist (*khuluww al-makan or al-balad or al-diyar min al-mujtahid*). The territorial lack of jurists occurred more than once in Islamic history, in Sicily and Spain for example, and did not constitute a historical precedent that could be seen as a basis for an answer to the question of the fatigue of the Shari'a. A questioner in late medieval Spain could travel to Tunisia and seek the opinion of a qualified jurist, as much in Wansharisi's (d. 914/1508) *Mi'yar* attests. The question of the absence of jurists in the whole world is different, because this is a situation that requires certain answers to a basic question: How may someone who is committed to living by this Shari'a apply it, given the lack of those who can teach that person how to do so?

The Arabic term *futur* by itself denotes lack of vividness. In common usage, water is characterized by *futur* when it is neither hot nor cold (i.e., lukewarm). A more abstract usage allows *futur* to be a quality applicable to poetry. The irreverent poet Ibn al-Rumi (d. 282/896) criticized the poet and government official Ibn Abi Tahir (or, Ibn Tayfur, d. 280/894) for producing flavorless poetry (*fatir*), that is, lacking in vigor and art (*'adimtuka yabn^{a} abi at-tahir^{i}, wa ut'imtu thuklaka min sha'ir^{i}; fa ma anta harr^{un} wa la barid^{un}, wa ma bayna dhina siwa-l-fatiri*: Oh, Ibn Abi Tahir, may I lose you, the kind of poet you are; Your poetry is neither hot nor cold; what is left between these two but the lukewarm!)[1]

Once it acquired a technical, legal meaning, *futur*, as Ash'ari theologians propagated it, denoted the absence of the qualified jurist (*mujtahid*). As the Ash'aris' interlocutors (Mu'tazilis and Hanbalis) characterize the issue differently, this term will remain central but never decisive in capturing all the arguments in the debate. When the moderns enter the debate, they also apply new terms. The game of terminology is never easy to play. In the heated debate on the creation of the Qur'an in the second–third/eighth–ninth century, terminology was most of what it was about. This debate is similar. Added to the inherited conflicts of terminology, choosing English as the language in which to discuss this issue will make it something different from what it could have been, had it been discussed in Arabic. But this is an inevitable limitation; nothing could be done to eliminate all versions of this difficulty.

Inquiries and Tools

One of the basic insights that guide any discussion of the debate on the Shari'a today derives from the multiplicity of issues under the rubric of the fatigue of the Shari'a. There is the question of the *future prospects* of the Shari'a and the question of its *current status*. In each case, there is the question of how to decide the health and vitality of the Shari'a or lack thereof. Is this dependant on the jurists who produce its rulings, the populations' consent to these jurists' authority, the governments in the societies where both these jurists and laypeople live? And how should one judge the jurists' capacity to represent the Shari'a, the populations' support for it, the importance and degree of governments' support for it, the impact of forces outside of Muslim societies on all of these factors? Within each one of these questions, therefore, many inquiries and methods to answer the different inquiries are covered.

The first question—the future prospects of the Shari'a—could be addressed with different tools. One may conceptually see fatigue as *mutation* and stipulate that no fatigue (as death or extinction) occurs unless one could imagine that a group's collective memory is capable of full cleansing. Against this view, one may (also conceptually) differentiate *regular functioning* of a system of norms from *eclectic reliance* on a system of norms that may have existed previously. One may also harbor theological beliefs that necessitate the survival of a given system of norms, based on belief in God's justice and consistency or mercy. Against this, one may have theological beliefs that the fatigue of divine norms entails no contradiction with God's justice and mercy and might even be beneficial to humanity. One may also answer the inquiry on the future of the Shari'a with a sense that it is likely or unlikely that a given system of norms will collapse in the near future, given recent developments. Conversely, it might be hard to imagine an argument from probability that argues against the fatigue of any given system of norms, unless something like a prediction of the nearing end of the world based on cosmic destructive events is at work—hence no sufficient time for the fatigue of current norms.

The second question, the current status of the Shari'a as a system of norms, can also be addressed using different criteria. Apparent functioning of norms in modern society is taken from assessments that often rely on political and social sciences. Ultimately, it is "observation" that is behind these assessments, coupled with generalizations that attempt to extend the limited area directly covered by the observation, since observation in this case is never comprehensive. This, with disanalogies, is also more or less true of the premodern methods—in this context, in the medieval Muslim world—used to assess the status of adherence to the Shari'a. That is, an *a posteriori* answer to the question of the vigor of the Shari'a at a given point relies on a generalization from observations by a jurist, such as Shatibi (d. 792/1390), who argued against the fatigue of the Shari'a based on the broad dissemination of the Qur'an and the *hadith* in his time, despite the fact the abode of Islam was slowly losing its Western European frontiers.

The fact that the discussion could take many directions should not be surprising. The Shari'a stands on a network of relationships, involving social standards and political organization and knowledge of the world—that is, a fully functioning Shari'a would still require the support of many people and institutions. Beside its producers, the jurists, it needs the aid of many human agents as well as an array of ideas and modes of understanding—the sciences of the day. Or, if we abandon our excessively suspicious, postmodern vernacular, it has to fit with the laws of nature, which one might learn gradually, and which must be in accordance with God's teachings at any given moment. The Shari'a, in addition, has many affinities to social standards and political structures. The *emphasis* in a debate on the life and health of the Shari'a could thus be *placed on* different aspects of its network of relations.

It is true that the question could be greatly narrowed down by following the old characterization of the fatigue of the Shari'a as an issue of vacuum in authority, authority being so narrowly and cleverly defined by the same participants in the fatigue debate as people like themselves. Yet, even when delimited this way, it remains multifaceted and multitracked. Is there an environment within which the education and generation of these authorities is possible, while other environments would not be conducive to the generation of such authorities? What happens when we disagree on the qualifications of these jurists? Is there a minimum standard one might accept for a qualified jurist? And since jurisprudence is an art, not in itself capable of being fully defined based on a concept that grows within a guild or a professional class, what are the guarantees that the inquiry on the survival of jurisprudence does not degenerate into an assessment of claims by individuals or groups that they are the inheritors and practitioners of this jurisprudence?

Chapter 2

Open Questions

"Complex systems are not made *ex nihilum*."[1] As one such system, the Shari'a, whose vigor or fatigue has been repeatedly debated, must be seen in terms too complex to be ruled functional or otherwise as if it were one simple unit. Since its infancy, the Shari'a appeared a puzzling entity, and it has certainly continued to be a complex reality ever since.

The task of the practical side of the Shari'a is to provide normative categories for human actions. These actions are all obligatory, prohibited, or something in between. From a certain perspective, this task could not fail. From this perspective, all human actions could be judged according to the Shari'a, since each act is at least, on balance, good, bad, or neutral. From a practical juristic perspective, however, it could be questioned whether the availability of these categories is intelligible without a measure of human interaction with these judgments or categories (to raise the questions from the worshippers' perspectives). For example, one could ask about the degree to which "intention" affects the action's normative category or value. Another problem is whether conflicting considerations may render a simple normative value of an act (to discourage or encourage it) difficult. The difficulty of denying the availability of knowledge of the values assigned to actions and the complexity of juristic vacuums, remain relevant to any debate on the death of the Shari'a.

In the medieval debate on the fatigue of the Shari'a, the issue was surrounded by other inquiries of legal and political philosophy. The "fatigue" question could be seen as part of a cluster of debates about the sources of the Shari'a before and after Muhammad received his revelations, the questions of legal and moral vacuum, the survival and extinction of the memory of the past, and the role of government in the establishment of law and custom, among others.

The "revelations" received by the Prophet Muhammad (d. 11/632) raised questions about the destiny of the previous laws and teachings of prophets and authorities, whose names were circulating at the time—Abraham, David, Moses, and Jesus.[2] The Arab polytheists among whom the Prophet Muhammad was raised did not think that life must necessarily be conducted according to any particular divine revelation, and many other nations at the time similarly lived by nothing that claimed to be revealed teachings of divine origin. It would not be far-fetched in this context to think about the possibility and consequences of living with unrevealed laws.

I will sidestep the issue of how the Qur'an itself addresses these and related questions as I am more concerned with how Muslim theologians and jurists debate the destiny of revelation-based norms, which involves much interpretation of the Qur'an and the Prophet's statements, but also involves something more: an interpretation of Islamic history. I will thus move to the systematic approach of the theologians and jurists to the overall inquiry into whether and how life may be conceived without the Shari'a.

* * *

After religious philosophy (*kalam*) and Islamic legal theory (*usul al-fiqh*) developed as discrete fields, four distinct inquiries emerged. These are:

1. Is reason, unaided by revelation, capable of arriving at binding answers to moral and religious questions (*al-hukm qabl wurud al-shar'*; *al-tahsin wa al-taqbih al-'aqliyyan*)?
2. Do the previous laws of Abraham and Moses (etc.) (*shar' man qablana*) continue to be sources of Islamic norms after Muhammad's revelations, which are the final revelations?
3. Is it possible for the Shari'a to be silent about a given question even during its normal life of functioning as a theoretically comprehensive system (*khuluww al-ashya' 'an hukm al-shar' ma'a baqa' al-Shari'a 'ala nizamiha*)?
4. Is it possible that pre-Muhammadan revealed laws (the latterbeing the final revelations) will experience fatigue or fading away (*futur al-Shari'a*; also enlarged into *futur al-shara'i'*), and what happens then?

Theologians and jurists disagreed on all of these questions, but their disagreement on each one of these questions tells a different story. I will attempt a sketch of these here.

Reason Unaided by Revelation

The question of the authority of "unaided reason" is addressed by Mu'tazilis through an insistence on assigning reason a role in inferring and deciding moral and legal norms, before and, it would appear, after the final revelations. This is a philosophical issue, prone as many philosophical issues often are to the misunderstanding and parallel conceptualization of the questions. (The difficulty of parallel conceptualization is addressed in the literature as verbal disagreement or *khilaf lafzi*, which means a disagreement that would disappear upon the clarification of terms and concepts.) But the disagreement in this issue is verbal (*lafzi*) only to some extent—some of it is resolvable upon the clarification of concepts; some of it persists. The persisting part is that one side (the Mu'tazili) are reported to believe that "unaided reason" is capable of generating binding norms, which carry the result of divine reward or punishment. The other side (the Ash'aris) denies this last part of the assertion—they deny that these reason-based norms could result in any divine reward or punishment.

Juwayni stated that Ash'aris had no qualms about the idea that "unaided reason" could correctly recognize and identify goodness and badness in actions; the question is what to do with this recognition,[3] The Ash'ari argument is straightforward: How could one be sure that God would reward or punish without a messenger from God conveying this information, where the divine message, one would assume, includes some *specifications* about the reward or punishment (even if you believe, as some Muslim philosophers did, that paradise and hell are mere metaphors). Subki's (d. 771/1369) subsequent summary of legal theory clearly stated this distinction between Ash'aris and Mu'tazilis as the point of the disagreement, not on reason's capacity to figure out the good or bad character of actions but to hold any beliefs about rewards and punishments based on the occurrence of these actions. The Ash'ari position, therefore, simply distinguishes between (a) any moment that precedes an available divine revelation from moments after that revelation, and (b) reason's capacity to recognize *good and bad* from its (alleged) capacity to think through the consequences of the recognition of *good and bad*.

I have a lesser degree of confidence about the Mu'tazili position(s), which seems to have a measure of untidiness, but I will delay my attempt to make sense of the Mu'tazili family of positions to chapter four. Suffice it now to say that Mu'tazilis thought that God's revelation was not the only way through which humans could acquire an understanding of what is good and desirable and what is not. Ash'aris believed this was the shortest of all shortcuts; God's assignment to humanity is much more complicated. An

Ash'ari is always suspicious of statements that describe the world God created with a sense of comprehensiveness. The notion that *this world is a perfect world* since God (who possesses all the attributes of perfection) created it raises Ash'ari suspicion. Who is going to tell us the details of the perfection of the world? Is not this perfection supposed to be beyond human capacity? How could the imperfect human explain perfection of any sort?

This disagreement is relevant to the question of how to handle a vacuum in humankinds' knowledge of God's norms, which were known through His revelations. The Mu'tazilis could easily resort to this same unaided "reason" in the case of the unavailability of the Shari'a; the Ash'aris will strike a different tone, ultimately vacillating, but will hardly acknowledge their failure to provide a full answer to the question of how to handle the absence of the Shari'a. Some of the Mu'tazilis ventured to propose that the very idea of the fatigue of God's norms was impossible, as it contradicted the perfection of God and His creation. Some of them did not go that far, but held the doctrine of the sufficiency of unaided reason in certain conditions, which is consistent with their trust in God's justice, while not committing all the way to the most perfect or "best" world. The weak point of this view is that it is too ambitious about reason's capacity. . At this turn in the argument, the Ash'aris have an easier assignment to take on: To show the weakness of the Mu'tazili stance. As for the Ash'aris' positive views on the questions of perfection of the world, they made no commitment to such doctrine; nor did they accept that God's justice could be understood in terms of human justice. The fatigue of divine norms is a problem, and its solution may not be easy, Ash'aris acknowledge; but we will not attempt to get out of the way of a faint wind by moving into the vicinity of an active volcano.

Revelations before and after the Prophet Muhammad

In an era in which the final Shari'a (of Muhammad) has experienced fatigue, people's relationship to the Shari'a of Muhammad would be the same as the position of those who lived by it when they think of pre-Muhammadan laws and revelations. The main difference is that there will be no replacement for this final Shari'a before the end of the world. There are, therefore, analogies and disanalogies.

The inquiry at hand, the post-Muhammadan utility of pre-Muhammadan revealed laws, involves philosophy and history. Some Sunni legal theorists argued that Muslims have a duty to follow all pre-Muhammadan laws that (a) have not been abrogated in the Qur'an or the Sunna, and (b) have been reported in these two sources.[4] This position is beset by potent objections, but its adherents defended it with much originality and skill. Among the objections are the fact that pre-Muhammadan laws have inconsistent doctrines (*mukhtalifa*), that they may have included instances of abrogation unknown to us (*al-nasikh wal-mansukh*), and that to apply these laws, one must assume a duty to conduct extensive "research" to unearth the correct forms of these laws, a duty one could not find in the Qur'an or the Sunna.[5] A position accepting the authority of pre-Muhammadan laws must first and foremost attend to the objection that pre-Muhammadan laws originate in suspect sources, the distorted Torah and Gospels. The best answer to these objections are ultimately to accommodate the objections; hence, one need not rely on any sources for pre-Muhammadan laws other than those of the Qur'an and the Sunna as stated in stipulation (b) that was mentioned earlier. If one fails to identify an indisputable source for a given legal doctrine in pre-Muhammadan teachings, the duty to adopt this doctrine does not fall on one's shoulder (*li-anna la nasil*[u] *ilayh*[i] *min tariq*[in] *yuthaq*[u] *biha, wa ma kan*[a] *hadha hukmuh*[u] *fa-qad saqat*[a] *'anna taklifuh*).[6] One might reasonably read into this position a sense of resignation to the fact that divine laws before the Prophet Muhammad have been lost to us, for all intents and purposes; they have undergone a full process of fatigue.

In theory, the Hanabila adhered to using available pre-Muhammadan laws more than others; in practice, the disagreement is thin, given the scarcity of the sources (though those familiar with *fiqh* will know that it is not just a half dozen issues, since the examples given in *usul al-fiqh* texts are not exhaustive). Both pre- and post-Muhammadan laws, however, share the exposure to the encroachments of time and the susceptibility to abandonment. This makes the question of the survival of pre-Muhammadan laws after the Prophet Muhammad received his revelations a foundation for the larger question of the fatigue of divine norms. Indeed, in Juwayni's (d. 478/1085) *Burhan*, one of the first prominent treatments of the topic (of the fatigue of the *shara'i'*), which influenced later treatments, the issue of the fatigue of the Shari'a is discussed as part of the issue of the fatigue of all divine *Shari'a*s. Juwayni introduces his arguments in opposition to those of the Mu'tazili Ka'bi (d. 319/931), who is credited with a denial of the possibility of the fatigue of divine norms and who is reported to have participated in debates about Mosiac and Muhammadan laws and was deferred to in one such debate as a final arbiter.[7] Following Juwayni, the Ash'aris will accept that all divine revealed norms—the divine *shara'i'*—were equally capable of undergoing fatigue, regardless of the status of this Muhammadan Shari'a as the last one.

In other words, the debate on the status of pre-Muhammadan revelations, which throws in much relief the idea of divine norms' susceptibility to erosions of different types (abrogation; abandonment and neglect), could not be forgotten when the destiny of the final revelations were debated. Not only that, Ka‘bi's ghost, with his argument tying the notion of the fatigue of all divine laws and revelations to the impolite notion of (a sort of) divine failure, hovered over the debate across the centuries. Ka‘bi, the butt of Ash‘ari jokes, had provided not only an argument for an overall perfection of God's creation coupled with faith in the human reason, but he also defended pre-Muhammadan revelations as persistent and immortal (until subsequent revelations that fill the gap created by their absence are available). Note also that an outcome similar to the teachings included in God's revelations may live in us, via reason. These divine teachings have the capacity of persisting in the social world, owing to God's justice and support for humanity. It may be the laziness of those who think otherwise that cause them to doubt these abundantly corroborated facts.

Vacuum in Divine Norms

The third question, whether vacuum can obtain within the realm of the Shari‘a during its normal life, invited disagreements once again involving parallel systems of conceptualization—that is, jurists and theologians disagreed because they characterized their questions differently; they were ultimately asking slightly different questions. The issue is already twofold. First, is there an indication in religious sources that the Shari‘a can be silent in some cases? And second, are there logical and descriptive arguments establishing that the Shari‘a can be and is indeed silent in some cases? The second aspect of the question is the most relevant here. To put it in a more elaborate way: Does the Shari‘a have answers to all questions; and is it capable of categorizing each and every human action as desirable, undesirable, or at least permissible? Or does it allow gaps and vacuums? The standard Sunni juristic answer is "no," it could not bear vacuum; and the reason is the potency of analogical reasoning. Analogy is meant to cover the area of ostensible Shari‘a silence by extending the logic of its explicit regulations to those areas where the Shari‘a "appears" silent. This is not taken to be a mere presumption; in reality, it seems to work.

If this is the case, then the Shari‘a's silence is only something of an optical illusion, suffered by those who have not developed good Shari‘a lenses. Analogy will always work, and it will always find a category for every human action, and actions will at least be encouraged, discouraged, or remain "*open*" to individuals without fear of punishment or looking forward to a reward (open, i.e., allowed), which is a broad legal category encompassing most human actions. This view seems to come from as early a treatment of the subject as those of Shafi'i (d. 204/820) and Ibn Surayj (d. 306/918) in his book on analogy,[8] and may be traced to earlier sources.

The same question was cast differently as a question of whether a human act can be devoid of a single or decisive *basis* for its categorization. Take the example of a person in free-fall who will end up killing someone by falling on that person. This could be proposed as a case of Shari'a silence, since this action could not be categorized as prohibited, reprehensible, permitted, recommended, or obligatory. But this supposed vacuum could be countered by saying that *free-fall ending in killing* is a prohibited act, but the one who seems to perform it is not responsible for its result, given her/his lack of choice. This fits within the scheme of impediments to responsibility and competence (*'awarid al-ahliyya*), which considers the impact of infancy and compulsion (among other conditions) on moral and legal responsibility. In this scheme, one must distinguish between the availability of a category for an action (which is always there) and circumstances removing or mitigating the responsibility of a given individual who may have been embroiled in an action.

One might still accept this clever solution (i.e., classifying an act as bad and denying the actor's responsibility for it) and come back with another argument. How could an act be characterized as good, bad, or even open or permitted (still a value judgment) when it is occupied by equal considerations that push its normative value in different directions? Will we then decide to prioritize some of these considerations arbitrarily in order to simply find a category for it? Take, for example, the act of evacuating a land one has occupied unjustifiably. This act requires moving about the land in order to evacuate it, but *moving about* a usurped land is prohibited and *evacuating* it is obligatory, and *these two* could not be separated. How could divine laws solve this problem? Would not these laws have to remain faithful to their values that push in different directions? The answer is that this is an *obligatory* act that *involves* a prohibited act. And there is a practical solution to this contradiction: the withdrawal from the land is required (corresponding to the obligation) while the occupant remains responsible for violating the body of the land until the withdrawal is complete (as this motion stems from a transgression on the usurper's part, which entails all requisite responsibilities that go with transgression). That is, any destruction during the evacuation should be compensated by the occupants without attention to the excuse that they were engaged in the *duty* of evacuation and hence should not be responsible for any inadvertent destruction that went with it, for example. As stated earlier, the silence of the Shari'a here is based on a scenario where it is fully functioning—as Zarkashi (d. 794/1392) put it, *fi taqdir^i khuluww^i waqi'at^{in} 'an hukm^i Allah^i*

ma'a baqa' al-Shari'at 'ala nizamiha.[9] The silence of the Shari'a may (theoretically) be said to exist or not, but there are practical solutions to the problems caused by that silence.

The Fatigue of the Shari'a

The fourth question, our central one—the question of the fatigue of the Shari'a, its susceptibility to senility, let us say, was debated in tandem with the first (the unaided reason's ability to make moral and legal judgments) and reflected a split among theologians from the third/ninth century into what is known as the Mu'tazili view affirming the unaided reason's capacity to provide binding answers to moral and religious questions (*al-tahsin wa al-taqbih al-'aqliyyan*) and the Ash'ari view answering this question in the negative. Other doctrines, such as believing that God is bound to do what is best for humanity (*al-aslah*), also affected the debate. Hence, as we said, the Mu'tazilite al-Ka'bi believed that the fatigue of religious laws (including those preceding the Muhammadan Shari'a, addressed in the second question) was impossible, because God is bound to do what is best, which includes making His guidance available, since the unavailability of divine laws is inferior to their availability.[10]

Following Juwayni's refutation of Ka'bi, the Ash'aris acknowledged the possibility of the fatigue of Shari'a norms over time. The same Ash'aris were also comfortable with the idea of the abrogation of specific laws within the Shari'a system, as long as these were replaced by other laws. But the Ash'aris did not accept the implication that God simply changed his mind (the so-called *bada'* doctrine). The Mu'tazili Abu al-Husayn al-Basri (d. 436/1044)[11] rejected attacks on the idea of abrogation of the laws of God as (logically and theologically) inappropriate. He argued that some limitations might be placed on abrogation by the lawgiver, but abrogation in principle remains a desirable and natural strategy for laws to address life's constant change. There is another thin disagreement here, boiling down to whether "change" is in itself an imbedded law in the functioning of the world, even governing revelation itself (Mu'tazili view), which has practical implications, or whether a good deal of change must be governed by higher laws, as most Ash'aris would say, while they resign to God's will, if it seems that He wanted change to end humanity's access to good norms.

Given the Ash'ari prolific production in legal theory and theology, theirs became the dominant view in the literature. That is, the dominant view among legal theorists, caused by the proliferation of Ash'ari writings on the subject, was that the fatigue of both previous laws and the

(Muhammadan) Shari'a was possible. I refer to this view as the majority view without any attachment to it, since I argue that all three medieval positions on this issue enjoy relative strength, and I also think that they are at least partly reconcilable.

The large, practical umbrella for these discussions is how the silence or absence of God's law should be handled. The solutions range from (a) going back to the unaided reason (many Mu'tazilis and some Ash'aris) to (b) referring to the memory of God's law based on governing principles, given the absence of the details (Juwayni's solution). And there is always insisting that neither silence nor absence can be demonstrated to have befallen or be about to befall God's law—the fatigue of the Shari'a could only happen at the very end of time, in which case one has very little time to do anything about it (the view attributed to the Hanbalis').

Lacunae in Actual Shari'a Models

The issue of lacunae in the Shari'a, whether while young or old, is at the heart of the inquiry of the fatigue of Shari'a norms. In a *conversation* between Muhammad Zahid Kawthari (1296/1878–1371/1951) and Abu al-Ma'ali Juwayni (419/1028–478/1085), divergent readings of Islamic legal history (partly, though not only, influenced by their *madhhab* affiliation) caused these two jurists to see the matter differently. Their research on the lacunae in Shari'a models before and after the *madhhabs* clarifies another aspect of the fatigue question and hence merits attention.

One of the insights to be gained from the Juwayni/Kawthari polemic is the following. The absence of specific laws within a developed system composed of reported sets of views, whether it be the Shari'a that was available to the companions or the one in the era of the schools (*madhhabs*), does not qualify as a case of *futur* or absence of law in the general sense. This must be recalled later to show that a modern argument about the inability of premodern Sunni law to provide immediate answers to modern questions is not an indication of this law's inability to answer these questions and address the vacuum at a later moment. Reflection on new questions does take time, and a temporary absence of law is not an outright absence of law. This has been how things worked all along.

Juwayni has distinguished between "the *madhhabs* of the companions" and those of the four Sunni systems (Hanafi, Maliki, Shafi'i, and Hanbali) by saying that the former have too many instances of vacuum, at least in reporting if not in development, which makes adhering to them unacceptable. Juwayni then moves on to the assertion that no one should pretend to follow a companion's *madhhab*, according to the consensus of advanced scholars (al-*Muhaqqiqun*). Between the schools of the companions and that of Shafi'i (d. 204/820), whom Juwayni follows, there is an intervening period of development, which includes Abu Hanifa (d. 150/767) and his students. Kawthari, who was angered by the way Juwayni belittled Abu Hanifa's school as less-developed than that of Shafi'i, attacked Juwayni for his "impoliteness" with the companions as well as with Abu Hanifa but could not provide a new, full account of the concept of the schools of the companions, their history and development, or their reporting to later generations. (It is important here to note that I am not interested in the complacent assertion that such a thing as the schools of the companions never existed, often presented as caution not to assert the existence of something one does not know existed. If one is not sure, one is not sure, but "not sure of a presence" and "sure of an absence" are not the same.)

For my purposes, the Juwayni/Kawthari (virtual) debate raises the question of vacuum in a manner that goes beyond the discussion on whether analogy always fills in the gaps of the Shari'a. The ultimate value of the Juwayni/Kawthari polemic is that it shows that distinctions between the companions' model of living by divine norms and the subsequent models (of the *madhhabs*) seem to evaporate the longer they are considered. Reflect on the following exchange.

> *Juwayni*: The general principles (*usul*) developed by the companions were not sufficient to address all cases (*waqa'i'*). Hence the questioner in the age of the companions had the option of taking the view of [Abu Bakr] al-Siddiq in one question and that of ['Umar] al-Faruq in another. This was not the case in the post-*madhhab* era (*'ahd al-a'imma*), because their [*madhhabs*'] principles were sufficient.
>
> *Kawthari*: This needs no elaboration! A lack of general principles for the companions means that they lacked a basis for their answers of the questions they received, which leads to the conclusion that they should not have given answers or opinions at all, rather than authorizing the questioner to choose from their [diverging] opinions. Claiming that the [companions] lacked comprehensive principles is a claim of their ignorance and an impolite position toward them, in addition to indicating [Juwayni's] ignorance of their affairs... Yet, we know that Abu Hanifa was indecisive in some issues, and Malik (d. 179/795) also hesitated in answering some questions and would even give a flat "I do not know," and Shafi'i gave two opinions in one and the same question and said that "if a report from the Prophet was deemed valid, it would be my view." None of this takes away their status as leaders of jurisprudence, since humans are not meant to know everything, and it is appropriate for a person to be silent when they do not know.[12]

Juwayni has an understanding of the difference between the work of Abu Hanifa and Shafi'i as that of an inventor of *the categories of the questions* versus a cautious evaluator of the evidence supporting any position *on these questions*. Juwayni claims that:

> Abu Hanifa (d. 150/767) spent his life in instituting the questions [of jurisprudence]; so, he did not have the time to evaluate and distinguish [the possible answers]. This is why [his two students] Abu Yusuf (d. 182/798) and Muhammad [Ibn al-Hasan] (d. 189/805) disagreed with him in many of his positions, as they distinguished valid from invalid views. [Abu Hanifa] denied the institution of endowments (*waqf*), stating that there was no such a thing as "endowment"; only a category of "wills" (*wasiyya*), and it could only be binding after a judicial decision. Similarly, on the question of measuring a *sa'* [a volume-based measure, equivalent to 2.75 liters today]: [Abu Hanifa] disagreed with Shafi'i when he said that it was equivalent to four *mudds*, which is 1.33 Iraqi *ritl* (around 400 grams). The same was true of Shafi'i's view that an in-mosque call to prayer (*iqama*) consisted of unrepeated sentences in disagreement with Abu Hanifa.[13]

Juwayni indeed claims that in all of these three questions (endowments, the exact value of the measure, and the nature of the in-mosque call to prayer), Shafi'i's view was corroborated by the companions' descendents who lived in Medina at the time of Harun al-Rashid (d. 193/809), as they related that Shafi'i's views coincided with the tradition of the Prophet. Kawthari refutes these claims by correcting Juwayni both on the substantive doctrine of Hanafi jurists and the historical events he relates. Both authors, however, agree that vacuum exists only when one considers the actual articulated doctrines and not the theoretical foundation of these doctrines.

Now we turn to Juwayni's *Burhan*, where he draws the subtle distinction between the possibility of vacuum and the actual occurrence of vacuum.

> As for the possibility of the absence of a ruling (*hukm*) in a case (*waqi'a*), no intellect would argue against it. As for it actually happening (*wuqu'uh*), I find that not likely (*unkir*[u] *dhalik*), since previous generations did "attack" queries with answers, despite the abundance and variety of queries given to them; [they attacked the questions] as if they believed there was no limitation to their capacity to answer [all questions]. And if it were possible that some cases had no rulings/solutions, that would have already happened and it would have been apparent. Since this did not happen, this indicates that such absence did not happen. As for their argument that the sources of laws are limited while events are unlimited, this does not indicate [the absence of law], since those who reflect on the Shari'a find it vacillating between two ends, one limited and the other unlimited: impurity (*najasa*) is limited

and purity (*tahara*) is not; prohibition (*tahrim*) is limited and permission (*ibaha*) is not—hence, when a case hangs in between the two ends and does not fall in the realm of that which is limited; it is judged to belong to the other area, the unlimited.[14]

The point of these discussions is that a *madhhab* or a legal system (or a worldview of an individual follower of the Prophet) consists of principles that may govern many cases, and the claim that a case could not be governed by the principles would likely not be conceded easily. This debate, however, could hardly be resolved in any easy way. Any system of laws and norms must stand the test of practice; otherwise its potential for completion (while it sustains apparent gaps) will amount to nothing but mere potential. The reason this system of norms or any other may be said to not suffer from lacunae is that it did function in practice. The practical functioning relies on more than the intellects of those who can extend the system's principles through analogical reasoning or similar tools. Norms need populations to have a healthy life. This leads to the last link I will consider in this chapter, the link between the fatigue of the Shari'a and another question, the question of the connections of political and social life to the Shari'a.

Political Science and Jurisprudence

Moral and social norms cannot be separated from society. This and the assumption that societies work under an umbrella representing "power" within each one take us into another element in this discussion. We don't need to take this in a Foucaultian sense where power even allows knowledge to be knowledge; medieval Muslim jurists speak of government as an element of life in normal circumstances. Governments need not be a presence that allows things to exist the way they exist. They are only an element of society.

One of the open questions that are adjacent to the question of the fatigue of divine norms is these norms' interaction with social customs and with government. The same (Ash'ari) theorist who refuted Ka'bi's optimistic stance of the endurance of Shari'a norms, now serving as a political theorist, wrote about the end of ideal government and the end of all functioning government, stating that the only resort of people with no functioning government is scholars and notables. But what happens when these scholars themselves are absent. This is the true question of the fatigue of Shari'a norms, and in Juwayni's view, memory of the good norms must

> JUWAYNI'S BREAKDOWN OF <u>MUSLIM SOCIETY</u>
>
> STATE GOVERNMENT (legitimized by contract with representatives of the people ahl *al-hall wa-l-'aqd*)
>
> ↓
>
> LOCAL GOVERNMENT (deputized by state government)
>
> ↓
>
> LOCAL LEADERS AND SCHOLARS (emergency replacement for local government)
>
> ↓
>
> <u>INDIVIDUALS</u>

be employed to recover as much as possible of these forgotten norms.

Before Juwayni, different social and political contexts have surrounded the debate medieval Sunni legal theorists had about "what happens when the Shari'a fades away, for lack of access to qualified jurists?"[15] Attending the philosophical and legal question were events such as the rise of the Umayyad state (40/660–132/750), which itself started to ignite another set of questions about legitimate government. The conflicts that involved 'Abdullah Ibn al-Zubayr (d. 73/692), who was seen as the legitimate leader and given a *bay'a* (consent to govern) by many, and other revolutionaries throughout Umayyad and 'Abbasid times (40/660–132/750; 132/750–656/1258) gave rise to theories about what legitimate rule was and how it was established. The achievement of Mawardi (d. 450/1058) in his Ordinances (*al-Ahkam al-Sultaniyya*) was not so much inventing as articulating theories (in the mould of the religiolegal language of Muslim jurists) locating the basis of legitimacy in government in a contract between the sovereign and the notables or people's representatives (*ahl al-hall wa al-'aqd*) or an act of succession from a previous ruler. Mawardi also simultaneously justified ruling based on control, absent a contract. The latter position (accepting control as a basis for government, absent a contract or a succession act), whether or not it justifies Saljuq rule in Baghdad, could indeed be found as a theory *in embryo* in the Sunni legal tradition of the previous three centuries.

Yet, medieval Sunni political scientists continued to be at variance about handling the usurpation of power without a contract establishing the legitimacy of rulers, or the lack of an ideal, legitimate government similar to that of the four rightly guided caliphs (Abu Bakr, 'Umar, 'Uthman, and 'Ali, r. 632–660). Many medieval jurists accepted the caliphate as an ideal, while adopting a realistic approach to the actual exercise of power in their societies. The decentralization of power was the decisive factor, and though many Muslim jurists considered the actual rulers as representatives of the caliph, these jurists by and large accepted that the craft of politics generated its rules, and that structuring the caliphate was by no means the most significant concern of the organization of a Muslim society.[16]

Is a Muslim government a source of support for jurists or is it a rival? *Rebellion and Violence in Islamic Law* demonstrates that there cannot be a neat answer to this question. The answer then is: it depends—indeed on many factors. This frustratingly terse and ostensibly insubstantial answer promises to be more exciting, the closer we get into the details. Theories of the regulation of rebellion reflected that the diversity of opinions was caused by many considerations.[17] Does this mean that government is totally irrelevant in an inquiry about the silence of qualified jurists? My answer is no. Chapter eight offers the details and discusses the implications of the relationship between government and jurisprudence as conceived by Muslim legal and political theorists.

The Shari'a ultimately has a dual presence in Muslim society, one relying on governmental concession and one on popular concession to its authority. But these are not unrelated. Sunni jurists, by and large, believe that these concessions are, in practice, concessions to the authority of jurists, whose absence is equated with the fatigue of the Shari'a. Further reflection on their writings and the Mu'tazili and Hanbali positions on the subject, however, will cause us to pause. Chapters four–six attempt to offer the details.

Two Arguments for the Fatigue of the Shari'a Today

The strongest arguments that the Shari'a lost its coherent presence in the modern era draw on the two elements sketched in this chapter: breaking with past reasoning and the presence of lacunae in Shari'a models. The first argument is surrounded by a family of ideas: for example, that modern juristic research sustains a weak connection with the unusually rich medieval juristic thinking, that the modern Hanbali law governing Saudi Arabia and other areas in the Muslim world, for example, does not qualify as continuity in Shari'a models. The second argument highlights the "incursions" of modern governments into areas where traditional Shari'a jurists used to offer their opinion comfortably, while the same jurists are now increasingly comfortable with "referring" their questioners to government regulations.

Both arguments have elements of strength and weakness, although both of them only describe situations that are not completely unprecedented in Islamic history. What must be questioned is the final assertion that, notwithstanding all apparent indications to the contrary, today's Shari'a presence is in essence an absence. For one thing, we have no sufficient indication of the volume of nonbinding fatwas operating in today's world, irrespective of whether these fatwas ultimately cover all the new lacunae created by the modern condition, and whether these fatwas govern people's lives today to degrees larger than that to which these lives are governed by modern laws.

The issue of government and modern laws' incursions introduces another difficulty: How much of the new realities of "codification," "the nation state," and "centralized political power" is capable of creating a totally new situation? Ibn 'Abidin (d. 1252/1836), as I noted in a previous work,[18] cited Nawawi's objection to Baybars's attempts to impose uniform evidentiary standards for the ownership of property, which would have deprived the populations of controlling aspects of establishing ownership within the community itself.[19] One may argue that Ibn 'Abidin was indeed the latest, or one of the latest, jurists to be able to draw reasonably on an earlier argument in this issue, given that the continuity of medieval juristic thinking may be extended to the end of his lifetime, the 1830s. The problem with the confident assertion that all governments following Ibn 'Abidin's time have (gradually) functioned under new circumstances, presumptively incompatible with the Shari'a, is that it begs the question of whether *madhhab* reasoning is a tool for the Shari'a or is itself the Shari'a.

No one could argue against the idea that the nation states have arisen as powerful entities whose relationship to traditionally trained jurists has come to be that of the powerful vis-à-vis the weak. But traditionally trained jurists have also influenced government thinking in many issues, as they offered even better solutions to issues where the Westernized and secularized elites were thinking in one direction and had to think differently after realizing the untenable nature of a simple application of Western norms in their societies. It is this back-and-forth, even in countries such as Egypt and Turkey, supposedly early players in strengthening nationalism and centralized, codified laws, that needs to be studied before one commits to a simple assertion that governments in the Sunni world have been agents of weakening the Shari'a throughout the last two centuries (since, say, Muhammad 'Ali and Mahmud II). And one needs to keep in mind that nationalism could also begin to lose ground in the near future and be replaced by new affiliations, some of them larger in scope and some narrower than the nations of the thirteenth/nineteenth and fourteenth/twentieth centuries, even the ones whose history could be traced within similar borders to an age earlier than the modernity of the last three centuries.

Chapter 3

Ijtihad Theory

This elastic term *ijtihad* has pushed both Sunni jurists and historians of Sunni jurisprudence to the point of exhaustion. The more you consider it, and the longer you investigate how both participants in jurisprudence and its observers have understood its ranks and functions, the more elusive it seems to become. *Ijtihad* denotes a capacity to exert oneself to produce a legal opinion. This production may be through devising an opinion by the jurist who answers an inquiry, or it may be through conveying a recorded opinion this jurist has the authority to convey, customized as it may be to the case of the questioner. In either case, the jurist may arguably be called a *mujtahid*, someone who possesses the capacity of *ijtihad*. [To digress briefly, the elasticity of terms indicating high authorities such as *ijtihad* is not unique to the status of an authority in law; the term *hafiz* (expert in *hadith*) received similar treatments, and the same is true of the lower (or more generic) rank of *muhaddith*.)[1]

Many "typologies" of *mujtahids* speak of classes of jurists, sometimes three, sometimes four or five, and sometimes seven. It is not clear, however, how meaningful these classifications are, and whether it is easy to fit known jurists into the proposed classes in each typology. Consider Shaykh Muhammad Bakhit al-Muti'i's (d. 1354/1935) scathing review of Ibn Kamal Pasha's (d. 940/1534) classification of Hanafi jurists into seven ranks. The accusations Muti'i levels against Ibn Kamal Pasha include the following:

1. Failure to articulate the difference between Abu Hanifa's (d. 150/767) first three followers, Abu Yusuf (d. 182/798), Muhammad Ibn al-Hasan (d. 189/805), and Zufar Ibn al-Hudhayl (d. 158/775), on the

one hand, and the founders of other schools of law, such as Malik (d. 179/795) and Shafi'i (d. 204/820), on the other.

2. Misclassifying many jurists by placing some jurists of high ranks in lower ranks and vice versa.

Other serious accusations are also given. The seventh rank in Ibn Kamal Pasha's typology, for example, describes a person who is not really deserving of the title "jurist."[2] Given that both Ibn Kamal Pasha and Muti'i are deemed advanced jurists and legal theorists, one should ask:. Why would their classification of jurists diverge to this extent? My best answer is that the task is simply hard.

If classifying "famous" jurists can be hard, harder still is producing an account of the ranks of less-than-famous jurists and deciding whether they should all simply fit in the lowest ranks of these typologies or whether they should remain "unclassifiable" for lack of information about them. It is indeed close to impossible to account for the qualifications of jurists fully or nearly fully. These jurists' disagreement among themselves, their ability to be "harsh" with one another, and our inevitable reliance on secondary sources to study some of their activities all make it difficult for us to obtain secure knowledge of their talent and juristic capacity.

There is an inherent difficulty in deciding whether qualified jurists have simply disappeared at a given time or age, based on an opinion that well-known jurists may not qualify as "qualified" by one's standards.[3] This judgment requires comprehensive knowledge of the state of the knowledge of jurisprudence in a given age, which even if limited to circles where this knowledge is likely to be available would still be a hard task to undertake.

What of contemporary jurists, our contemporaries, that is? We could certainly know more about them. Some of them may be our teachers, colleagues, or students. Yet, if the typologies of jurists is our way of figuring out whether we are witnessing an end to jurisprudence, the results we are able to reach will be quite shaky. In addition, every age is characterized by a sense of "loss" of knowledge, knowledge that used to be available to previous authorities. These previous authorities (as they present themselves to the imagination of their successors) are always better, more knowledgeable, and closer to some "origin" than their scholarly heirs. This is behind the saying that "contemporaneousness serves as a veil" (*al-mu'asara[tu] hijab*)—it makes scholars belittle the achievement of their contemporaries, perhaps for no good reason other than the fact that they share the same "corrupted age."

But why should we demand more than approximate knowledge of the juristic capacity of scholars we attempt to judge? It is obvious that the judgment on someone's ability in this area would be passed only by those who are engaged in the same task of jurisprudence: thinking of categories for human behavior—that is, judging actions to be lawful or unlawful, calling an act obligatory, recommended, reprehensible, or prohibited. Only jurists can judge other jurists in this regard. We do not expect engineers or physicists to judge jurists as capable or incapable, competent or incompetent in their jurisprudence. This judgment of jurists, beset as it is by the possible influence of "jealousy" and the impact of opposed views on issues, is the best possible indication of the presence of qualified jurists. Challenges remain, including in the case where the standards of good jurists are lowered universally, and where those charged with "policing" the high standards become themselves unable to observe the lost high standards in their own work. There is nothing you can do to fix that, however, unless you can assume that someone will be able to identify this problem from outside—that is, this nonjurist observer will be better in assessing the capacity of those involved in the production of jurisprudence than all those participating in it, so as to see the participants' low standards and make note of the death of qualified jurists, of the end of *ijtihad*.

We are left then with two options: one is to continue to participate in the game with the rules as they were set up, with all the deficiencies and the potential of repeating the scenario of the Ibn-Kamal/Muti'i disagreement. Or, we could try a new approach, a judgment from the outside.

The Judgment from Outside

The jurist/*mujtahid* is at the center of the medieval debate on the fatigue of the Shari'a and serves as a "standard" in this debate in two important senses. In the Ash'ari position in the debate, the absence of qualified jurists is itself equal to the fatigue of the Shari'a, and the arbiters of whether the qualified jurist exists are qualified jurists themselves. In chapter seven, when we discuss how jurists coped with second-class status in modern social and political life, it will become apparent how the shift in the debate (from focusing on jurists as subject and criterion) made insisting on this version of the discussion harder (though not devoid of insights, which is an underlying assumption in my project).

As if the aforementioned complexity of how the *mujtahid* could be discussed were not sufficient, we are thrown into further complexity whereby the status of the jurist as subject and arbiter for the Shari'a can be contested. The contesting voice would sound something like this: Who cares about the traditionally trained jurist? Was not this type of people the source of all the problems of the Shari'a? The destiny of the Shari'a should never be tied to the availability of this so-called traditional jurist; we are beyond that now. What we should focus on is the resources of the Shari'a of today and tomorrow, and perhaps we ought to be thankful and relieved (rather than distraught) that the old standards are less and less accessible and intelligible to us today.

To be sure, modern assessments from the outside (i.e., by nonparticipants) of how the Shari'a (with *ijtihad* as its tool) should be understood are not without precedent. About a millennium ago, Miskawayh (d. 421/1030) attempted to solve the ostensible paradox that *God clarified everything in His Revelation yet jurists' disagreement seemed to persist* as follows. Miskawayh asserted that there was no contradiction, because no one could come up with any Shari'a ruling that has no basis in the Qur'an. However, he continued: "Ijtihad, which is a means of worshipping God and a declaration of obedience to Him, or a way to establish the very benefit of reflection and research in itself, not for the sake of any conclusion, could not lose its value due to mistakes after the effort has been exerted and the task properly executed."[4] Miskawayh moves on to draw a simile between *ijtihad* and an exercise to move about the bell-scepter (*sawlajan*) for the sake of sport without intending to hit the bell, which could not be said to be devoid of value in the instances in which it does not hit it. The process or the search, rather than the conclusion, is what matters; even a non-*mujtahid*, such as Miskawayh, could see that clearly, as he could see that juristic disagreement was natural.

Be that as it may, in our modern context, calls abound to limit the discussion to the modern Shari'a's tools and potential for survival on new terms. But let us not forget potential calls for an opposite stance. If the old standards were less than certain, any alternative standards have lower chances of working. Time is not on the side of new standards—time here raising its ugly head from the past, not the future. Time, that is, legacy, is not on the side of new standards, since standards need time to acquire stability. In other words, some could also reasonably argue that the old standards, inadequate as they may be, are safer and have higher chances of working than any newly developed standards.

If the debate on the fatigue of the Shari'a could shift away from linking the Shari'a to *ijtihad* during much of the last century or century and a half, and only a memory of this medieval debate with jurists at the center could be found today, then should we (to be at least on firm historical grounds) limit ourselves to discussing the old sense of *ijtihad* that is intelligible to those who appreciate the qualified jurist, the *mujtahid*, as the representative of the Shari'a? Or, should we move on and leave the old *mujtahid* to his time, which is decidedly different from our time? Neither question could be answered in the affirmative, and the reason is twofold. First, the old debate is still very much alive, despite the introduction of many new elements to the Shari'a itself and its surroundings. Second, a new, confused sense of *ijtihad* accompanies the shift in understanding the health and illness of the Shari'a, and though this confused sense has not succeeded in creating a new standard in real life at all, it created significant noise and allowed the old sense of *ijtihad*, hard as it may be to study, to become even more blurry. Some observers do believe that there is no difference between the ambiguity of the term among medieval jurists and among today's brave discussants who debate the health and frailty of the Shari'a with no reference to the activities of jurists. That is (thus goes the bad argument), since it all seems to bear disagreement, it must be the same.

I will not engage this position here. I should focus on explaining how this new discussion of *ijtihad*, or simply the thing that qualifies people to have views worthy of discussion about religious obligations, changes the discussion. I should hasten to say that this development is also twofold. First, there is an ease with which people arrogate to themselves the right to say what they think about religious obligations from an Islamic viewpoint. Second, there is a lack of discipline in the terminology, an almost opportunistic use of the term *ijtihad*, as opposed to a commitment to a standard.

What then is the status of what qualifies as new ideas about *ijtihad*? First, access to education about fields that became known as the natural, social, and human sciences created a new language for thinking about the world, society, and humans, which occupy the same space as that occupied by (old) juristic debates about the world, society, and humans. Verbal disagreements abound. But there are significant moments at which the debaters reach very telling moments of frustration. Those on the side of "old jurisprudence" insist that the new educated people still have many bad intuitions about how this thing (the Shari'a) works. They have not read the whole Qur'an, let alone memorize and spend hours reflecting on its possibilities, and many of them would not even recognize well-known and abundantly reported *hadith*s. The legal reasoning of the founders of the Sunni school sounds foreign and outright simple to them (but they will not always confess to that). How could these be the inheritors of Islamic jurisprudence? By contrast, adherents of the old jurisprudence, even while aware of their weak position in the ranks of economic, social, and political existence in the world, genuinely do not think that those who received "good, new" education are actually capable of being togged up in the mantle of Islamic jurisprudence. These "old-fashion" jurists are of course dissatisfied about their own status in the world and the investment they put into their long and unrewarding education, but they are still able to see that the new education is no replacement for the old one.

Those on the other side feel frustrated by the "narrow" angle from which old-fashion jurists see things. They think these jurists (who are modern only in body but not in mind) make frequent mistakes about the natural and social phenomena about which they, who are on the side of modern education, know more. In short, the champions of modern education feel doubly superior to the inheritors of old jurisprudence. They simply can't learn from them. In some cases, they spend years studying under these jurists of traditional education only to come back a few years later to attack them. In other cases, they get transformed, but then they can't adopt their older views with passion any more. And they can't easily serve as mediators.

Another debate about *what share the Shari'a should claim* in any society takes place in "the circles of power." The result of this state of affairs is that the old Shari'a gets squeezed and forced into corners of various degrees of narrowness, and old-fashion Shari'a jurists breathe only through new forms of traditionalism, which they are fully aware bear many elements unlike the old tradition. .

If my diagnosis of this shift is more or less accurate, then the new *ijtihad*, which only requires something like being "smart" and college educated, could not be the issue any more. It will only be part of the noise surrounding the real issue, which is how much the culture and social structure of Muslim societies is shifting to an extent where the old arguments of old jurisprudence will no longer be intelligible. Did this already (partly) happen? Is this condition behind the move beyond an argument about whether the Shari'a maintained some presence vis-à-vis a changing Muslim society and government (say, for the sake of a rough assessment, from 1850 to 2000) and into speaking of an epistemic shift. This will be revisited in chapters nine and ten.

Forgetting the Foundation

The idea that *ijtihad* is tied to its history as well as its own textual foundation is not a foreign idea in Sunni jurisprudence. It is not simply a consequence of some recent salafi assertion that Muslims should keep looking toward the past in search of true guidance. Constant reflection on the history of the activities of *ijtihad* (without calling it the history of the activities, if you think this expression is too modern) is almost at the core of *ijtihad*. But there is a curious feature this reflection generated, which we cannot ignore when we discuss the fatigue of the Shari'a. I will label this feature, for the sake of simplicity, being self-conscious about the beginnings. Again, if you plan to understand it, do not impose modern salafi meanings on this idea.

According to Ibn ʿAbidin (d. 1252/1836), Ibn Nujaym (d. 970/1563) argued that analogy within Hanafi law should not be based on cases decided after 400 AH.[5] That is to say, a case decided after the first four centuries of the hijri calendar is not by itself suitable to be the basis for a new ruling extending the rationale of the post-400 case via analogy into new cases. The context for this, in Ibn ʿAbidin's writing, is a discussion of whether one may hire and provide compensation to others to perform religious recitations and chanting for an occasion that causes celebration. This, Ibn ʿAbidin argues, must be prohibited, since it is ultimately compensation for an act of ritual. Ibn ʿAbidin rejects an argument that Hanafi law allowed, after previously prohibiting, compensation for teaching the Qur'an. In this context, the question arises whether permitting an act (compensating for recitation) belonging to a prohibited category (compensating for worship) becomes itself a new norm and can be further extended to new cases. The argument Ibn Nujaym levels would reject an extension based on an extension, or an easing based on a previous easing. True, the principle of easing austere or difficult laws remains functional, but it may be applied more stingily and strictly—and, in all cases, an exception could not derive from another exception; the new (suggested) exception must be considered on its own merits.

This should be understandable in principle. Every legal or moral system must place limitations on its capacity for generating new norms, which is achieved here through juristic activities. Without limitation on juristic activities, any system of legal reasoning would move *faster* beyond its foundation. The move beyond the foundation, to a limited extent, remains natural and inevitable; it must simply be made more slowly and cautiously. Ibn Nujaym's warning is consistent with mechanisms that aim at bolstering this caution and creates limits on juristic activities. These mechanisms include the idea of juristic consensus, whose substantive claims (e.g., jurists unanimously agreed on proposition P1) can be reconsidered, but only when thorough effort and a crisis meet up. The crisis creates the condition for the desirability of reconsideration, and the effort allows for a fresh look at the consensus and an attempt to narrow down its limit in order to make room for new views within an area that used to be governed by the consensus. Ibn Taymiyya's many attacks on perceived consensuses provide good examples, but I will provide another example presently.

In certain ways, a reconsideration of a previous consensus is a "clarification" of that old consensus, as one must prove that the previous consensus was never as broad as some have understood. Take an attempt to reconsider the consensus on punishing an individual "*murtadd*" (apostate) by death by showing that the initial consensus took place during the *ridda* (apostasy) wars in the years 11–12/632–633, which were a punishment of "collective *ridda*" by war, while jurists remained reluctant to apply one standard on the individual *murtadd*, with many of them thinking of the case of the individual *murtadd* as a case of collective *ridda* in embryo (i.e., the individual *murtadd* who must be taken seriously is the one who is practically engaged in a preparation for collective *ridda* by calling others to join him).[6] What remains within the "jurisdiction" of the old consensus (what does not change here) is hence thinner than it once appeared. The *ridda* punishment that is the subject of consensus is for collective *ridda*, which is essentially "war" against a Muslim community. The stuff of which previous consensuses are made are ultimately the basics known in the texts of the Qur'an and the Sunna, coupled with very limited principles, which the early generations of Muslims adopted.

If this solution gets us out of many problems, it generates problems of its own. Aside from sounding self-satisfied, as it favors the subjective judgment of the same jurist/participant whom we keep asking to explain to us the rules of their game of jurisprudence, it seems to display a measure of contradiction by insisting on legal reasoning and then retracting it when it is no longer desirable. And ultimately, one must answer this question: How could it be true that (a) the ultimate foundation against which the Shari‘a should not deviate are the texts of the Qur'an and the Sunna, and that (b) these texts are insufficient to provide the basic skeleton of this same Shari‘a?

Unfortunately, there is no answer to this question, as far as I know. Yet, what is certain is that emphasis on the foundation (Qur'an, Sunna) goes beyond a solution to random problems, such as the one that engaged Ibn ‘Abidin here. No matter how steep the jurist in his *madhhab*, no matter how argumentative this jurist could become when claims of his *madhhab*'s faults are introduced, the jurist remains tied to the Qur'an and the Sunna of the Prophet as the foundation of his thinking. Not only that, many of these jurists are ready to turn the table upside-down when their interlocutors argue that the *madhhab*s are the perennial Shari‘a or even suggest that *madhhab* collective efforts could become a replacement for the foundational texts of the Qur'an and Sunna.

No one could argue with a good jurist that the difficulty and inaccessibility of the Qur'an and the Sunna are higher than the difficulty of the texts of the *madhhab*, which paved the way to access the Qur'an and the Sunna more easily. Muti‘i, whom I mentioned earlier (and who studied, among other *madhhab*s, the Hanafi school that has been accused of doing away with many texts), argued that to the layperson access to the Prophet's language remained easier than access to juristic language:

> How could a man with the least degree of reasonableness and fairness allege that an individual who is not equipped to understand a statement by the Prophet and apply it, such as the Prophet's statement that a prayer-leader (*imam*) is set up to be followed; hence when the *imam* utters the *takbir* [declaring the beginning of the prayer], you [the followers of the imam] should do the same, and when he kneels, you should follow him, and when he stands up after the kneeling, you should do as he did, and when he shouts "*sami*^{u}*-Allah*^{u}*-l*^{i}*-man-hamidah*," you should say "*rabbana-w*^{a}*-lak*^{a}*-l-hamd*'" and the *hadith* transmitted by 'UbadaIbn al-Samit: "the Prophet prohibited exchanging gold for gold, silver for silver, wheat for wheat, barley for barley, dates for dates, salt for salt—unless the exchanged are equal and the exchange immediate; if one increases [the exchanged] or asks for an increase, one has engaged in usury" and like texts—how could one allege that the person in question would not be able to understand these Sunna texts and their like, that only a qualified jurist (*mujtahid*) understands them, and then claim that a non-*mujtahid* understands the [technical] language of the *mujtahid*.[7]

Comparing the relative difficulty and ease of the Qur'an and the Sunna to that of juristic texts is part of a discourse that caused significant confusions in the *ijtihad* debates, especially in recent centuries. The emphasis on the foundational texts of the Qur'an and the Sunna and their persisting accessibility has become both an anchor for the discussion and a basis for misleading statements. If *ijtihad* is supposed to be, in essence, understanding the revelation and applying it in a given age, then the value of previous juristic debates is always in question. On the one hand, no reasonable person, certainly no serious participant in Islamic jurisprudence today, for example, could suggest that we must ignore a millennium of juristic production to "preserve" the foundation of the system. On the other hand, no one could allow previous juristic thinking to become a replacement for the Qur'an and the Sunna. Expressions of the different positions in the middle to avoid the unacceptable extremes often lead to confusion. It is precisely this confusion that besets what was to be known as the position of the Hanabila on the question of the future of *ijtihad*—rejecting the possibility of the end of *ijtihad*, that is-which was supported by many non-Hanbalis as we shall see, such as Ibn Daqiq al-'Id (d. 702/1302), Shatibi (d. 790/1388), and later Shawkani (d. 1250/1834).

One of Shawkani's arguments that the fatalist Ash'ari position (that the fatigue of the Shari'a was inevitable) has been misguided was based on the idea that this position may have fallen into the trap of "forgetting the foundation." Shawkani tackles the assertion of the absence in a given age of a qualified jurist or *mujtahid* (which as we said could mean someone of the caliber of Abu Hanifa, Shafi'i, and the founders of schools of law or someone who at least understands these founders' reasoning). There are multiple ways to argue for this assertion, one of which is to point to the loss of access to profound juristic understanding over time. This, Shawkani argues, is nonsense, because juristic knowledge has become even more organized, more accessible than ever before, as centuries passed. He states that commentaries on the Qur'an are now numerous and accessible, and the same can be said of knowledge of the Prophet's reports, which early generations used to have to travel to learn about. *Ijtihad*, he concludes, is now easier (*aysar*) rather than harder than before. Those who object are misguided, since they "have dedicated their energy and skill to 'emulating' and following other authorities and occupied themselves with knowledge far afield from the Qur'an and the Sunna and hence judged others to be incapable of that of which they were themselves incapable."[8]

Shawkani attempts to identify specific *mujtahid*s for every generation, which some assumed did not have a *mujtahid*. The question, again, is one of assessment, the judgment whether someone's juristic activities were a sufficient indication of this person's capacity for independent juristic thinking, whether this person identified himself with a school or decided to remain unaffiliated. This inevitable aporia—one must accept that assessing individuals will differ from one "judge" to another—leaves us where we started. *Ijtihad* will remain elastic, no matter what we do to fix its meaning. The attachment to the foundation will only produce confusions, unless all the employed terminologies are fully explained.

It is easy, on this account, to see how confusion could arise about what exactly is expected of someone who aims to reach the capacity for independent reasoning (*ijtihad*). However, the accessibility of a specific argument or the ability to engage each single text of juristic debates could never be seen as a criterion for reaching *ijtihad*. *Ijtihad* is a faculty by which a participant in jurisprudence understands juristic positions and converses with them based on principles that are themselves not simply derived from any school of law. This means that an intelligent person may study Islamic jurisprudence for a long time and still fail to be a participant in it, given his or her focus, his or her emphasis on trying to understand and evaluate arguments from outside, having relinquished the responsibility to engage in evaluating these arguments for himself/herself. This may be a subtle or obvious point, depending on one's understanding of the nature of Islamic legal reasoning.

Ijtihad and the *Madhhab*

To understand *ijtihad* in the language of legal theorists, one must think of it as an activity that was available to all generations of Muslims before and after the founding of *madhhabs*, both followed and extinct. As a term, *ijtihad* appeared at a certain moment in history, was popularized among a certain group, and denoted the activity of working toward an informed opinion. But the historical progression of the term itself is irrelevant to understanding the fatigue of the Shari'a as the absence of *mujtahids*. It is also irrelevant to understanding the use of the term in the language of Sunni legal theorists, by and large. How would someone who insists on the period-strict standard understand a term like "*ijtihad al-sahaba*" or the *ijtihad* of the companions?

It may have been anachronistic of Ibn Taymiyya or other medieval jurists to use that term *ijtihad al-sahaba*. But this is not an issue for our inquiry. Anachronism is a problem because it causes people to confuse the meanings of words by letting them travel backward and forward in time, but insisting on strict periodization of terminology is even more problematic here, because it prevents us from understanding what is going on in juristic debates. It is in fact nonsensical to impose our modern, academic fear of anachronism (which has become something of an equivalent to judizing before an inquisition panel) on a discussion by Muslim jurists who did not employ an ideal version of the term *ijtihad* to a moment before it came to indicate an activity within a *madhhab*.

The pseudoargument from caution, that lack of records of comprehensive systems before the four schools and bad recording of extinct *madhhabs* such as those of Awza'i (d. 157/774) and Ibn Abi Layla (d. 148/765), muddies the water further. One does not need to generalize about the companions' era from the examples one finds documented, and this is the sense in which one might understand Juwayni's report of a consensus that no *madhhab* for the companions should be followed. But a series of skeptical stances about everything one could learn about the first centuries of Islamic legal history would likely be replaced by an alternative narrative drawn from the imagination of the skeptic. It will be difficult, for example, to understand how the followed *madhhabs* evolved, and how a discussion of consensuses from the time of the companions was even possible without some concessions to the "loose" usage of terminology by the legal theorists.

There is a strong similarity between pre- and post-*madhhab ijtihad*, even if the detailed circumstances of each one of these two stages are very different. One of two mistakes is often made here: (1) insisting on the difference to the exclusion of similarities, or (2) conflating the two. Acknowledging the similarity has many advantages; for one thing, it helps us understand the new arguments about the survival of the Shari'a despite the end of the *madhhabs* by pointing to the old experience of pre-*madhhab ijtihad*.

One of the disadvantages of going too far in the direction of "inferences" is a degree of comfort with assertions of what the companions' juristic activities were like from their reported views here and there, an equivalent to the behavior of salafi optimists who believe that all you need in understanding the Sunna is to figure out *hadith* criticism methods. (It cannot be denied, however, that this optimism played a positive role in an important revival in *hadith* studies and in fact in enlarging the study of companions-history too. But I also find more than one disadvantage in lacking all historical sensibility.) What I am after here is what may be called "under-historicizing" and "overhistoricizing." In one case, the presumed persistence of themes prevents any meaningful understanding of these themes. In the other case, the degree to which an idea or a practice changes as it moves from one era to another might be so insignificant in the big picture that insisting on the distinction leads to distorting as opposed to clarifying what happened.

A conversation with both preschool and postschool juristic thinking is thus inevitable, and there is room for disagreement about how it can be done. Zarkashi (d. 794/1392) discusses the condition of "*nazar*" in a *mujtahid*—the ability to evaluate arguments—by cautioning that this condition may be misunderstood and made into a tool to simply perpetuate engagement with a given school or *madhhab* as opposed to encouraging understanding. Guided by insights from Ibn Daqiq al-'Id (d. 702/1302), Zarkashi argues that Ghazali's (d. 505/1111) famous stipulation of knowledge of (Greek) logic as a prerequisite for *ijtihad* widens the circle of conditions for *ijtihad* without sufficient basis, since we know that early *mujtahids* did not engage in Greek logic yet were able to perform their duty of answering all questions of how to characterize behavior as acceptable or unacceptable, desirable or otherwise.[9] The capacity for reasoning is what is required here. On the linguistic tools needed for *ijtihad*, Ibn Daqiq al-'Id insists on a similar distinction between knowledge of the language of the Arabs, where one is justified to insist on a high standard of scrutiny for the *mujtahid*, and knowledge of language research and inquiries that may border on philosophizing about language.[10]

The knowledge that allows someone to be able to answer every question is presumed not to exist. Original *mujtahids* such as Malik and Shafi'i themselves either hesitated or refrained from answering some questions. Here one encounters the well-trodden edict: only the insane could answer all questions given to him (*man afta f*^{i} *kull*^{i} *ma su'il*^{a} *'anh*^{u} *f*^{a} *huw*^{a} *majnun*).[11] As we discussed in the previous chapter, lacunae in any juristic systems do not in themselves indicate the failure of this system to grow into its "silent" areas, as long as the system is latently functioning in these areas, that is, latent with principles that can immediately be applied to these areas.

Relativity in *Ijtihad* and the Fatigue of the Shari'a

Does this divine Shari'a allow any degree of relativity in *ijtihad*? How could a divine Shari'a allow that? The answer to the question of whether the Shari'a accommodates a degree of "relativity" must be obvious enough to those who think that God's law could not be relative in any sense (i.e., that it is obviously not possible to reconcile relativity and the Shari'a). This simple understanding, however, is far from useful or illuminating. A Muslim jurist and legal theorist would need something like *ijtihad*-relativity to understand the life of the Shari'a in the world throughout its history.

The definition of *fiqh* itself sets the tone for any discussion of this issue. *Fiqh* is a type of "knowledge" (*'ilm*), and knowledge, unqualified, is akin to certainty rather than probability, but the legal propositions of *fiqh* are of only probable value; thus, what elevates *fiqh* to the level of knowledge is only the certainty that one must follow what is probable, because it is the best available among all available alternatives. Even on this abstract level, the Shari'a, with the exception of the thin area of consensus, could not consist of anything more than *probability* that *must* be followed.

These are the degrees of access to knowledge in this scheme:

1. *'Ilm* proper (certainty; knowledge) enjoys both certainty and conformity with the truth. For example, my judgment that my (white) shirt is white qualifies as *'ilm* or knowledge.
2. *Zann* (correct judgment by probability) enjoys conformity to the truth but not certainty. For example, my judgment that my white shirt is probably white is *zann*.
3. *Shakk* (suspending judgment)—I have no idea what the color of the shirt is. This happens in the case of conflicting, equal evidence as opposed to no evidence at all.
4. *Wahm* (judging incorrectly based on probability)—I think that the shirt is yellow, when it is really white.
5. *Jahl* (judging incorrectly while being certain; ignorance)—I am sure the shirt is yellow, when it is indeed white. There are qualifications for *jahl* that divide it into two categories, one being simple ignorance

or *jahl basit* (I have no idea about the color of the shirt, e.g., I do not even know what it is like) and the other is complex ignorance or *jahl murakkab*, which is this class—that is, judging incorrectly with certainty.

Fiqh may be based on probability, but does this establish that the *ijtihad* of the Shari'a bears relativity? Many will assert that Shari'a and *fiqh* are not identical. Moreover, the uncertainty of rulings does not mean that they are relative. Finally, consensus makes some of the rulings permanent and definite. Let me take these three objections, one at a time.

Shari'a and *fiqh* are indeed not identical, and the (good) attempts at fully distinguishing them reflect their complex relationship. In certain contexts, the two terms are indeed interchangeable, especially when adjectival forms are applied. *Al-hukm al-shar'i* and *al-hukm al-fiqhi* (*shar'i* or *fiqhi* ruling) can mean the same thing. When they are used to indicate different things, they still do not indicate distinct realms, only overlapping ones. For example, *fiqhi* maxims or *al-qawa'id al-fiqhiyya* belong in the realm of generalizations from opinions and doctrines of a given school or *madhhab*. *Al-qawa'id al-shar'iyya* or *Shar'i* principles are less clear. It could denote timeless principles such as preferring a practice proven to descend from the Prophet to another that was agreed on by later generations, even while acknowledging that there may be arguments to adopt the later practice. Sometimes the distinction between clusters such as *al-qawa'id al-fiqhiyya* and *al-qawa'id al-shar'iyya* benefits from the flexibility of the term *al-qawa'id*, which could mean maxims, foundations, principles, among other possibilities. My point is that a simple, conceptual distinction between Shari'a and *fiqh* is not likely to be successful, unless one may also decide to impose a standard distinction among *al-qawa'id al-shar'iyya, qawa'id al-shari'a,* and *qawa'id al-shar'*. And the more relevant point here is that the Shari'a, in practice, could not fully get out of the probable (*zanni*) character of *fiqh*.

As for the objection that uncertainty does not lead to relativity, again, yes and no; mostly no. The disagreement among jurists and the practical presumption of both the correctness of all for the purposes of the lay populations and correctness of only one for the jurist who is involved in the search for God's law lead to practical relativism. True, a judge's decision creates practical certainty and leads to no further "juristic" consideration of the matter for the purpose of adjudication, and I will address this in a second. But this is evidence of juristic relativism, if you will, rather than the opposite.

Consensus, adding to its limited realm, may be seen mostly as a coincidence of agreement on readings of a host of texts of relevance to a given issue. The consensuses that survive are based on foundational principles that new generations of jurists could not do without. But this is outside of the realm of the exercise of lawmaking, strictly speaking. Consensus signifies what is shared by all jurists, not the details of the Shari'a. The Shari'a, the same divine Shari'a, is a man-made Shari'a, despite what the rhetoric of God-made and man-made laws might lead some to believe. While their language sometimes gives the impression that they may have felt inspired in their juristic research, major medieval jurists did not believe their work was the outcome of direct "inspirations"—unlike Ibn 'Arabi (d. 638/1240), who believed that when he wrote his *Futuhat*, he was led to say certain things or that his hand was led to write certain things. *Ilham* or inspiration-based judgment is practically rejected as a source of law among Sunni legal theorists. Shari'a *ijtihad* is indeed as relativistic as *fiqh* is.

There is a disagreement as to whether the correct view in a given issue is one or many, with distinctions among theological questions and questions of the essential principles (*usul*) from practical issues asserted.[12] Focusing on practical issues, disagreement persists as to whether those disagreeing are all correct or only one is correct. An assertion of the correctness of one's view (while acknowledging others' possible share in the truth) governs the *practice* of *ijtihad*. In his *Nusrat al-Qawlayn*, for example, Ibn al-Qass (d. 335/946) argues that allowing opposed opinions to be considered all "correct" in one and the same situation might lead to allowing one woman to be legally married to three men (based on a Maliki *fatwa* and two Hanafi court decisions in an example he offers) or allowing two people to have the right to exact retaliation from the other and be both within their legal rights.[13] (Yes, Ibn al-Qass's assertion here may have to do with him being a follower of Shafi'i, but his basic point appeals to a trans-*madhhab* principle.) Based on this, no one should argue that the Prophet's statement that different jurists may receive rewards for their effort is an indication that opposed views could all be correct.[14]

At any rate, practical certainty is presumed in a court decision, which prevents us from revoking it, but this certainty stems from the decision's judicial nature—the fact that it supports claims to a physical property or to fatherhood or the like. However, the main argument against revoking a judicial decision confirms its epistemic insufficiency; the argument being that since the revocation can be further revoked and so forth, the first decision must stand. That is, the decision should stand because neither this decision nor any alternative could be deemed superior after a comparison. This confirms that, when certainty is unavailable, probability replaces it as the desired standard. In sum, these two features (multiplicity in correctness and practical insistence on one correct view) show that denying relativity by clinging to the divine source of the Shari'a is not compelling.

One must also remember that the Shari'a manifests itself in real life, which is naturally full of contingencies. Difference in the circumstances attached to a given question turns a correct answer to it irrelevant when addressing what appears to be, but only appears to be, the same question. The apparent similarity between two questions could be denied if the customs and social standards of relevance to the questions under consideration differ. Knowledge of custom and social standards is hence part of the knowledge of the correct law.

In this context, one may understand the arguments for and against the disappearance of juristic authority as engaging the inevitable qualities of contingency and relativity. The arguments presented by the Mu'tazili theologian Ka'bi and by Hanbali legal theorists for rejecting the proposition of the fatigue of the Shari'a adduce God's fairness among his creatures, which necessitates that He offer them a baseline of access to knowledge of Him and how to worship Him, thus contradicting the fading away of the Shari'a. Dissenting with these positions, the (Ash'ari) majority accepts the fatigue of the Shari'a as a possibility with nothing to contradict it; it does not contradict God's justice to leave no guidance for humanity (He will treat them fairly, anyway). When the Shari'a experiences fatigue, people are not expected to do what is impossible, that is, to seek the advice of jurists who do not exist. They should only do their best, and this is all that is required of them.

Ijtihad is a tool to generate knowledge of the categories of human actions. This tool, therefore, is a prerequisite to the availability of the practical knowledge of the Shari'a as guidance for human behavior. The difficulty of judging *ijtihad* from the outside, that is, by nonpracticing jurists, is a formidable obstacle in the path of any death-of-the-Shari'a assertion.

Part II

Jurists and Nonjurists

A virtual debate among Mu'tazilis, Ash'aris, and Hanbalis on the fatigue of the Shari'a determines the nature and parameters of the issue in pre-modern times.

Chapter 4

Suppose We Forgot the Law

The fourth Islamic century (roughly the tenth of the Common Era) opened with scattered arguments about the destiny of the Shari'a. By the end of the fifth century (eleventh CE), three distinct positions on the subject have been formed. These same three positions will dominate the debate until its virtual end (in its traditional phase) in the 1250/1830s [As I said, I am thinking here of Hasan al-'Attar's (d. 1250/1835) supercommentary on Mahalli's (d. 856/1453) commentary on Subki's (d. 771/1369) *Jam' al-Jawami'*], and a new debate, or a new phase of the debate, slightly overlapping with the old one, championed by Shawkani (d. 1250/1834) began. What happened between the beginning of the fourth/tenth and the end of the fifth/eleventh centuries that caused the fatigue of the Shari'a debate to evolve in this way?

In the beginning, there were two views on the subject. One, later to be systematized and stated as the view of Ash'ari theologians and legal theorists, held that there was neither a rational nor a textual basis for asserting the Shari'a's eternal vigor. In other words, on this view, the Shari'a could indeed experience fatigue. This view may arguably be called the anti-Mu'tazili view, if one considers Mu'tazili thinking responsible for raising the question of the beginning and end of the Shari'a first [although there are many good reasons to be unsure about the exact starting point; and a perusal of (the Shafi'i Mu'tazili) Abu al-Husayn al-Basri's (d. 436/1044) *Mu'tamad* raises questions about any assertion that this was an issue Mu'tazili theologians and legal theorists strongly emphasized). Shi'i (especially Isma'ili) thinking in the fourth/tenth century may have exerted some influence on bringing the issue of the "end of time" to the fore. But it was Abu al-Ma'ali al-Juwayni (d. 478/1085) who provided the most influential articulation of the Ash'ari (or anti-Mu'tazili) view. Somewhat contemporaneously with that, a Hanbali view, ultimately embracing the Mu'tazili conclusion with something like the opposite of its theological foundation, came to be articulated. This was provided by authors such as Abu al-Khattab al-Kalwadhani (d. 511/1116) in his *Tamhid.*

Juwayni's choice of Ka'bi (d. 319/931) as an interlocutor—Ka'bi being a Mu'tazili who argued against the fatigue idea—should not detain us for long. Ka'bi is credited with the extreme view that God, being bound to do what is best for His creation (*wujub al-aslah*), will not allow the fatigue of the Shari'a, just as he never allowed the fatigue of previous *shara'i'* (revelations and divine laws) before He revealed His last message. This view denies that human history has ever experienced a lapse of God's revelation and laws. It bears reflection whether this view, in this form, may be traced back to an earlier generation of Mu'tazilis. But this could also take us further afield and would generate more controversy than would be helpful in illuminating the concrete debate on the life and destiny of the Shari'a. A few remarks will, therefore, suffice.

Khayyat's (d. 299/912) *Intisar* suggests connections between the question of the fatigue of the Shari'a and other issues, which shows the Shi'i relevance to this debate from an early date. These issues include the question of "who conveys the divine law" and "whether this conveyer must be infallible." The Rafida (Shi'is), Khayyat reports, insist that the conveyer of God's message must be an infallible *imam* (thus lowly *mujtahids* are not sufficient), while Hisham al-Fuwati (d. 217/833) and Abu al-Hudhayl al-'Allaf (d. 235/849) held that God will not deprive the world of pious conveyers of His guidance. These pious individuals' conveyance of God's message is a sufficient basis for their contemporaries' responsibility to follow His guidance—regardless of whether these pious conveyers are identifiable to all (people) to be such conveyers.[1]

The same Abu al-Hudhayl al-'Allaf (d. 235/849) is credited with what was (later) considered by Ash'aris a standard Mu'tazili view—that before revelation, the unaided human reason is sufficient basis for ethical and religious responsibility. Shahrastani (d. 547/1153) lists this in his *Milal* as the seventh of ten principles or doctrines, which distinguished 'Allaf from other fellow theologians. This involves his insistence that reflection before revelation leads to knowledge of God, that those who fail to reach that recognition deserve punishment, and that through the same unaided human reason, one should be able to (independently of any revelation) identify good and evil actions and qualities, such as lying and injustice.[2]

If one considers the question of God's guidance and temporal authority over the human population in a society, one may consider the Shi'i position as lying at the center amid multiple possible extremes. The Shi'is insisted on an infallible imam to solve the problem of the availability of divine justice through a representative of God's divine revelation. This insistence on the infallible imam could be contradicted in different ways. One might argue, as the two aforementioned Mu'tazilis (Fuwati and 'Allaf) did, that infallible conveyers of God's message are not necessary, as it seems that most of the time people lived without prophets; only in certain moments and places were prophets available. If prophets were the only path to knowledge of God and good and evil, this would lead us to the absurd conclusion that God's guidance was unavailable in the majority of human history. This is clearly irreconcilable with God's justice. Against this view, and still in rejection of the Shi'i theory, one may argue that these instances of the absence of prophets have occurred but do not contradict God's justice, since one may still believe that when these lapses happened, they were not complete, and traces of early revelations could be accessed. Accordingly, one must not see these lapses as an indication of the death of revelation—death and illness are not the same thing.

The latter position, which might appeal to (jurists' or peoples') memory of previous divine revelations as a basis for God's guidance, did not seem to square easily with these famous Mu'tazilis' views and was hence not deemed attractive. The emphasis on the survival of reason-based knowledge and the availability of reason-based norms can be found in much Mu'tazili literature. Other statements by Mu'tazili writers establish the sense that each age has its own guides and leaders. The language of these ideas is less than indicative of how these Mu'tazilis would attend to our specific question. Take, for example, an assertion by Jahiz (d. 252/866) that every age has always had its scholars who distinguished wisdom from "that which mixes with, and is hence mistaken for, wisdom," and authored for subsequent generations works in different branches of knowledge and arts (a thought that will be echoed by the Hanbali Abu Ya'la al-Farra' (d. 458/1066) as we will see in chapter six).[3] This may or may not be taken as a commitment on the part of Jahiz to the view that God's guidance will never experience any lapses in the world, regardless of historical evidence of the fluctuation of people's attachment to what may be seen as God's guidance, and regardless of the rise and fall of the power and following commanded by ideas and authorities (which could occur even within the span of one generation).

In fact, Jahiz seems to accept the view that knowledge will dwindle with time, and that this will be a function of people's laziness, rather than any "natural" or supernatural cause. Even in his time, there were signs of lost knowledge, and common perceptions and beliefs that are contradicted by the views and beliefs of the *salaf* or early generations. At the end of time, ignorance will prevail, it seems. It is known that leading scholars will not survive until the end of time (*ila akhir al-zaman*) and that those who will succeed them will not represent sufficient and adequate replacement for the earlier ones (*man yaji*[u] *ba'dahum la yaqum*[u] *maqamahum*).[4] In the same treatise, Jahiz had proposed that at the end of time people would be busy about *daqiq al-kalam* (abstract epistemological questions) without mastering *jalil al-kalam* (detailed knowledge),[5] which leads him to reiterate the lamentation of the gradual loss of knowledge.

The one willing to deny that these lapses ever occurred was Ka'bi. As his views are reported by others in this debate (most of his writings are not extant), Ka'bi appears in the writings of Ash'ari theologians and legal theorists not as a real philosopher or theologian, but almost as an ideal straw-man, or worse, as the butt of jokes, and with this unfortunate status, his memory survives among Ash'aris for the subsequent millennium.

In this debate, Ka'bi sets himself up for criticism by holding (a) the view that God's revelations and laws never experience fatigue in the sense of disappearance with no replacement, and (b) explaining this by God's commitment to doing what is best (*aslah*). Each one of these invites refutation, and the result was a virtual fest of polemics, which endured for a long time. Juwayni outlined the basic flaws in Ka'bi's position on the fatigue question and then shifted the discussion to "what to do" when divine guidance is in short supply.

When Juwayni addresses pre-Muhammadan revelations, he notes that even according to some of the Mu'tazila, these revelations could and indeed did experience fatigue. Again, Ka'bi here stands with less than full backing by other Mu'tazilis. He believes in what he calls the divine duty of doing what is best for people (*ri'ayat al-aslah*), adding that if people accepted the path of their shari'a, then it is best for God to let this shari'a survive. Its fatigue would be a cause for deviation, which is the opposite of what is best, *al-aslah*. Juwayni wonders whether other advantages and benefits may be drawn from letting the Shari'a experience fatigue, such as allowing people to use their own "reason" to learn about their duties and obligations.

As for the final revelation (*shari'atina*), its fatigue would be denied by those who denied the fatigue of any previous shari'a. Those who disagreed about the destiny of previous revelations disagreed about this one, since some of them believed that they were all the same, that is, they all undergo fatigue, but some of them said this one was different. The distinction is based on the fallacious notion that since this Shari'a is the last one, its fatigue would create a gap (of no-guidance) at the tail of our world and before the end of time. If the argument here is that gaps simply do not occur at the tail of any divine shari'a, whether or not it is followed by another, those who accepted the fatigue of previous shari'as would disagree. But if the argument assumes that a gap at the end of the world would be qualitatively different from any gap that may have occurred historically between any two previous shari'as, this distinction needs to be explained (and it could not be explained). A person living during the gap between two shari'as and one living between the last Shari'a and the end of time have the same challenge.[6] Therefore, one can only believe that all revelations face the same destiny—they all survive or all experience fatigue.

In the absence of the Shari'a, one is led to either holding that human responsibility ceases to exist or that it is founded on something else. If human responsibility remains despite the absence of the Shari'a, a Mu'tazili has an easier time, since a Mu'tazili believes that "human reason" may serve as a basis for norms, binding norms that lead to reward and punishment on the Final Day.

Reason, *Ijtihad*; Reward and Punishment

The Mu'tazili position would be unfairly treated if it is left with this lukewarm representation, especially that the aforementioned representation is partly derived from the refutation of this position. As I said in the introduction, there are many points of strength in the Mu'tazili view. The "comical" Ka'bi and other Mu'tazilis would not be able to defend themselves if we leave this task to their refuters, whether these be Juwayni or others. To be sure, Ash'aris believed that Mu'tazilis were formidable adversaries, and Ka'bi (Abul-Qasim al-Balkhi) was praised for his amazing intellect and grasp of issues by his enemies in the debate. One might even say that it is because of his particular achievement that he was attacked and made into a joke. The relationship between the strength of a view and opposition to it is indeed often a direct rather than an inverse relationship.

And as I showed in chapter two, each position is best explained by "related" positions. In the remainder of this chapter, I will attempt to address these related positions that make sense of the Mu'tazili theory on the fatigue question rather than stress its weaknesses. In this respect, the Shafi'i Mu'tazili legal theorist Abu al-Husayn al-Basri presents himself as a good resource.

Basri's teacher 'Abd al-Jabbar (d. 415/1025) has argued before him that both prophets and guides/imams/sovereigns may be absent in certain generations[7] and that *fatra* (absence in authority) has been established by the Qur'an and other sources (*qad thabat^a bi-l-Qur'an^i wa ghayrihi ^{a}l-fatrat^u bayn^a al-rusul*).[8] Those who insist on the availability of the *Imam* as a sign of God's constant guidance to humans do indeed try to establish something that could not be established, since humans could live without messengers (*yajuz^u khuluww^u al-mukallafin^a min^a a'-rusul*), and if imams are representatives of these messengers, their absence could *a fortiori* be established.

Basri came to the scene with a major contribution to legal theory. His *Mu'tamad* raises multiple issues surrounding *ijtihad*, the tool to guarantee survival and vigor for the Shari'a, which the Ash'aris made into the essence of the question of the fatigue of the final revelation. Basri's conceptualization of *ijtihad* emphasizes the flexibility of the process of reflection about both (a) conclusions about norms and (b) their foundation. In essence, a qualified jurist could reconsider any inherited doctrine or reasoning with very few restrictions. Note that Basri was known to be a Shafi'i, but he seems to assume no contradiction between his Mu'tazili and Shafi'i affiliations. The *furu'* rulings he mentions in his *usul* are clearly influenced by Shafi'i's rulings and reasoning, but he does not set out to defend many practical juristic doctrines in detail.

In Basri's scheme of *usul al-fiqh*, reason seems to hold full sovereignty before revelation. The categories accepted by reason even survive after the revelation is given, since the latter does not contradict the former in its broad categories. The revelation itself must be accepted based on principles provided from reason—hence the wisdom of God justifies accepting His Revelation, and the infallibility of the Prophet and the Muslim community as a whole justify submission to their rule.[9]

Basri's understanding of *ijtihad* is particularly thrown into relief in his discussion of the nature of consensus. Consensus is an agreement of jurists, which ought to be rare. Why does it even happen at all? It could be because there is only really one possible reading of the foundational texts of the Qur'an and the Sunna in some cases. Some legal theorists suggest that consensus may be an indication of a missing text, a statement by the Prophet Muhammad that reached earlier generations and could not hustle its way to later generations. But why should a coincidence of views exist; why should there be an agreement despite the possibility of disagreement, and despite the presence of reasonable readings of the foundational texts and multiple "good arguments" for these? Could consensus be founded on an agreement on argument? In other words, could *ijtihad* be the basis of consensus?

The answer is "yes." Basri allows *ijtihad* to be the basis of consensus. The mystery of previous generations' agreement is thus resolved, not as caused by lost revelation, as some legal theorists argue, but by an agreement of the minds.[10] This serves as a demystification of consensus, believed to be an infallible source of law by later legal theorists, whether it is based on the missing texts or on a blessing by which God endowed this final nation, which makes it possible for some of them, but never all, to get it wrong in any particular issue.

Basri's scheme is also complemented with other important doctrines. No one should restrict later generations to either the reasoning or the conclusions of previous generations of scholars. If we are able to do that, we should be able to force anyone who agrees with Shafi'i in one case to agree with him in all of his opinions. This is untenable (there is indeed a consensus against such a claim).[11]

Based on reason, Basri argues that God asks us to follow *ijtihad* as we seek knowledge of how to worship Him correctly. God could have asked all prophets to make the very exercise of reasoning (*qiyas* and *ijtihad*) the foundation of their religious commitments (*ta'abbud*). But God asks us to worship him based on "texts" sometimes, and based on analogy in other times. Why should free analogical thinking and other forms of reasoning not be available to the prophets themselves, Basri asks? Some argue that this is because the prophet is different; he is a vessel for God's knowledge, and hence should not simply act like another agent in search of guidance, such as ourselves. This is dismissed with an assertion of the similarity between prophets and nonprophets as *mukallaf*s, humans with responsibilities toward God who essentially follow a search for God's guidance.[12]

It must be true, then, that God could have asked any prophet to devise laws based on his own reasoning from a limited foundation (or perhaps from the innate capacity of reason itself). We know He did not do that; so, why should believing in this assertion matter? Because this is ultimately the basis of all commitments—period. Even if one did not adhere to the doctrine of God's duty to do what is best, or the idea that the world is indeed perfect (because God's way is the perfect way), one may still believe that human reason will provide a rescue from error were a certain revelation to wither away.

This level of clarity about how *ijtihad* occurs and its capacity to create norms (nay, something close to universal norms) presents a fresh view of the meaning of the question of the fatigue of divine revelations. The burden of proof is now firmly placed on the shoulder of an adversary who insists that humans are likely to lose this capacity to live by norms that basically derive at least partly from their human reason, when this happens through *ijtihad* all the time. The analogies between the position of a prophet and a nonprophet powerfully limit all attempts to go back to employing the mystery of revelation to undo the complex picture that demands of humans to think as humans constantly—whether to generate reasoned agreements or reasoned disagreements. The argument against Basri, it seems, must be that humans could simply lose their humanity, or this aspect of it anyway, and could hence cease to have any success in engaging with the world to the extent they have thus far.

For all Mu'tazilis, God does not abandon his duty of justice—these are the people of *'adl*, God's *'adl* to be specific. It does not necessarily follow, however, that reason-based norms create responsibilities that are identical with those norms known by the aid of divine revelation. Reason-only norms may simply invoke praise for those who observe them and place blame on to those who disobey them, but this does not have to be equal with the same reward or punishment of which God's revelation speaks. After all, those who have never heard of the revelation could not be expected to bear any responsibility with regard to its content, whether they accepted the responsibility and deserved to be rewarded for that or rejected it and incurred divine punishment for their rejection.

The question of what type of reward or punishment results from these binding norms is secondary, compared to the question of reason's capacity to engage in generating norms, with and without revelation. Ibn 'Ashur (d. 1393/1973) makes this point in his commentary on Qarafi (d. 685/1284). He states that a Mu'tazili could, without contradiction, deny any commitment to the view that God's punishment is deserved by the failure to live in accord with *tahsin* and *taqbih*, the evaluation of behavior based on bare reason. A Mu'tazili who believes that value judgments can be issued without the benefit of revelation does in fact accept that knowledge of heavenly reward and punishment is given through divine revelation and not from the unaided reason. Hence this Mu'tazili may hold any belief about the type of reward and praise or reproach and blame to be deserved for following or ignoring the norms of the unaided reason, so long as these are not exactly the same as those spoken of in this divine revelation, lest this be taken as an imposition of impossible tasks (*taklif ma la yutaq*)[13] on humanity, that is, the task of learning the content of the revelation that was simply unavailable.[14]

One must finally distinguish different types of Mu'tazilis (and even different types of early Mu'tazilis) as regards their interest in the details of the questions of reason's rule before and after revelation. Some early Mu'tazilis who had what may be called a theological orientation and those who may have had a literary orientation engaged in this question differently, and their modes of expression varied. All these views and expressions would still differ from the treatment of a Shafi'i, such as Basri, who understood the application of what is good or bad in the judgment of reason (*hasan, qabih*) in terms of legal categories—the obligatory, the recommended, the reprehensible, and the prohibited. Different again is the Zaydi Abu Talib Yahya Ibn al-Husayn Ibn Harun (d. 424/1033), who provided a crisp presentation of *tahsin* and *taqbih* in his [supposed commentary on Ibn Khallad and Jubba'i's (d. 321/933)] theology,[15] and who by the way does not provide a satisfying path as to how to address the question of *futur al-shara'i'*.

Later Shi'i Mu'tazilis, who identify *'aql* as a source of law with the Qur'an, Sunna, and consensus, also offer a different flavor (even someone such as al-Hakim al-Jashmi (d. 494/1101),[16] who was said to have started as a Hanafi and ended as a Zaydi, can be separated from those before and after him). These Mu'tazilis could all polemicize against the Ash'aris, accusing them, for example, of failing to recognize the terms *husn* and *qubh* outside of their revelation-based meaning and hence could never debate these terms outside of the context of revelation.[17] Be that as it may, the Mu'tazili view distilled from these sources is that reason can devise categories for actions before and after revelation, and that *tahsin* and *taqbih* will always be available, whether jurists are around of not.

God's Duties and Those of Humans

To complete the picture, one must also remember that while thinking of the Mu'tazili view in this subject, the issue of God's duties should never be marginalized in this or related debates. The Mu'tazili master commentator Zamakhshari (d. 538/1144) spoke of God's responsibility to provide guidance for His creation through accessible, clear instructions and laws. Zamakhshari comments on the Qur'anic verse 92/12, where it is asserted "Indeed, guidance is incumbent upon Us" by saying: "guidance to the truth is a duty for Us, [which is fulfilled] by establishing guiding indicators and clarifying the law" (*inn^{a} al-irshad^{a} ila ^{a}l-haqq^{i} wajib^{un} 'alayna binasb^{i} ^{ad}-dala'il^{i} wa bayan^{i} al-shara'i'*).

The Qur'an thus supports the notion that God has duties, the main difference between these duties and those of humans being that God's duties are self-imposed. There are other significant disanalogies between divine and human duties, nevertheless, as Zamakhshari's discussion of "worldly pain" shows,[18] but this again will take us far afield.

The Mu'tazili Position

Despite the scantiness of the evidence, which will encourage many to argue for suspending judgment, one could understand a Mu'tazili view on the subject. We certainly have the option of remaining silent, but this reflects a higher desire to win arguments with contemporaries than a desire to make sense of the position that may have provoked the whole fatigue debate. I have operated in the realm of "*lazim al-madhhab*," that is, inferences of positions from known positions, rather than explicitly stated positions, but this is all I could find. I hope this does not invite predictable debates about whether it would be better to say nothing here, but I welcome "better" ways of understanding the Mu'tazili position in this and related inquiries.

Ka'bi's rejection of *fatra* and his obscure view of "what is best" do not seem to be echoed by many Mu'tazilis. But you do not need to agree with Ka'bi on these tenets to be a Mu'tazili; nor do you need to agree with him to hold a reason-based solution to the question of how to deal with the end of access to revelation. The essence of a Mu'tazili position that is based on *tahsin* and *taqbih* is a version of the acceptance of human responsibility as a constant, as the degree of access to divine revelation varied.

Though expressed differently by different philosophers and theologians, the Mu'tazili position can thus be restated as an expression of the triviality of the fatigue question. The fatigue of the Shari'a, defined as the absence of jurists, is nothing other than the loss of a profession; our capacity to learn about good norms is a different matter. The latter is always available because of God's justice, and in practice, lack of jurists who teach the norms in certain ways takes us back to something of an original position (parallels with Rawls's not intended), where we are all naturally responsible for our own actions, not only acting on the good norms given to us, but also identifying what is good to begin with. This is said without any assumption that humans will have been created equal in their capacity to identify these norms; only that humanity is overall charged with this responsibility and cannot be relieved of it.

An insistence that the Shari'a can never experience fatigue should be understood in these terms. The Baghdadi school, and notably Abu al-Qasim al-Balkhi or al-Ka'bi, did not mean to offer a simple prediction of the future that the profession of jurists will never die. This question in his time was hardly as meaningful as it has subsequently become. Many in his age and after him may have harbored a sense that this profession was not going in the right direction from the start; that it started on the wrong foot. But this, in an important sense, was not an issue. The only real challenge to God's justice was an absence of the sources of norms, one of which being the human intellect, which is unimaginable. Changes in human history are ultimately trivial; they can't touch what matters; they cannot affect God's justice.

Many Mu'tazilis take for granted that God's last revelation has been available and that the role of reason was to engage this revelation rather than reject it or subvert it. Many late Mu'tazilis, who were also Shi'is of different types, take *'aql*/reason to be a source of the divine law itself. The question of the lack of access to divine norms may not have been taken seriously by many of them, and the question can indeed be averted in several clever ways. But a true Mu'tazili is bound to apply the doctrine of *tahsin* and *taqbih* to the question of *futur al-shari'a*, which will distinguish their answer from an Ash'ari counterpart. *Suppose we forgot the law*—a Mu'tazili is asked. The answer would likely be: There is no such thing as forgetting to reason, and reason is a source of God's law all the time.

The issue of what question is raised is behind much of the disagreement about what is attributed to Mu'tazilis or others, whether this attribution is gained through the writings of Ash'ari theologians and legal theorists or through a direct consideration of the Mu'tazilis themselves. One could go from simply copying Ash'ari texts in their descriptions of Mu'tazili views to being certain that Ash'aris have been wrong, and neither position is commendable. 'Abd al-'Azim al-Dib (d. 1431/2010) says that the majority of legal theorists (*mu'zam al-usuliyyin*, who are Ash'aris, I add) claimed that Mu'tazilis believed that "reason" was a source of norms. After consulting the original books of Mu'tazilis, he added, he could not find that to be true in this general form (*bi-hadha* *a*l-*itlaq*); rather he could find the Mu'tazila to have answered the question of the authority of the unaided reason before divine revelations, but after these revelations, norms are derived from God only (*la hukm*[a] *illa lillah*), which is the belief of all Muslims.[19] I agree with Dib that there are ambiguities in the Mu'tazili position (and indeed am prepared to negate a simple Mu'tazili position). But on whether the Mu'tazili position could be seen as indistinct from the Ash'ari theologians, since all Muslims must believe the same thing about reason's authority at any moment after the divine revelation, there may be room for disagreement with Shaykh Dib here. (The disagreement may never be fully resoled or clarified, since Dib already passed away.)

Ibn Rushd

Non-Mu'tazili legal theorists would agree that prophets are needed as a means of conveying God's message to humans, and hence prophecy can be established by reason. This is an important foundation for any subsequent discussion of the deterioration of prophetic teachings. What if a philosopher, who is also a legal theorist, does not believe that prophecy is established by reason in the first place? Here there is a lesson that Ibn Rushd's case teaches.

Ibn Rushd took theologians to task for trying to pass off some "statements" as arguments to establish the necessity of prophecy. He then argues that the only foundation for establishing prophecy consists in the historical records of prophets, and the only test to distinguish true from false prophets are their success or failure to provide teachings and laws that survive the test of time. I shall reproduce the first part of this view where Ibn Rushd demonstrates that there is no argument for the necessity of prophets. In his *Kashf*,[20] Ibn Rushd says:

> No one could reasonably argue that the presence of messengers is established by reason, based on an argument that reason establishes the possibility [that God could send] messengers, since the *possibility* of which they speak is [in essence] *an ignorance of what transpires*, rather than any thing inherent in the nature of existing things, just as we say it is possible for rain to fall or not fall [tomorrow, for example]. The possibility that is inherent in the nature of existing things is accepted when experience establishes that a given phenomenon does occur some time and does not occur at another, as in the case of rain. At this point reason establishes some generality about the aforementioned natural law (that it belongs in the realm of *possibility*). The opposite of this is *necessity*, which is experienced all the time, which leads reason to categorically and decisively establish that a natural law could not be altered. If your interlocutor (the deniers of prophecy) were to accept the presence of at least one prophet at a given time, then it would be apparent that prophecy was possible. But since your adversary in this argument claims that this was never established by experience, the possibility we would claim is nothing but an ignorance of the two opposite possibilities here, that is, the possibility that it has occurred and that it never occurred.

Ibn Rushd then argues that claims of prophecies are simply historical facts and hence could not be denied. The truth of these prophecies' content is a different matter: Good prophecies must correspond to good philosophy. But prophecies are not the only indicator of good norms or the only path to the attainment of good life. The inaccessibility of the teachings of prophets would be a loss but cannot be elevated to an absence of the Shari'a. In addition, jurists are mere interpreters of the prophets' teachings and their survival could not be equated with the availability of divine teachings. On this understanding, first, one could hardly establish any claim about the possibility of the fatigue of the Shari'a, since this is a realm where only guesses and analogies between what was witnessed and what was never witnessed operate. Second, since reason and revelation lead to the same path, any articulation of good norms has to draw on what is true in both of these. Whether or not a given interpretation of good norms is found, the foundation is always there to recover a version of these good norms. One is led here to the conclusion that, despite the scorn Ibn Rushd had for Mu'tazilis, as he grouped them among other *mutakallimun* who could hardly distinguish true argument from rhetoric, Ibn Rushd's position would be similar to theirs in the fatigue question. In the case of the absence of jurists, we are left with no option but the use of our reason alone.

True, Ibn Rushd directly addresses the question of the lack of jurists at the end of his *al-Daruri fi Usul al-Fiqh,* a summary of Ghazali's *Mustasfa.* But even if our assumption that *al-Daruri* was written early in Ibn Rushd's career is wrong (we are operating on the assumption that it was written when Ibn Rushd was 37 years old, in the year 562/1166), the *Daruri*'s statement hardly constitutes a philosophical position about the issue to the extent that his *Kashf* and his philosophical writings (notably *al-Tahafut*) do. In the text of the *Daruri,* Ibn Rushd simply reiterates the ambiguous consensus that *ijtihad* is one of the collective duties that must be fulfilled by some; otherwise all fall into sin. Then he argues that the very presence of new cases by itself demands the presence of fresh thinking, which makes simple conveyance of old views insufficient:

> Since there is [currently] a group that resembles laypeople in certain respects and independent jurists in other respects, namely those called *fuqaha* in our time, we must inquire into how to classify this category, that is, into which category [laypeople or jurists] we should include them. It is apparent from their affairs that they are of the same level as laypeople. The difference between them and [regular] laypeople is that they [the *fuqaha*] have memorized the opinions of independent jurists and could convey these to the laity, without attaining the conditions of independent juristic reasoning. This makes them "conveyers" [of the law] from the jurists. If they stop there, that would be fine, but they sometimes "transgress" their limits and extend through analogy the ruling of cases by the authorities they follow to cases where nothing is reported from these authorities; hence inventing new principles (*yaj'alun^{a} asl^{an} ma laysa bi-asl*) and turn the views of the authorities into a foundation for their own views; a significant straying.
>
> Could it be that they should simply take the first position, that is, that they convey the doctrine they think (to the best of their knowledge) is the correct view of an authority, and the next generations would also do their best to do the same, which leads to thinking that those fulfilling the duty of independent legal reasoning are unavailable in our age, for example—rather only those who came earlier—and hence the duty would only be fulfilled by reference to previous generations, which should be sufficient, even if it was only one man or a few men, as we find the case to be with these schools, I mean Malikis, Shafi'is and Hanafis? What would indicate that this could not be the case is the consensus that, in each generation, all collective duties must be fulfilled, and only then no one is asked to fulfill them. In addition, queries (*nawazil*) are limitless, and it is not possible to convey an opinion from a previous generation's authority in each case [since the new cases would be different]. Hence we are left with one of three possibilities: Either (a) to make the views of previous authorities "foundations"

> for later views to be derived from them, or (b) that many issues would be left undecided—and both of these possibilities are untenable (*mumtani'*). We are then left with (c) that no age can be devoid of a *mujtahid*. You know that generations before us were this way, that is, that they lacked a *mujtahid*, which does not mean that no one in them reached the rank of the *mujtahids* [such as the founders of the school], but that those [who attained this level] decided to follow previous authorities.[21]

The problem of norm-vacuum seems to exist on a certain level in most generations. If we stipulate the presence of scholars of true competence (equivalent to the masters who founded the schools), the collective duty of *ijtihad*, true independent legal thinking, may not be fulfilled, in which case the whole Muslim population has failed to fulfill one of its responsibilities. The presence of the *fuqaha* who make their living "doing law" is not at all a guarantee of the fulfillment of this collective duty. Does this mean that the Muslim population has indeed fallen into sin for most of its history? Ibn Rushd's cryptic formula and insistence on solving the problem "logically" rather than historically does not provide a full answer.

There are a few complicating factors even with this already complicated and ambiguous picture, and some simple solutions to problems we face here. Many great jurists, who may have been just as good as the founders of *madhhabs*, have followed in the footsteps of these founders. These are *mujtahids*. Ibn Rushd's insistence that some of those who understand correct reasoning are found in each age leaves us with the thought that maybe one or very few are enough, and each age will be full of *fuqaha* and perhaps only one or two or three *mujtahids*. This solves many problems. First, the collective duty is fulfilled; second, the distinction between qualified and unqualified jurists is maintained; third, the following two absurd conclusions are averted: that (a) the jurisprudence of previous centuries will have to be stretched by those who do not know how to handle it to answer new questions; or (b) that we live in a legal and moral vacuum. The question remains whether Ibn Rushd allows for a state of affairs where human reason plays an ameliorative role that fills in the gap created by a malfunction in the old systems of jurisprudence. The 37-year-old Ibn Rushd may say that this could never happen. I think the older Ibn Rushd would say that should this happen, reason must assume a higher responsibility.

Law's Life in Potentiality

The Mu'tazili view and that of Ibn Rushd address the fatigue question more successfully in theory than in practice. I will refrain, with the exception of this concluding comment, from pursuing this point further in this chapter. The life of any given system of norms could not be fully theorized by an emphasis on *ijtihad*, an emphasis on the analogies between founders of a system and its followers, or even a historical observation about gaps in any given system of legal and moral norms. [That is, unless we think of the Shari'a as an equivalent to the Averroian intellect that appears to be nothing but pure potentiality (= *isti'dad^{an} faqat*).][22] In other words, the life of a system of norms must draw on many details of reasoning—God is in the details.

In the case of Islamic moral and legal norms as understood by "the participants," the function of law is to regulate actions. Its function is neither to establish "rights" nor defend them, nor is its ultimate function to create stability. Norms are needed for actions that occur and go away, disappearing into the realm of history. The vigor of norms hence consists in their "availability" rather than "possibility."

Any view of this law as a system of ideas, connected to life only by a capacity for application, or potential application, does not attend to this law's dependence on practice. This is further confirmed by another quality in the Shari'a: actions are judged differently when certain circumstances change. For example, eating carrion is prohibited, but eating it in a case of uncertainty of the availability of an alternative before the body disintegrates is allowed. This dynamic character of the Shari'a makes it capable of constant interaction with life. A fulfillment of the law, in this case, is thus meaningless or paradoxical. This law is also a step farther away from a case of law's potential force remaining in the state of potentiality for later application.

This is meant to dispel the notion that a Mu'tazili view of legal and moral norms based on the notions explained in this chapter could simply be extracted from Mu'tazili early writings in order to recreate a Mu'tazili Shari'a of a sort. The later Mu'tazilis, not unlike their Ash'ari counterparts, who have been jurists (of a Zaydi affiliation, for example) could only argue their *tahsin* and *taqbih* with complex references to their *madhhabs*. In order to justify a Mu'tazili intellectual lineage, neo-Mu'tazilis must shoulder the responsibility of systematic thinking and comprehensive interest in law.

We now turn to the Ash'ari view of the subject.

Chapter 5

The End of Jurisprudence

Had the Shafiʿi jurist and Ashʿari theologian Abu al-Maʿali al-Juwayni (d. 478/1085) not engaged Abu al-Qasim al-Kaʿbi's (d. 319/931) denial of the fatigue of the *Shariʿa* (or the fatigue of all divine *sharaʿiʿ*), we might well have found ourselves addressing different debates on the issue. It would be an exaggeration to claim that the debates would have been nonexistent. But their flavor would have certainly changed. Juwayni's contributions to the fields of *usul al-fiqh* and *kalam*, to the research in both theoretical jurisprudence and theological philosophy, in addition to his status in Shafiʿi law as a virtual second founder of the school, after its first founder Shafiʿi (d. 204/820), was responsible for his influence on the issues involved in our subject.

Juwayni's *Burhan*, a text in legal theory, is one of four *pillars* of the field of legal theory; Juwayni's student Ghazali's (d. 505/1111) *Mustasfa* being another; and a third being Basri's (d. 436/1044) *Muʿtamad*, which we mentioned in the previous chapter. The question of *futur al-shariʿa* and the debate with Kaʿbi appears in the *Burhan*. In another treatment of the topic the *Ghiyathi*, Juwayni discusses the implications of the absence of ideal government and of government altogether. This book climaxes in a discussion of the question of *futur al-shariʿa* (or the extinction of jurisprudence). The question is whether it is possible, after the Shariʿa has been known and has functioned for a long time, that knowledge of it—knowledge of its provisions, explanations, and arguments—simply ceases to exist.

The assumption here is that when Shariʿa jurists are not produced any more, people must live in ignorance of God's law. But could not one think about this issue differently? The extinction or end of jurisprudence may be due to different factors, including the lack of the jurists who promulgate it and know its provisions, but also including people's rejection of its authority, among a variety of other reasons. In Juwayni's treatment, the end of jurisprudence or the end of jurists is a condition that obtains without any questioning of its authority by the people. Juwayni addresses the absence of jurists and their knowledge with the understanding that people's need for this knowledge will survive, despite the unavailability of its scholars.

Before spelling out Juwayni's arguments in this section, I would like, on pain of some repetition, to give a general review of where Muslim legal theorists have stood on the issue of *futur al-Shari'a*. The questions of the fatigue of the Shari'a are essentially two: (1) whether scholars of the Shari'a could become extinct; and (2) does its obligatory force and applicability end if this happened? Some Muslim legal theorists answered the first question (whether the Shari'a could become extinct) in the negative, thus declining to answer the second question, (i.e., does its applicability end if this happened?).[1] Aside from the Mu'tazila and Ibn Rushd, whom we met in the previous chapter, and the Hanabila, whom we will meet in the next chapter, the (Ash'ari) majority of legal theorists and theologians seem to find no clear argument against the possibility of the extinction of the Shari'a, and some even make it sound as if such extinction may be inevitable. The Prophet Muhammad is reported to have foreseen a time when *two people would struggle to solve an inheritance question without any authority to guide them to the correct answer*. In his *al-Bahr al-Muhit*, Zarkashi (d. 794/1392) takes note of this tradition after reporting that the proper view is that this Shari'a, not unlike previous divine teachings and laws, could suffer "fatigue." Ghazali (d. 505/1111) reported a consensus held by previous jurists that pre-Islamic laws of the prophets before Muhammad had already experienced that fatigue. Ka'bi is mentioned as the only one who objected to this idea, based on his doctrine that God is bound to do what is best, the best of all alternatives (*aslah*)—for people, and that leaving people with no law is not better than keeping the law alive. Perhaps this Muhammadan law was placed, by God's providence, too close to the end of time for there to be sufficient time for its "extinction" to take place.

Despite the three centuries separating them, Zarkashi paraphrases Juwayni's "surmising" that the law is not likely to become extinct within 500 years, given the abundant availability of its scholars at the time. This could be used to address arguments leveled by people like Shatibi (d. 790/1388), who pointed to the abundance of knowledge of the law during the hundreds of years separating Shatibi's time from the time of revelation as a clear indication that such law is not bound to become extinct. Zarkashi then points that should life in this world continue for much longer (without specifying a thousand years, thousands of years, or even longer periods of time), then the extinction of the law is likely to take place.

There is, therefore, neither an argument for the necessity of the survival of the Shari'a nor one for the necessity of its extinction; all is possible.

Aside from the question of the possibility or likelihood of a given law's extinction, a legal theorist must be able to answer the philosophical question: how should subjects who are deprived of guidance, moral and legal, go about their lives in this condition? This condition (the absence of guidance) is hardly limited to the condition in which the law ceases to function or in which knowledge of the law becomes unavailable (after it has been available). As we explained earlier, one could imagine at least two conditions where the law may not be available beside the case of its loss over time. First, there is the condition of humanity before this law was available to them (*al-ahkam qabl al-shar'*).[2] And second, there is the condition of law's failure to regulate all human actions (*khuluww al-waqi'a 'an hukm al-shar'*)—thus suffering a gap while it is generally deemed to be operative, as we explained in chapter two.

The philosophical disagreement about the status of the law before and after knowledge of the law has become available hinges on the discussion of whether "reason," unaided by revelation, may reach judgments that would be binding in the absence of revelation (*al-tahsin wa al-taqbih al-'aqliyyan*), whether these judgments are (a) fully independent of the content of revelation, (b) similar but not identical to the revelation yet equally binding in the absence of God's law, or (c) whether these reason-based laws are another version of God's law, which reason is capable of discerning. The standard Ash'arite view, usually defended in the classics of Sunni legal theory, rejects the Mu'tazilites' idea that reason, independent of revelation, is capable of discerning binding laws that have the force of God's law.

One must remember that Ash'ari theologians are known for their belief in the causal relationship between knowledge and responsibility. When you receive the news of a prophet (whose prophecy is demonstrable), you are responsible for following that prophet, but if you do not receive the news, you do not have this responsibility, and this includes responsibility for believing in God and acting on the beliefs taught by this prophet. God has established an argument for His divinity and worthiness of worship by His revelations to prophets; hence a person who lives in a distant mountain and does not possess any knowledge of prophets is excused for not attending to all acts of worship and to faith itself (*ma'dhur^{un} fi tarki ^{a}l-a'mal^{i} wa-l-iman^{i} ayd^{an}*).[3]

The Ash'aris, however, resist allowing reason to be a virtual reviewer of God's plans in the world to vet them as just or fair. This Ash'ari worldview could be seen to allow God's abandonment of His creation, since God does not need to make His guidance available *just because* people think that He must do that. It is an easy target. Even the Hanabila, who argue against this abandonment (essentially) on a religious basis, may fare better than the Ash'ari irrational and undesirable "surrender" to a whimsical God.

But the Ash'aris believed their position was reasonable, not only in conformity with religious beliefs. Ash'aris believed that there was no equivalency between humans and God to make one a replacement for another. Their opponents who kept thinking "what human would usually do" and expected God to do the same were the ones in error.[4]

The Ash'ari view is a hard sell in our days, but one must at least give it its due defense. The world of the 15th Hundred of Islamic history includes strong support for a neo-Mu'tazili or even Rushdi (ascribed to Ibn Rushd) views of God's behavior. And many have internalized a Hanbali view on this and other issues, consciously or subconsciously. God has to make sense in His behavior, that is, He has to make human sense. If he fails to do that, he may be doubted or even defied. Some versions of these positions are a bit jocular, I must say, because if people are prepared to think that God exists, they should not worry about His evil (or good, or anything from his side; after all, he is only a concept; he does not exist). But if God exists (qua God), He may not be defied and, most importantly, He does not have to be like humans.

Still, this Ash'ari view, which seems to abandon reason for the sake of following revelation, remains problematic. The aversion to the Ash'ari view is not only an aversion to "Islam" per se. The idea that many laws and structures of order in life could not and should not be fully understood by humans is certainly available in different forms, and some type of it is necessary for socialization. If the essence of Ash'arism is "submission," listen to (one may say, *tongue firmly in cheek*, just to anger the anachronism police further) a statement by a seventeenth-century British "Ash'arite" John Selden (1584–1654):

> I cannot fancy to myself what the law of nature means, but the law of God. How should I know I ought not to steal, I ought not to commit adultery, unless some body had told me so? Surely 'tis because I have been told so. 'Tis not because I think I ought not to do them, nor because you think I ought not; if so, our minds might change: Whence then comes the restraint? From a higher power, nothing else can bind. I cannot bind myself, for I may untie myself again; nor an equal cannot bind me, for we may untie one another. It must be a superior power, even God Almighty.[5]

Ash'aris, as I said before, did not believe that they stood unsupported by reason. Many arguments that support the Ash'ari view have nothing to do with a religious or submissive temperament. When they are on the offensive, Ash'aris demand clarifications of the concepts that are consumed by their opponents, the concept of reason, for example. The so-called human reason in fact does not exist. Fihri (d. 643/1246) insisted that the dominant sense of judging something to be good or bad is based on culture and conventions (*'urfi*), and only in the case of abstractions (such as speaking of knowledge versus ignorance or justice versus injustice) should judging anything as good or bad be ascribed to human or universal reason.[6] This takes away much of the strength of an argument that "reason" could arrive at any binding conclusions and anticipates the argument from the contingency of reasoning hinted at in Selden's statement. The alternative to the decisive revelation is constant reasoning, argument and counterargument, and nothing stable; nothing like good-old "reason" emerges at all.

Could this argument reverse direction and be leveled against the Ash'aris? Laws change, and whether we see their change as "continuity" or "death," their change is inevitable. Would not the life of the Shari'a then be similar to the life of any law? In other words, could the stability assumed in God's law (expressed by jurists, who are what remains of prophets as Sam'ani[7] says) be another "assumption" not unlike the stability of reason? This would mean that by the time the fatigue of the Shari'a was debated, hundreds of years after the death of the Prophet Muhammad, this Prophet's Shari'a had already experienced fatigue multiple times. Could these Ash'aris have been unaware that even their *Shari'a* has changed over time and must have taken diverse shapes across geographic areas? Unaware of this issue they certainly were not; they may not have discussed it in the same terms in which it is proposed today. (The decisive issue remains, for our contemporaries, whether people have a say at all in these processes, and if the answer is "yes," then to what extent? I will come back to this point repeatedly.)

Najm al-Din al-Balisi (d. 729/1328), as Zarkashi (d. 794/1392) reports, struggled with the generalization that laws change due to the change of times (*taghayyaur al-ahkam bi-taghayyaur al-zaman*) and thought that at least one reading of this general rule must be wrong, namely, that *law* should change because people would gradually reject *its* authority. This is because God must have known that they would reject this law's authority when he first revealed it to them. To say that a "change of attitude" among people ends the law's jurisdiction over them would, thus, not be an acceptable legal problem to address. On the face of it, this (conservative) view must clash with Ibn 'Abidin's (d. 1252/1836) acceptance, in principle, that "changes in custom" affects legal provisions, if there is a way to reconcile law and custom, as I explained elsewhere.[8] However, once considered carefully, it becomes clear that these views are reconcilable, with gray areas left to juristic investigations on a case-by-case basis.

The Ash'aris who believed the fatigue of this last Shari'a was as inevitable as the fatigue of the Abrahamic or Mosaic Shari'a did not expect a revelation after the Islamic Shari'a before the end of time to provide proof of the fatigue of the Shari'a of Islam. They would then think that the equivalent of the new revelation is a submission to a life with no revelation-based laws, however one understands the nature of the end of time. Shatibi's sense that there was no sufficient time span before the end of the world for the Shari'a to experience any serious fatigue seems to presuppose that the very passage of time may be sufficient to wear out a system of legal and religious values. Note that the system of the Shari'a here is identified in terms of (at least in part) objectively discoverable principles and practices, rather than something open to infinite possibilities or interpretations. If the Shari'a were open to infinite interpretations, then those entitled to speak in the name of the Shari'a could simply all agree to provide a new system and call it by the old name. Is this possible? Would this be the same Shari'a? In the Theseus paradox, a similar question is raised as to whether piecemeal change of a ship until none of its original pieces survives makes the ship a different ship. If the ship is a metaphor for the Shari'a, and our answer is that the ship remains the same as long as it could be believed to be the same, we would argue that as long as there is a claim that the Shari'a is the same, then it is the same. All you need then is a confident group of people who claim to offer new interpretations of the old Shari'a, no matter what their substantive claims are.[9] Ash'ari theologians would probably be amused by this line of thinking.

The constant-interpretation Shari'a thesis will clearly fail to provide any type of description of the changes that befall the Shari'a. It will also contribute nothing to an understanding of the Ash'ari position, in whose articulation Juwayni played a major role. The most that one can extract with certainty is that the survival of the Shari'a through its qualified jurists is not a given, in Ash'ari doctrine.

Juwayni on the Extinction of Jurisprudence

Juwayni addresses the question of the extinction of jurisprudence in two different contexts. The first is what we already referred to, an attack on the Mu'tazili rejection of the fatigue of the Shari'a and a defense of God's justice and perfection (the *Burhan* discussion). The second came in his discussion of the absence of ideal government, whose replacement he suggested must be scholars and notables, where he ends his discussion by considering what a Muslim community should do when these scholars themselves are lacking (the *Ghiyathi* discussion).

In his *Burhan*,[10] Juwayni shows the limitations of any acceptance of the fatigue of the Shari'a without a basis for religious and moral obligations.

(This paves the way for his attempt, in the *Ghiyathi*, to "detail the extinct law" from a few general principles.) In his effort to establish the possibility of the fatigue of the Shari'a, Juwayni says that there is no rational argument against the fatigue of laws of any type; and no distinction among different laws is needed. This was stated explicitly, he says, by our master Abu al-Hasan [probably Mujashi'i (436/1071)], who garbled his position by the doctrine that humans remain responsible for their actions, despite the absence of any basis for their responsibility, which emanates from a view that accepts requiring the impossible (*taklif ma la yutaq*). Abu Ishaq al-Isfrayini (d. 418/1027), by contrast, had accepted the fatigue of laws but denied requiring the impossible, ultimately adhering to the Mu'tazili view of making reason (*mahasin al-'uqul*) the basis of religious and moral obligations.

In the *Ghiyathi*, Juwayni's analysis establishes a paradigm of thinking about law in the Ash'ari view, which will survive the centuries. In this view, the question of the extinction of the law is twofold, one concerning the loss of knowledgeable jurists and the other concerning the loss of their authority, since the life of law depends on the two agents of lawmaker and the law-abiding individual. Juwayni addresses the tasks assigned to jurists (those on the serving end) and individuals (those on the receiving end) of the law. He then enters into the familiar debates about the qualifications of jurists and the degree of "reflection" individuals must do to apply the law in their lives—given juristic disagreement.

In his two works, Juwayni then argues that the jurists may disappear, and the populations may need to rely on remnants of the knowledge of jurisprudence. The production of law, which used to be the work of jurists only when they existed, may now be given to those who were only concerned with the consumption of the law. In the last section of the *Ghiyathi*, where I think Juwayni's achievement is most conspicuous, he goes over the main doctrines of the existent law, the Shari'a, arguing that its basics and general principles from revelation and from reason can offer the means to detail the law, even after it becomes extinct (basics here mean bare-minimum rules, such as the idea that marriage was the norm and families were based on it, despite the disappearance of the detailed knowledge of how it was practiced). The assumption of a "dormancy" of the Shari'a is also not excluded in this discussion, with interesting questions that result from a revival of knowledge of the Shari'a after it has become unavailable.

Juwayni's position, already discussed in chapter three, about the law before the schools (*madhhabs*) is also presented here. The Prophet's companions have enjoyed knowledge of the law and employed valid methods to acquire an understanding of what was obscure about it. But after the schools have been established, we are not expected to reach for the companions' legal views. Thus, the law seems to mutate yet live on. An analogy may be drawn between the conditions of the law's absence before the revelation and the condition of its absence after the revelation. What is less obvious is whether an analogy may be drawn between the law's infancy (companions' era) and its old age or senility.

As the law progresses, earlier raw *madhhabs* (such as that of Abu Bakr, d. 13/634) become unusable, since people of later generations (such as Shafi'i, d. 204/820) have sifted through these raw *madhhabs* and developed more complex ones. This shows the limitation of the value of early precedent and the limitation of earlier thinking in general. However, no extreme paradigm of constant superseding of the old by the new is suggested here.

The Argument against Reason's Unqualified Sovereignty

What distinguishes the Ash'ari position from that of both the Mu'tazilis and Hanbalis is its insistence that reason's *rule* is limited. It is on the basis of this that Ash'aris, first, could have no qualms about the idea of the fatigue of the Shari'a. Were someone, such as Ka'bi, to object that God must do what we believe is best, the answer would be that God does not have to attend to our reason's expectations; only we have to attend to His expectations of us.

The same limitations imposed on reason also lead to the idea that judging actions to be good or bad based on the human reason could not become a *default position*. If anything, it is a limited tool to address conditions of necessity. *Norms* do not *normally* come from reason. Rather, they spring from revelation, or in extreme circumstances could be discerned with the aid of not-perfectly-accessible revelations. This also shows that Juwayni's position in the *Ghiyathi* is in tune with Ash'ari theology, despite its potentially distinct formula.

One may object that Ash'aris argue against reason's unlimited jurisdiction with the aid of reason itself. Could this be justified on the basis that human reason is indeed capable of showing its own limitations? Qarafi (d. 684/1285) articulates this argument:

> We argue that the world is created in time (*hadith*). Either there was good in it (*masalih*) or not. If the former, then God had delayed creating this good for infinite ages [between eternity and creation]. We then could not say that "God does not fail to do what is good." And hence human reason could not assert that any norms (*ahkam*) existed before the divine revelations (*shara'i'*)

> [since this same reason could not explain the delay in the creation of the world, which is a delay in the creation of its benefits or *masalih*]. Nor could one assert that God observes the good (*mura'at al-masalih*). If the world was devoid of the good (*masalih*), and [hence] God did that which did not include the good [by creating it], then the human reason could not assert that God does only what is good; rather, based on their view, God could do what is devoid of wisdom, which violates their principle [that God does only what includes wisdom].[11]

It is one of the peculiarities of the human reason that it could discover its own limitations—it does that constantly. Accordingly, an argument based on *reason* to disqualify *reason* itself does not include any contradiction. The attempt to reason about "creation" (its nature and timing) betrays this strong limitation in the human reason. The argument against Ash'aris' critique of human reason as an attempt to use one thing against itself, to disprove reason by the aid of reason, may thus not be as clever as it sounds.

The Survival of the Truth and the Survival of Scholars

Does the Ash'ari position allow for any separation of the question of the survival of the truth from the survival of scholars? If not, their position would sound irritatingly doctrinaire. When Hanbalis emphasize the prophecy that a group of the believers will always maintain the truth (*la tazal*^{u} *ta'ifa*^{tun} *min ummati zahirin*^{a} *bi* ^{a}*l-haqq...)* against another prophecy that knowledge of God's ways will be removed from the world by the death of scholars, Ibn al-Hajib responds:

> We grant that the [prophecy of the survival of the truth] indicates that the "absence" [of the truth] will not occur [in actual life], but where is the negation of the logical possibility [of its absence]? And even if it is granted [that this negation of the occurrence is a negation of its possibility], our argument [that *ijtihad* may disappear; that scholars may become unavailable] is stronger because it explicitly states the end of knowledge (*qabd al-'ilm*), while your text speaks only of the prevalence of the truth, which does not entail the survival of scholars, and if this were to be granted, then the [two texts] would be contradictory, and the first possibility, i.e., the possibility [of the absence of *mujtahids*], prevails, since [possibility as opposed to impossibility] is the default presumption [which should be followed when contradictory considerations cannot be reconciled].[12]

Ibn al-Hajib here argues that all prophecies of the survival of the truth are irrelevant to debating the fatigue of this specific Shari'a. In fact, even a prophecy that something will not occur does not establish the logical impossibility of that event. He goes further and argues that should one assume that the two texts are mutually exclusive, the *possibility* of the end of the Shari'a (standing as a default position) tips the balance in favor of the text prophesying the end of knowledge of the Shari'a. The prophecy of the demise of the Shari'a through the demise of its scholars is hence decisive in establishing a prediction of the fatigue of the Shari'a, defined as the absence of jurists. What remains to be ascertained is what is to be done when this situation arises.

This distinction between the truth and the specific Shari'a is confirmed in several other discussions of this issue. Ibn Amir Hajj (d. 879/1474) asserts that negating the survival of scholars (*'ulama*) implies a negation of the survival of the narrow circle of qualified jurists (*mujtahids*), but negating the survival of the truth does not indicate anything, since it does not entail the survival of *mujtahids*.[13]

A Matter of Profession—An Academic Turf?

There is no way to deny, however, that the Ash'ari position stands in this field with some peculiarities, despite the fact that I characterized it as the majority view, based on its abundance in the genres in which I am most interested. The first peculiarity is the bizarre *clarity* of the characterization of *futur al-shari'a* as the absence of *mujtahids*. This, as I indicated, can be taken by some of our contemporaries as proof of collective or professional self-absorption, as these jurists reflected on the end of jurisprudence, the end of the profession of jurists, as a theological and theoretical question. Second, in the Ash'ari view, there is nothing wrong with the end of the Shari'a as a juristic product; all good things come to an end. The reader may be susceptible to the wrong impression, things the way they are in Ash'ari thought, that these legal theorists and theologians had clear-cut definitions of the fields of jurisprudence and theology in the way modern departments in universities have attempted to (and some still) define the borders of their fields so as to guarantee a certain level of acquaintance with a certain body of scientific or literary prose products (*the field's literature*) or experience for its faculty. This impression should disappear when the reader learns that what was at stake was ultimately the quality of the mind a jurist possesses, associated as it must be with the possession of certain kinds of information and technical vocabulary. In fact, in his commentary on Iji's (d. 755/1355) *Mawaqif*, Jurjani (d. 816/1413) digressed as he discussed the definition of *'ilm* (knowledge; science) into a discussion of the often artificial, though defensible (*istihsan*-based), divisions of the sciences. He says that, in theory, divisions of the sciences unlike those in use are possible, that hybridization from existing sciences is equally possible, and that even considering *one inquiry* to be a separate science is also possible. Topics can vacillate between one science and another. He then adds the important insight that the history of a given science or field of inquiry is one of the reasons it is divided and *bordered* the way it is.[14] *'Ilm*, its borders and formulae, then includes many arbitrary elements. The capacity to perform the task of a jurist must be something else.

The end of jurisprudence, or the end of the profession of "jurist," is therefore not an end of an academic fad or tendency. It is the end of a capacity to solve certain problems. This Ash'ari claim will continue to be interrogated. Why would not the human mind solve (differently) these problems that used to be solved a certain way in the past? The Ash'ari answer would be that there is such a thing as "lost knowledge" that could not be replaced, even by clearly intelligent and original solutions to what seems to be the same problems the old knowledge used to address.

Chapter 6

Ijtihad for All

In a treatise known as *al-Furqan bayn[a] al-Haqq[i] wa [a]l-Batil*, Ibn Taymiyya (d. 728/1328) attempted to produce a sketch of the history of heresy, starting with the Kharijis' excessive labeling of most Muslims as non-Muslims, passing by Shi'i reconsideration of the status of the Prophet Muhammad's two companions (Abu Bakr and 'Umar), and the Qadari (Mu'tazili) views about grave sinners' middle state (*al-manzila bayna [a]l-manzilatayn*; residing neither in Hell nor in Paradise), and moving into other heresies such as those of the Murji'is with their excessive skepticism about the nature and stability of "belief" as well as the impact of actions on faith.[1] The Mu'tazili heresy can be dated, according to Ibn Taymiyya, to as early as the end of the age of the companions or thereabout.[2] This heresy, the denial of qadar (hence the label Qadari and Qadariyya), is best understood broadly as a failure to accept God's will without mixing its apparent elements with human (Mu'tazili) reasoning, tinged as it is by foreign ideas—as Ibn Taymiyya explains in other writings.[3]

Ibn Taymiyya thus thought of the Mu'tazila as among the earliest heretics. This may not be contested, but some might dispute whether the Mu'tazilis were indeed the earliest to propose, based on their doctrine of God's justice, that the fatigue of the Shari'a inquiry (what should people do when the Shari'a is no longer accessible) could not be a meaningful one, since it is based on an impossible presumption, that is, that God's law (based as it is on both prophecy, which is a manifestation of God's justice, and human reason) may experience fatigue. The fatigue of the Shari'a indeed, they would argue, could not happen, since God's justice contradicts abandoning his creation in this way, and what is less obvious yet could be distilled from their discussion of the fatigue debate is that the fatigue of the Shari'a contradicts the basic assumption that human beings will always possess their capacity to employ their "reason" in order to discern good norms to live by—as long as they remain human.

To digress briefly, Ibn Taymiyya, a figure who fascinates Western scholars, still serves as a tool for generalizations about the Muslim world today and historical Muslim societies' failings (which Western scholars generously try to help Muslims work on). New generalizations replace the old ones, but the new scholarship is reminiscent of the old. Worse, now "old" notions that we thought were debunked to no return are coming back (perhaps some of today's Islamicists feel guilty that erudite Orientalists had been mistreated). We often seem to go back to the drawing board. We still face simple assumptions about the nature of Islamic legal and theological reasoning, and attempts at making sense of this reasoning to learn from it, to benefit from it, are rare.

It is usually attempts to "understand" (note this) the evolution of Muslim philosophical, theological, and legal thinking. Neat narratives can be found; for example, Ghazali (d. 505/1111) killed philosophy in the Sunni Muslim East, and Ibn Rushd (d. 598/1196) was the last philosopher of the Sunni Muslim West; tradition ends up prevailing in the Muslim world as modernity's impact on the world is confirmed; the Mu'tazilis rose at the end of the companions' era, trying to introduce some primitive philosophy to Islam, but were set back by Ash'aris who favored tradition, and Hanbalis came with even a stronger emphasis on tradition, and so on. These and similar assertions can be only be praised for their clarity, rather than for being informative.

Not only was the Sunni Muslim world large enough to encompass traditionalists, rationalists, and various other grades of "others," the political triumph or dominance of one variety or another of the various views (always much more limited in real life as can be gleaned from many sources than is presented in these neat narratives) was not paralleled by weakness or lack of development of other positions. One of Islamic intellectual history's great features is that many positions have been preserved and even further developed by their opponents. Mu'tazili doctrines continued to be studied and investigated until Muhammad 'Abdu (d. 1905) came to the scene, allowing him to borrow freely from them, not necessarily (at least in the start) based on Mu'tazili earlier sources, but on Ash'aris' studies of the Mu'tazili view. Mu'tazili ideas were also simultaneously alive in Shi'i intellectual production.

I am not interested in pursuing the question of who knows more about the Mu'tazilis, and whether their history amid the Shi'is is where we should start or any similar question. Nor will I make the juxtaposition of a Mu'tazili and Hanbali theologians and legal theorists the subject of this chapter. This chapter will complete the picture of the fatigue debate by explaining what counts as the Hanbali position, which is in agreement with Mu'tazili theorists that the fatigue of the Shari'a may not be a defensible position, but which also could not adopt a Mu'tazili stance on the nature of divine guidance and humans' need for it.

Dissent—For or Against Reason?

In the beginning, there was the generation of the companions. The dissent of Wasil Ibn 'Ata' (d. 131/748) and his moving way (giving us the term *i'tizal*), to be the head of a school of his own, established a predecessor to the Mu'tazili school of the next century. Should this be seen as a rejection of tradition and siding with reason? The tradition of the Prophet's early followers has already been unwieldy. Wasil's view that grave sinners must occupy a state between the two states (*manzila bayna al-manzilatayn*), contrary to the apparent sense of the Qur'anic language, does cling to other forms of tradition, rather than represent a view based solely on reason. The Mu'tazili Jubba'i's (d. 302/915) position that "the unaided human reason" could discern the patterns of God's justice and divine balance need not be seen as mere adherence to reason; it seems to be more hybridized of reason and revelation. Similarly, the Ash'aris' rejection of Jubba'i's insistence on human reason's ability to understand God's justice, which is the founding myth of Ash'ari theology, is followed by Ash'ari attempts at assimilating, rather than undermining, the Mu'tazili valuing of reason. Hanbalis did not simply advocate a return to tradition against Mu'tazili and Ash'ari excessive emphasis on reason; they used reason differently. What is most important is that these strands all survived both in the literature and in oral public knowledge (and found their way in some version to popular knowledge), the myth of the death of Mu'tazilism notwithstanding.

What we are left with is not a simple evolution, it is an accumulation. Detecting and discussing accumulation and continuity, across geographic and historical planes, has not been Islam Western scholars' strongest suit. Recent insistence on disjunctions and discontinuity in Islamic history react to (and parallel) the extreme of neat and simple (evolution) narratives of past Orientalism, and they both fail to see a picture of accumulation and hybridizations.

The relationship between the Hanbali and the Mu'tazili views on the fatigue question illustrates the case for a complex picture that does not preclude continuity. From what if not a diametrically opposed theological worldview then the closest to it, the Hanbalis argued something like the Mu'tazili position we discussed in chapter four. The Hanbalis did not hold

God to be bound to any sense of justice they themselves or other humans may be able to *discover* or articulate or even *develop* on their own; nor would they dare to understand God's plan for the world from any point of view independent of God's revelation. Yet, they held the same position on the fatigue inquiry as that of the Mu'tazilis', namely, that it is meaningless to think of such a thing as the fatigue of the Shari'a; that inquiring into what should happen when humanity has no guidance (and hence on some views no access to knowledge of their duties) is an unjustified indulgence into an inappropriate hypothetical; and that the best answer to the question "what happens when we wake up in the morning without conveyers of God's law" is "there is no answer, because this does not happen."

If it is neither God's duty of justice, nor the persistence of "reason" as a tool for learning about good and evil, then what makes the fatigue inquiry inappropriate? What is the twist by which the Hanbali position agrees with the Mu'tazili rejection of the fatigue of the Shari'a without accepting many of the Mu'tazili premises? It is the Hanbali sense that "*ijtihad*," in principle, is both a duty and a right for all. This will not be twisted back into a "reason-reigning-supreme" position, since *ijtihad* is not simply the capacity to reason; rather, the ability to reason within the parameters of divine revelation. Well, this begs the question of how untrained individuals could get it right when they reason within the parameters of God's revelation. And the answer is that when their *ijtihad* is possible, if they get it wrong, they are wrong, but they remain in possession of their "right" to try (to use the word in a modern sense here), absent better options.

This "right to try" begins from the basic question of belief itself, where many Hanbalis find themselves, in my view, closest to Maturidis who considered belief based on imitation (*iman al-muqallid*) an exception to the rule, rather than a natural position for most believing Muslims. Hanbalis even go beyond Maturidis and say that untrained practicing Muslims are ideally expected to understand as much of the Shari'a as they can (and different Hanbali jurists disagree on how to broadly understand this) and that laypeople are hence the default initiators of their own religious commitments. I will come back to this soon.

This view lay centuries in the making, and the early Hanbalis paved the way for it with two important distinctions. *First,* they addressed the question of the absence of norms before the Shari'a (*hukm al-ashya'^{i} ^{a}l-muntafa^{u} biha qabl^{a} wurud^{i} ^{a}sh-shar'*) in conjunction with the question of lacunae in the functioning Shari'a. How could the void be filled? One possibility is to resort to a default position of prohibition. This, apparently stringent view, springs from a sense of caution not to transgress into an unknown area that may be part of the realm of the prohibited. Prohibition is preferable to other options because it is the safest, but many jurists have argued for permission or for simply suspending all judgment in the case of the unavailability of Shari'a norms. Again, some Mu'tazilis shared this Hanbali view of resorting to a default prohibition before revelation, but the Mu'tazili governing principle remained judging behavior to be praiseworthy or blameworthy, which is not reconcilable with a Hanbali cautionary prohibition of uncategorized behavior. As Ibn 'Ashur explained, the main difference between the "jurists" who judged actions to be prohibited before revelation and the Mu'tazilis who had a default category of actions uncategorized in the Shari'a is that the jurists committed themselves to a specific ruling (*hukm*^{an} *wahid*^{an}), whether it is prohibition or permission, for all actions, while the Mu'tazilis made this judgment for behavior whose qualities of goodness or badness are undiscernable (*ma lam yuttala' fih*^{i} *'ala sifat*^{i} *husn*^{in} *aw qubh*).[4]

Second, Hanbalis thought of the tasks of jurists as an important contribution to the Shari'a but not a *conditio sine qua non*—a condition without which the Shari'a itself does not exist. The Shari'a, that is, is not fully contingent on jurists. This is also a rejection of the Ash'ari view, which strongly hesitated to allow practicing Muslims to simply pick and choose from the opinions of available jurists. Hanbalis hence reject both extremes of Mu'tazilism and Ash'arism. For them, the human reason is there to be guided by revelation, and it should not overstep its authority by becoming an independent designer of norms. The craft of jurisprudence, in addition, should not claim a monopoly on norms by overmagnifying the laity's incapacity to think "semi-systematically" and engage meaningfully in discerning norms.

Before All Revelations

Could this "optimistic" position be thrown into doubt by a question about what happened before all revelations? If Hanbali legal theorists could claim that God would not leave Muslims with no guidance in the future, could not it at least be claimed that He did that already to other nations before he sent His revelations? What happened before all revelations? As they rejected the notion that absence of guidance as a possibility to be taken seriously, Hanbali legal theorists cited arguments that such absence simply never occurs (echoing the general statements Jahiz made about each nation having some scholars at any given age). This current nation, the nation of Muslims or followers of the Prophet Muhammad, have additional confirmation that knowledge of their "way" will remain available. This may not be a guarantee that its scholars will survive until the end of time, but it is a confirmation that knowledge of divine norms itself, with or without the scholars, will survive. Even the time of Adam was not devoid of divine guidance; the Qur'an speaks of God's instructions to Adam (eat this; avoid this), and the same must be true of all ages. The question about the absence of guidance "before revelation" is hence unintelligible, since such time as "before all revelation" does not exist.

The language of Hanbali legal theorists shows a degree of caution about how one may argue that revelation has always been available. But since the thrust of the argument is theological, this caution dissolves into fairly strong assertions. Abu Ya'la al-Farra' (d. 458/1066), for example, attributes to "others" the view that there was no human time before all revelations, but he fully adopts that view. Those others, he says, held that each generation must be given a path or law (*shar'*), because God would not allow a generation to be devoid of that, as he did when he created Adam who was given the instruction not to approach the forbidden tree. Hence even the question of what people should do before all revelations is itself wrongheaded (*w^{a} idha kan^{a} kadhalik^{a} batala an yuqal^{a} ma hukmuha qabl^{a} wurud^{i} ^{a}shshar'*).[5]

What "Conditio Sine Qua Non"?

The Hanbali divergence with the Ash'ari view that the absence of *mujtahids* and the fatigue of the *Shari'a* are the same condition still demands elaboration. In his *Tamhid*, Kalwadhani (d. 510/1116) understands *ijtihad* as an activity in which both specialists and average worshippers are engaged, but to different degrees. If scholars were to disagree among themselves about an issue, a layperson may simply pick one of their views, if the lay questioner sees them as equal in their knowledge. Some suggested that the piety of jurists should be made a consideration in a layperson's search to determine which one to follow among them, but this is not a defensible position for many.[6]

Should the jurists be equal in every respect, in their piety and knowledge, it would be hard to tell the questioner what to do; the layperson has nothing but self-reliance, as it were: she/he must simply apply her/his own *ijtihad*. Kalwadhani states:

> Were they (jurists) all the same for him/her (the questioner), and were one of the jurists to offer him/her a *fatwa* that prefers the heavier commitment and another a lighter one, the questioner gets to pick, according to the apparent reporting of al-Husayn Ibn Bashshar (d. 286/899 [editor has it

> Yasar], because [the questioner] had the right to choose either one of the two disagreeing jurists for counseling before asking one of them. This [choice] to follow either one of them after they declare their opinion (*fatwa*) is not unlike his initial choice.[7]

The obvious objection facing this view is that this questioner might simply end up choosing the "easy" *fatwa*, a strange and unacceptable position in the eyes of 'Abd al-Jabbar (d. 415/1025) and some Shafi'i legal theorists, on the ground that "truth is heavy" (*al-haqq*[u] *thaqil*) as the Prophet's tradition has it. The report (that the Prophet said the truth was heavy), however, is dismissed as a suspicious piece of tradition (since it is a report by the few—*khabar ahad*), while stronger traditions emphasize that God likes His licenses to be used, just as he likes His regular duties (*'aza'im*) to be taken seriously. In the final analysis, there are good reasons to take the "lighter" view as there are reasons to take the "heavy" one. This being the case, the questioner enjoys the freedom to "pick" in the case of unresolvable disagreement.[8]

The Hanbali family of doctrines on the fatigue of the Shari'a, the individual's normal duty of *ijtihad*, and the higher responsibility of the individual in cases of indeterminacy, was not simply a response to the Mu'tazili or Ash'ari view. In any case, the Hanbalis could cite previous authorities dating back to the companions' generation. According to Abu Ya'la (d. 458/1066), Ahmad Ibn Hanbal (d. 241/855) said: "All thanks be to God who made at the tail of every messenger's message (*fatra min al rusul*) remnants of those of knowledge (*baqaya min ahl al-'ilm*)."[9] One should not read too much into the context in which Ahmad Ibn Hanbal made this statement (which is after he was released from jail), since Hanbalis will take this statement to be a statement of doctrine that could not be dismissed regardless of the psychological state its author had at its utterance. The same statement found its way to Kalwadhani's *Tamhid* and is followed by a clear assertion from the author: "Thus he (Ahmad) believed that no age could be devoid of a messenger or a scholar to be followed (*'alim yuqtada bih*)."[10] This statement, as cited in both sources, addresses the debate on the default characterization for individuals' actions when the guidance of God (*shar'*) is unavailable through either messengers or scholars, where, as I said, some Hanbalis hold the view, similar to some Mu'tazilis, that this default position is "prohibition" (rather than permission).

The *ijtihad*-for-all paradigm remains a curious position with multiple possibilities. In this paradigm, *taqlid*, following an authority, is simply not an option in all issues, whether these be issues of belief or practice. There are types of "knowledge" that could not be gained from authority. Examples include "knowledge" of God and His oneness, and knowledge of the correctness of the message of the Prophet Muhammad. This goes against the assertions by some (Ash'ari) Shafi'is that such following of authority may be sufficient.[11] The Ash'ari view, accepting faith based on emulating a trusted example, *iman al-muqallid*, hence could be attacked from different perspectives, ranging from a Mu'tazili to a Maturidi to a Hanbali. In the end, they all think this notion of "emulation" in something so basic, and as our contemporaries would say, so personal, as faith is suspect.

Interestingly, the same Shafi'is hold that no one could believe that their daily prayers and annual fasting is a duty based on someone telling them that these were duties. As they exclaim, how could the knowledge that is the foundation of this duty be simply a matter that could be delegated to authority?[12] This distinguishes between general knowledge of the foundation of the rituals, where a layperson's sense of the need for God is at work and may be fulfilled by common knowledge, and an understanding of how an argument for the existence of God could be defended. On the Hanbali view, laypeople and scholars share much more than what appears to be the case. Note the tone of this argument:

> It is not true [that laypeople know God less than scholars do]! With scholars laypeople share knowledge of God and the basis for His oneness and revelations through prophets, because these are matters one could realize through her/his basic senses and reflect on by her/his intellect, and with this "know" [that there is a Maker] through God's acts, His creation of the Heavens without need for pillars, and what He infused them by [that is]: the Sun, the Moon, and the stars, which he made to move; He smoothened the surface of the earth based on water, while a building would not stand on water, and created the human from a *nutfa* (semen) and made her/him pass by stages until she/he could sustain knowledge and the capacity to organize and learn crafts.[13]

Kalwadhani then moves to knowledge of the impossibility of multiple Gods, based on what is known as *dalil al-tamanu'* (the impossibility of equal multiple "owners" of the universe who control it with harmony). Knowledge of the details of the rituals is also based on abundant reporting of these details and neither bears much doubt nor requires arguments, just as laypeople do not need to learn how to argue about the presence of old nations whose traces are amply attested.[14] Kalwadhani is hence confident that laypeople and scholars share what matters: the basic knowledge and capacity for understanding that are needed to both build the foundation for the beliefs and the practices of the Shari'a and thus make the life of this Shari'a independent of extensive Shari'a technical discourses possible. In normal circumstances, it is the abundant (and somewhat obscure) details of the Shari'a (*the furu'*) that requires the specialists, but even in these the relationship between questioner and "authority" is not as simple as it might seem.

Ibn Taymiyya's Attacks on Reconciling Reason and Revelation

In many of his writings, Ibn Taymiyya dedicated much energy to attacking the view that in order to be accepted, the truth of God's revelation needs to be reconciled with "fashionable" knowledge. This attack is also melded with another attack against obscurantism and against haughty, unrealistic assertions of the capacity of either "reason-based" or "inspiration-based" knowledge to provide an enduring understanding of the essentials of the world. In one of his answers to the question on a report that the Prophet indicated the primacy of the creation of "reason" (*awwal^u ma khalaq^a Allah^u al-'aql*), Ibn Taymiyya rejects the claim that the Prophet could have uttered these words. In this context, Ibn Taymiyya leveled one of his long attacks on the notion that reason and revelation must be reconciled.[15]

The main tactic employed by Ibn Taymiyya in this discussion is asserting that the burden of proof in this matter must be shouldered by those who claim a need for the reconciliation between revelation and reason. All the involved issues are disputable: What is reason, how does it relate to essential and a priori knowledge, how does it relate to empirical knowledge, how does it relate to other types of knowledge, what is its function and relationship with the reality of the world—among other questions. In addition, ambiguity and lack of correspondence between revelatory language and philosophical or mystical language (presumed parallels between words such as *qalam*, pen, and *'aql*, reason, for example) all add a burden to those who claim to work on reconciling reason and revelation and leave their position even more precarious.[16] In return, perhaps, Ibn Taymiyya accepts the burden of refuting traditions that seem to lend support to the need for a reconciliation of reason and revelation. He also accepts other burdens, such as providing simpler interpretations of certain traditions to replace their obscurantist or convoluted interpretations.

The reconciliation of revelation and reason predictably goes through stages, starting from saying that the apparent meaning to be taken from the language of revelation was meant to agree with the expectation of the average person (which is saying that revelation lies, Ibn Taymiyya says; note that the Mu'tazila may have done that from time to time) and ending with full doubt about all that God's revelation teaches.[17] Ibn Taymiyya hence holds that the Shari'a, the path of God, both in beliefs and practices, bears some complexity, but does not bear the burden of reconcilability with all human inventions. Saving revelation and its knowledge is hence tied to learning and preserving it rather than subjecting it to constant transformation through these reconciliations with reason. The fact that Ibn Taymiyya's contemporaries (as well as predecessors) produced many of these suspect reconciliations, which led him to his long refutations, did not after all cause him to prophesy the end of time or the fatigue of the Shari'a. He stopped after refuting all bad experimentation and tampering with divine knowledge and left us with an assertion that God's hand will prevail at all times.

The Hanabila's Recruits

Whatever the exact influence of Ibn Taymiyya among other factors, the post–Ibn Taymiyya world seems to have shown added adherence to the Hanbali view on this subject. The Shari'a that requires much involvement from its practicing followers is protected by more than its scholars. The position, known as the Hanbali position, however, did not always come only from Hanbalis. It was strongly supported by many non-Hanbalis, the most famous of whom if you rely on Ash'ari sources is *Ibn Daqiq al-'Id* (d. 702/1302), whose name pops up in *usul al-fiqh* sources that discuss the issue during the subsequent five centuries (roughly between the 700s/1300s and 1200s/1800s). *Ibn Daqiq al-'Id* became famous for his distinction between the absence of jurists in *normal* history and their absence in *eschatological* time, the very end of time, when natural laws themselves do not seem to apply any more (e.g., when the Sun rises from the West). But there are many non-Hanbali supporters of the Hanbali position who deserve our note. One of these is the great Shatibi (d. 790/1388).

Shatibi assumed a distinction between this *Shari'a* and previous *shari'as*, it seems, before he could fully articulate the distinction. The distinction he finally discovers is this: contrary to previous *shari'as*, which were given to their people to preserve, the preservation of this *Shari'a* was made a task for God Himself. The answer, courtesy of Judge Abu Ishaq Isma'il Ibn Ishaq (d. 282/895), corroborated by Abu 'Abdillah al-Mahamili (d. 330/941), refers to the same verse about preserving the *Dhikr*, understood to be the Qur'an, which contrasts with the *Torah*, whose preservation was deemed a failure by the Qur'an itself.

Shatibi's second leg of the argument is empirical. Observation seems to confirm that rushing to learn the foundation and applications of this

Shari'a was on the rise. Detailed knowledge of the Qur'an, nay of each one of its letters, was becoming more abundant. Meticulous analysis of Arabic texts and study of its laws was equally abundant. The same could be said about reporting the Prophet's tradition, about the effort dedicated to distinguishing what belonged in his tradition and what was a deviation (*bid'a*), and even about refuting fallacious attacks (*shubah*) against this tradition and the correct religious beliefs. The Qur'an, the Sunna, and the Arabic tongue, being the foundation of this *Shari'a*, and being afforded much support from divine providence (also reflected in empirical evidence) provide the guarantee for this *Shari'a*'s survival. Shatibi thus concluded that the inquiry into the fatigue of the Shari'a was an unnecessary indulgence, meriting only the courtesy of quick dismissal.

As I said earlier, it was the early Hanbalis who paved the way for this view. They did that, most crucially, when they characterized, as we showed in the case of Kalwadhani, the tasks of jurists as an important contribution to the Shari'a but not a condition without which it does not exist. They also did that when they distinguished the question of the absence of norms before the *Shari'a* (*hukm al-ashya' al-muntafa' biha qabl wurud al-shar'*) from the question of filling the gaps after the Shari'a (the lacunae discussed in chapter three), as Abu Ya'la did.[18]

Ibn al-Najjar

The Hanbali view continued to be represented and articulated in later *usul al-fiqh* texts. The Hanbali position found an articulation in the tenth/sixteenth century by Ibn al-Najjar al-Futuhi (d. 972/1564). Ibn al-Najjar states the doctrine as follows: "there can be no absence of all *mujtahids*' according to our fellow [Hanbalis]." Ibn al-Najjar cites Ibn Muflih (d. 762/1361), who added that some non-Hanbalis held the same view, including Qadi 'Abd al-Wahhab al-Maliki (d. 422/1030). The arguments for this position include the Prophetic assertion that a group of his (the Prophet Muhammad's) followers will remain in adherence to the truth (and triumph with it). Ibn Battal (d. 499/1105) reminds us that this is the very last divine revelation, the one that will witness the end of time, and even if the signs of the end became apparent, and the religion was getting weak (*wa in zaharat ashratuha wada'uf[a] al-din*), there will remain some who adhere to the Prophet's teachings. The counterargument from the prophecies about the end being associated with the spread of ignorance and evil is dismissed as these prophecies "are *general* in language but *particular* in intent" (Juwayni's dismissal from the other side claimed that the prophecies that knowledge would wither away were more relevant to the discussion and the counter-prophecies were too *general*, hence less relevant to the discussion). The prophecies about the cessation of knowledge, Ibn al-Najjar says, must be about specific geographic areas, since those who will adhere to the truth, prophesied in the earlier texts, could not be among the evil prophesied in the other texts.

Ibn al-Najjar then acknowledges Subki's (d. 771/1369) support for the Ash'ari position. This is followed by the familiar general discussion of *ijtihad*, which falls into the confusion about the nature of the lost *mujtahid*, independent or affiliated. The ease with which *ijtihad* tools are acquired in later times is contrasted to later generations' lack of determination and energy to do less and attain more than what earlier generations have had.[19] But the fatigue of the Shari'a, as the end of guidance, is dismissed without any qualifications.

* * *

The lessons of the medieval debate are multiple. After considering the Hanbali contribution to the debate, one is bound to think of this assignment. Define the Shari'a as a path in whose design the observant participates, and imagine its extinction while the observants are alive. The medieval debate on the fatigue of the Shari'a, in fact, leaves us with many questions, most importantly: Could an empirical assessment from a privileged, external viewpoint be conducted to determine the vitality of the Shari'a?

Pessimistic, Optimistic

From opposite ends, both Mu'tazili and Hanbali legal theorists rejected the notion of the fatigue of good norms. Though very different in their expression, both groups can be said to have insisted on continuity, the survival of the basics, the supremacy of certain ideals above history and above the human capacity for change. The Ash'aris (the majority of legal theorists who took the pain to present a concrete position in the debate) lowered their level of analysis to "observed" history and accepted the fatigue of divine norms. They may be better readers of history, but the Mu'tazili and Hanbali camp would find the Ash'ari microanalytical stance philosophically and theologically deficient.

It is up to the reader to impose a notion of optimism about human nature at least on the Mu'tazili version of the macroanalysis of history, consistent with what is stable and what is true in our *world of becoming*. I know many think that there is no such thing as God's norms, but they could still understand this argument as one concerning the survival of some basic human norms. The reader can also, with reason, impose a sense of fundamental divine providence on both the Mu'tazili and Hanbali versions of this analysis. And, perhaps, a degree of pessimism, realism, or something like these can be super-fitted onto the Ash'ari analysis. I have no quarrels and no approvals for these characterizations. I find these positions to be reconcilable and ultimately diverging to an extent because they answered slightly different questions. My observation is that this question of the fatigue the Shari'a can bear disagreement, but it can also bear "hidden" agreement—the type medieval theologians and legal theorists call "verbal disagreement" (*khilaf lafzi*), disagreement in terms, not in assessments.

Ijtihad for All in the Fifteenth Hundred

The "*ijtihad* for all" paradigm picked up tremendous steam in the thirteenth Islamic century with Shawkani's (d. 1250/1834) argument against the fatigue thesis and became what may today be called, for a lack of better characterization, the Salafi position (what a medieval legal theorist—*Maturidi* or *Ash'ari*—would call the Hanbali position). In the Shawkani version, God's invisible hand has manifested itself by making the *Shari'a* ever more accessible, by facilitating knowledge of the Prophet's tradition (the Qur'an's transmission having been secured a long time prior) and by facilitating a basic understanding of the instructions of God and his messengers to all in the later centuries.

Part III

Modernity and Its Questions

A change in the status of traditional jurists, coupled with an emphasis on the foundation of the Shari'a and with modern state transformations, shifts the debate.

Chapter 7

A New Picture

In a dramatic depiction of the changes that took place in Egypt between 1860 and 1900, *Muhammad al-Muwilhi* imagined a conversation between a deceased pasha who had stood at the helm of the Ministry of War during the first half of the nineteenth century and a character like *Muwilhi* himself, living at the end of the nineteenth century, who speaks for the author (*Muwilhi*) much of the time. The pasha's interlocutor, named *'Isa Ibn Hisham*, took it upon himself to explain these changes as the circumstances allowed. In one section of the book, *'Isa* tells the pasha about a major change in attitudes toward the role of the Shari'a in public life, at least by the Egyptian elites, and perhaps many others who aspired to be like them.

In this section of *Muwilhi*'s book, one hears of the unbelievable existence of an imperial law unsupported by an occupying army representing an empire. But this bizarre state of affairs is described after some preparation for the poor pasha, who failed to witness this development that took place over a couple of generations, since, for better or worse, he had been dead. The deceased pasha's misfortune leads him to have to make a court appearance. The pasha naturally expects to find himself in the same Shari'a court with which he is familiar. His companion, *'Isa*, explains that the court that will handle his case is a *civil*, rather than a Shari'a, *court*. This leads to a further explanation by *'Isa* that there are now different types of courts in the Egypt of the second half of the nineteenth century. The pasha could only see this as a sign that the country had ceased to be one—that it is now fragmented and no longer functions as one unit. *'Isa* comes back with another explanation, correcting the pasha and stating that the jurisdiction of Shari'a courts has simply been curtailed and is now limited to some areas of family law. In reaction, the pasha issues a lamentation of a people who lost their ability to live by their laws and adopted another people's as their own. There is no military occupation, and the fact that French laws rule many aspects of life in Egypt has nothing to do with a return of the French who had invaded Egypt in 1798 but had to leave the country three years later. It is a choice by the Egyptians themselves, *'Isa* asserted, as he explained that the presence of the imperial law, rather than the *Hamayuni* law of an Ottoman sovereign who at least shared the populations' religion, was *because of us* (Egyptians, that is). How could this imperial law, being in disagreement with God's law, be adopted by Muslims? *'Isa* surprises both the pasha and the reader with an assertion that one *mufti* in the ministry of justice said that this French law was not really irreconcilable with Islamic law (*anna hadha al-qanun al-faransawi ghayru mukhalif li al-shar' al-Islami*)[1] and hence may simply be today's *shari'a*.

The idea that the *Shari'a* can be reconciled with other laws of different types was known to medieval Muslim jurists; juristic discussions of *ahkam al-dur* (the world's legal abodes) address the conflict and reconciliation of Islamic with non-Islamic laws, for example, in cases where Muslims live in non-Muslim lands. (Some reconciliations are also found when non-Muslims live among Muslims.) But the idea that reconciling different laws is an easy task (or that reconciling most of the *Shari'a* with whole legal systems of different sources is possible) is a modern aspiration. This is the high burden of the effort to "reform" Islamic law.

To assert, however, that non-*Shari'a* laws has nothing good in them would be an extreme that could probably not be promoted by any Muslim jurist who had strong contacts with non-Islamic laws. In the modern era, Muslim jurists saw good and bad in non-Islamic laws. For example, *Jabarti* (d. 1251/1835), who chronicled the French occupation of Egypt (1798–1801), had more than one chance to praise French bureaucracy and regulations. In describing one of the turning points of the French occupation, the assassination of Kleber (Napoleon's replacement as leader of the French expedition in Egypt) at the hands of Sulayman al-Halabi in 1215/1800, Jabarti favorably compared French legal practice with some practices claiming to represent the *Shari'a*. The French whose laws are based purely on reason, he said, were more careful in their investigation of the assassination of their top officer, Kleber, even though clear circumstantial evidence was on the side of the apparent claim of assassination. Between *Jabarti* and *Muwilhi*, the shift was going in a direction of change both for traditional jurists like Jabarti and the new (Western-educated) lawyers who appear in Muwilhi's book.

The Muwilhi court drama captures a shift in the status of the *Shari'a* from the twelfth/eighteenth century onward. To be sure, it was not only that new intellectual elites who grew up in Muslim countries happened to think that European laws were simply more worthy of following than the backward or less-developed laws of the *mashaykh* who represented old jurisprudence. The borders between insiders and outsiders of the Muslim community were blurred, even when those in question were the rulers of a Muslim community.

Ahmad 'Urabi (d. 1328/1911), the leader of the Egyptian revolt of 1882, related the following confusing picture in his court defense (in the face of claims of stirring up the army revolution against the *Khedive*):

> On July 11 [1882], the day Alexandria was pounded, a telegraph from the Prime Minister (*ra'is majlis al-nizara*) sent to all government agencies announced that the country was in a state of war and that the government would apply martial law, according to the known custom [in cases such as this], then any one who disturbs the public peace would be court-marshaled. Hence, a military court was formed by the War Ministry. The Khedive went to Alexandria under English military protection after the people of Alexandria and the soldiers went out of it. Now [the Khedive] was either a prisoner of war or he had joined the enemy of his country; and in either case, the country should not be left without a leader, according to Islamic law. If he was a prisoner, he could not be simultaneously prisoner and ruler, and if he joined the enemy, then God's Scripture rules him out of the Muslim community, in which case he could not be its leader.[2]

Was the Khedive a prisoner of war or was he a rebel who abandoned Islam and joined the English enemies of the Egyptian population? He was neither. He was a new category that generates as much confusion as the fact that the Egyptians simply seemed to prefer French laws to Muslim laws without being under French military occupation. The *Shari'a*, from that point and gradually, had to live a partial life in the public arena, and at times live underground, as support for it by the elites in society and their imitators was in decline.

* * *

The nineteenth century, a starting point for many of the developments we take for granted in the twentieth and early twenty-first centuries, can be divided into two halves, the first being the time when the seeds of weakening jurists started in places such as Egypt, and the second where toward its end, according to Hallaq, the death of the *Shari'a* may have taken place. The Hallaq thesis is that something like (what Charles Taylor would call) *a ratchet effect* befell the *Shari'a* where no return to its functional past was possible—just like a machine that has undergone major systemic breach could not simply be returned to its state before the breach. The calls for a paradigm shift (*qati'ah manhajiyya*) in reasoning and institutions in the Arab world, such as the ones proposed by 'Abdullah al-'Arwi,[3] became a reality that claimed at least Shari'a legal reasoning and institutions among its casualties.

I cannot support the assertion of the end of *Shari'a* either as a *culture* or as a *legal science* for several reasons. I think that social life in Muslim societies has absorbed and preserved much of the *Shari'a*. I also think that the *Shari'a*'s legal elites (who suffered major blows without question) have in fact timidly but effectively endured and influenced current thinking about law, morality, and their interaction to an extent beyond what the death-of-Shari'a discourse acknowledges. I will keep coming back to the end-of-the-Shari'a debate throughout the remaining chapters of this work; I start here by acknowledging the relevance of the reform discussion to that thesis.

It should be clear that I am not proposing, in this chapter, to write a short history of a century that has been studied repeatedly by scholars and continues to give new students more to ponder (some of the tremendous materials available remain obscure and even materials that are not obscure are simply understudied or so far poorly studied). I am proposing to outline *pro-madhhab* attitudes that became in effect *neo-madhhab* positions as well as *post-madhhab* attitudes about the *Shari'a*, whose presence itself signifies a new stage in understanding the fatigue of the *Shari'a*—all the while rejecting an equation of the new picture with a full divorce with the *Shari'a* of old times.

I start from the assumption that something happened in the nineteenth century in places such as Turkey and Egypt in the Sunni world and Iran in the Shi'i world that initiated a new stage in Islamic history. [A doctoral dissertation I am currently reading focuses on the 1878 (Ottoman) *Mejellet* and the 1949 Egyptian Civil Code and considers codification of the *Shari'a*, in the first case, and of European laws into an Egyptian law, in the second, to be an essential game-changer in the process of reform-as-transformation of the *Shari'a*.] We must remember, however, that since at least the eighteenth century, Muslim societies in India and maritime Southeast Asia had already encountered European expansion and begun a process of legal and social transformation. This can be detected in the tone and emphasis of some juristic treatments of old subjects. For example, the Hanafi Shah Waliyyullah al-Dihlawi (1114/1703–1176/1762) decided to start his short treatise on *ijtihad* with a reminder of a lesson we may have already learned from the medieval Hanbalis who hated the half-divinity imposed on the *mujtahid*. Dihlawi's tone is different from the medieval Hanbalis. As is understood from the definitions of scholars, Dihlawi says, *ijtihad* is an exertion of energy to arrive at detailed rulings based on the accepted foundations of these rulings, that is, the Qur'an, the Sunna, consensus, and analogy. This, he asserts, is *broader than an effort to learn what jurists have said before, whether to agree or disagree with them.* This (*ijtihad*) also encompasses effort with and without the aid of others as long as the one performing the search enjoys both the comfort of the heart (*yatma'inn*^{u} *qalbuh*) and an informed intellect (*'ala basira*). Those who believe that this activity does not count as *ijtihad* harbor a bad opinion (*zann fasid*)—Dihlawi asserts.[4]

I am told by my colleague Gurrinder Singh Mann that one should not assume that Dihlawi had any serious understanding of the nature of the British endeavor in Asia or sensed any imminent change in the status of Muslim populations' position in the world. Until further evidence is available to me, I will take this to mean that one must then not read into Dihlawi's reconsideration of some aspects of *ijtihad* and its relationship to jurists and laypeople a reaction to a new age or an anticipation of the need for reactive reform.

Dihlawi's full presentation of *ijtihad* shows that people are ultimately one of four types in their relationship to the Shari'a: (1) a founder of a school such as Abu Hanifa (and these are something of the past); (2) a follower of one of these; (3) a person with extensive but less-than-systematic knowledge of the *madhhab*; or (4) a layperson. There is no attempt at conflating the third and fourth categories, but the way Dihlawi lays out the types raises strong questions about exaggerated claims of the inaccessibility of understanding the Shari'a to the largest sector of its consumers (type 4). This tone, though traceable to some medieval forbears, brings up in the context of Dihlawi's full project a new look at the world that is connected to the Prophet's tradition much more than to the *madhhabs* that were seen by some to serve as mediators between this tradition and its followers.

In this mid-twelfth/eighteenth-century presentation, one could see the dawn of the project of reform or some reform-in-embryo. One must be cautious not to exaggerate the value of Dihlawi's position as an exemplar of simply either *continuity* or *change*. Moving forward in time, the century following Dihlawi, the thirteenth/nineteenth century, witnessed further action. What distinguished the thirteenth/nineteenth century were the two facts of (i) generalizing the situation (in India and Indonesia) to larger areas in the Muslim world and (ii) making the impact closer to the heart of the Muslim world. Later, in the fourteenth/twentieth century, the Arabian Peninsula itself, where it all started, was affected by the same virus. There is no question that a new phase of Islamic history has begun. But could not this simply invoke the seventh/thirteenth-century Mongol attacks on the Muslim world, which threatened to change the face of the Muslim world forever? Yes and no. Analogies abound, but, among many disanalogies between the two cases of the seventh/thirteenth and thirteenth/nineteenth centuries, Mongol leaders ended up embracing Islam after a period that was shorter than the time that has already elapsed between the end of the nineteenth century and our present time. Further, it seems that today an almost inverse situation may be in the making; some of today's Muslim populations may have started to embrace the religion of the modern Mongols.

I will, against some hesitation, place the story of the nineteenth century in a short chronology to attend to the question of the slow weakening of the Shari'a as it manifested itself in what is called the reform of the Shari'a. Dihlawi and Sanhuri will appear again in this chronology, which I hope will strike *the correct tone of the facts* and avoid exaggerations of different types.

Modern Reform of the Shari'a Revisited

What may be called a modern shift in the status of the Shari'a is heavily associated with changes and developments that originated outside of the Muslim world. These changes and developments (which have been differently explained as continuation, appropriation, or rejection of the philosophical, religious, and political ideals of premodern Europe[5]) did not affect the Muslim world equally or simultaneously. In the Sunni world, India, Turkey, and Egypt played a central role in the formation and distribution of reactions to this European impact on the Islamic East, but the Islamic West could tell its own story. India's vast resources were *discovered* by Europeans; Turkey was the center of the Caliphate; Egypt was on the receiving end of a French "expedition" in 1798 and was subsequently a center of many activities in the intellectual and political development of the Arabic-speaking part of the world. A more comprehensive association with Western ideas and institutions, coupled with a stronger objection to these, distinguished the Muslim West—North African lands west of Egypt. While influences originating in these (Eastern and Western Muslim) centers are undeniable, these centers of contact remain incapable of speaking for the Muslim world as a whole. The traditional *madhhab*, the natural representative of the *Shari'a*, came to be subjected to strong modifications and even explicit attacks by participants in Islamic jurisprudence. *Shari'a* jurists who participated in a reform of their system gradually came to accept a second-class status among lawgivers in their societies. The same will also be the case for jurists who rejected the idea of reform, while trying to keep as much of what was left of the *Shari'a* alive.

In the remainder of this chapter, I attend to these changes, which made the medieval debate on the fatigue of the *Shari'a* only part of the background for any discussion about the status of God's norms in the world today. Let us start by briefly recounting the "reform" story from the perspective we have been advancing (where reform is a catalyst of fatigue).

Reservations

Many reservations are raised when one applies the notion of "reform" to the recent episodes of Islamic legal history (roughly the last two or three centuries). First, reform may not be an appropriate term to describe a reaction to external (Western) control, in many cases aimed at assigning a role for Islamic law to play within a larger "global" legal and political structure from outside of it. Second, to identify a process of development within a given tradition as constituting "reform," one must be able to clearly distinguish it from other stages of development within this tradition. This requires a long justification, attending to difficult questions of how the long history of this tradition may be studied and analyzed. Considering a certain view to be truly novel or "reformist" faces narratives that trace this idea to its predecessors. Third, associating recent stages of Islamic legal history with reform also risks reducing this history to the events, movements, and ideas one associates with reform. For this reason, the 1996 *Oxford Encyclopedia of the Reformation*, for example, noted the harmful, reductive tendencies resulting from reading the sixteenth century, which also affects reading its aftermath, as the century of the Protestant Reformation (and Catholic reform) and Counter-Reformation, as if everything that happened in the sixteenth century can be understood as acts of reform and reactions to it.[6]

Despite these reservations, speaking of Islamic law and reform seems to have acquired sufficient legitimacy. This is because recognizing the global context in which modern movements speak of reforming Islamic law or recognizing conceptual difficulties in the study of reform does not negate its presence and importance. Reform in Islamic law consists in a complex series of events, movements, and ideas that deserve to be studied. Historians of Islamic law can therefore identify champions of Islamic legal "reform" as well as skeptics about it. But this should alert us to the danger of myopic readings of this history, of which students of reform histories may fall foul. Instance of over-reading of change or exaggerations in assessing the shifts in social ethics and legal and political institutions in Muslim societies also result from this posture.

Ijtihad and *Tajdid*

The idea of renewal (*tajdid*) in religion is hardly a modern invention in the Islamic tradition. The Prophet Muhammad is credited, according to Abu Dawud's *Sunan*, with the following prophecy: "At the start of each century God will send those who will renew for the people their religion (*li hadhihi* ^{a}*l-ummat*^{i}… *man yujaddid*^{u} *laha dinaha*)." This prophecy has been taken seriously by Muslim theologians, jurists, and historians long before modernity. Some Muslim historians offered their "educated guesses" about the renewers of previous centuries. In this context, names such as 'Umar Ibn 'Abd al-'Aziz (d. 101/720), Shafi'i (d. 204/820), Ibn Surayj (d. 306/918), Ghazali (d. 505/1111), Razi (d. 606/1210), and Ibn Daqiq al-'Id (d. 702/1302) were offered to identify the renewers of the first, second, third, and fifth through seventh Islamic centuries.

Another term of relevance to the question of Islamic law and reform is the one we reflected on so far the longest, *ijtihad*. In premodern times, *ijtihad* and *taqlid* were constantly debated. *Ijtihad* means exerting effort, and it was hence used as a legal term indicating a process of reflection by a jurist to arrive at legal norms regulating actions. *Taqlid*, or following the counsel of an authority, was seen by many as the natural path for the average followers of the religion to learn their religious duties. Medieval jurists still called for the laity to engage in a measure of nontechnical *ijtihad* and to take responsibility for the choices they make in their religious actions. *Ijtihad* is available to the believer, even according to those who champion *taqlid* as the default means of acquiring knowledge of religious duties, in some matters of law (as I mentioned in chapter six) and in matters of fact. Of the latter, it is common for jurists to mention that the layperson may exercise their own *ijtihad* in cases such as deciding where the direction of the prayer is, absent definite knowledge of that direction. If matters of reality (such as the direction of the prayer) can bear independent judgment, other issues of rituals and unlawful gain, for example, are contingent on the questioner's knowledge of themselves and of the world as they experience it, which allows them to exercise their ijtihad. Even after receiving a jurist's counsel, a questioner is left to his/her conscience as to whether to follow the advice they received. After all, an independent jurists' counsel is not typically enforced by the government and depends on the questioner's choice of which authority to consult and their decision to follow the counsel they solicited.

In modern times, a new *ijtihad*/*taqlid* controversy could be identified (addressing the degree to which an average believer should engage in *ijtihad*). The *ijtihad*-for-all paradigm we spoke of in chapter six gained much strength. The Yemenite jurist Shawkani (1173/1759–1250/1834) called for a rejection of *taqlid* and a (qualified) universalization of *ijtihad*. Though strongly affected by its context, Shawkani's call for *ijtihad* represented a theoretical or a philosophical challenge to the basis of *taqlid* in Sunni, Shi'i and Ibadi Islam.

Reform in Religion and in Law

The Protestant Reformation led by Martin Luther (1483–1546) and John Calvin (1509–1564) gave birth to modern concepts of reform. [In English, the verb "reform" (meaning to fix or improve, from the Latin *reformare*) precedes in existence the noun "reform" which appears only after the Reformation; thus modern "reform" of religions is born out of the Reformation.] But the term reform also came to apply to laws without any emphasis on their religious character. For example, the term reform is retrospectively applied to many ancient and medieval legal systems, such as Roman law and medieval European laws.[7] Applied to Islam in particular, reform is seen to encompass reforming its religiolegal system, or in other words be both a reform of religion and a reform in law. Modern reform, applied to Islamic law, can be compared to the Protestant Reformation (especially in what may be called a neotraditionalist variety of Islamic reform movements, which championed a return to scripture) as well as to renaissance humanism (in its modernist variety emphasizing Islam's acceptance of progress and new experiments).

Despite its being amenable to description as religious, Islamic law must be distinguished from religious doctrines and reflections, often described as theological, since these mostly concern relations involving God. Contrasting with theology, Islamic law governs human behavior in the market and in the family, among other areas. This might be a basic point at this stage of our inquiry, but its inclusion is justified. It helps us understand why much of Islamic legal reforms can be compared to early modern legal reforms in Europe more properly than it can be compared to religious reforms.

Muslim reformers such as 'Abd al-Razzaq al-Sanhuri (1895–1971) emphasized the distinction between the beliefs of Muslims and Islamic law as a legal system.[8] Reforming Islamic law, in this view, is an intellectual rather than a strictly religious project. After all, Islamic law governs relations involving non-Muslims, who affect and are affected by Islamic law as much as Muslims affect it and are affected by it. In this scheme, reforming Islamic law, therefore, must be approached as a universal project, aiming at stating rational and human principles, even if these did not in reality apply to all humans. Yet, as we shall see, not all Islamic law reformers championed rationalism. In fact many of them made their mark by attacks on rationalism and its advocates.

Reform in religious law is also akin to heresy (as reformers are sometimes labeled heretics), and heresy can be seen as a matter of theological rather than legal concern. The closest equivalent of heresy in Islam is the concept of *bid'a* (lit. innovation), denoting undesirable inventions in religion. The term is occasionally used to indicate inventions, plain and simple; hence, the term *bid'a hasana* or good innovation; in general, however, applying the term unconditionally implies an innovation not worthy of approval.

The term *bid'a* has recently acquired unprecedented currency among literalist reform movements in the Muslim world, most famously (to Western readers) in Wahhabism, which made ridding Muslims of *bida'* or innovations the hallmark of its reform call.[9] The focus of Wahhabi attacks on innovations is in the realm of beliefs, but they also use the term to refer to what they consider deviations in matters of legal practice. Thus, many of the views of modernist reformers would be deemed examples of *bid'a* from a Wahhabi viewpoint. One cannot, however, reduce Wahhabi reform to a call to abandon modern innovations, since, in practice as well as in theory, what we may call (with much license) Wahhabi Islam established a culture that accepted modern innovations not directly relevant to religious matters on a narrower definition of the latter. Modernists also employed the terminology of *bid'a* in their attacks on undesirable practices, such as those occurring in popular celebrations of mystics.[10] The idea of the evaluation of new practices, however, is old, and should not be seen as an invention of modern times.

Structure

Islamic law is a system of religious, legal, and moral norms, covering areas as far apart as rituals, trade, family relations, and it even regulates some generalities applicable to the realm of government. In the area of rituals, Islamic law prescribes for the capable (a) five daily prayers, (b) fasting during the daytime in the month of Ramadan, (c) annual and seasonal almsgiving, and (d) pilgrimage to Mecca once in a lifetime. These rituals address Muslims individually and collectively. For example, the daily prayers could be performed individually or congregationally, while the Friday Prayer is designed to be performed only congregationally once a week. Almsgiving can be fulfilled through the actions of an individual and can also be organized communally. Other aspects of Islamic law possess a different social quality, such as laws regulating marriage, divorce, child custody, sale, business partnership, bankruptcy, and so on. Muslim jurists also address matters of public law, such as crime, adjudication and the administration of courts, the legitimacy of revolution, among other issues.

In Islamic law, juristic production is not contingent on government enforcement. For example, a Muslim jurist may argue that certain transactions are "usurious" and thus prohibited, even if the government allows them. Therefore, the law may be said to exist as a discursive exercise of argument and counterargument, centered on a body of legal doctrines or rulings. Rulings concerning the already mentioned rituals, such as fasting, address *private* religious matters. But government also plays a role in enforcing many aspects of Islamic law. Thus, punishments for crimes such as murder and robbery, which are enforced by the government, are also part of Islamic law. Islamic law, ultimately, consists in "discourses" (supported usually by social practices) and "governmental orders." This broad scope of Islamic law is reflected in the story of modern reforms in Islamic law.

The categories of modernist and neotraditionalist reform movements have been an essential part of the story of reform in Western literature. Modernist reformers primarily addressed (a) political issues, such as the form of government in Muslim society and the need to adopt the principles of democracy; (b) economic policies, such as the prohibition of usury; and (c) rules regulating women's rights, from inheritance rights to participation in government. But all aspects of Islamic law came under scrutiny in modernist reform discourses. Take, for example, potential conflict between the daily prayers and regular daily work hours. In this issue, some modernist reformers call for relaxing the requirement of praying five times within certain limits, citing the need for a strong commitment to productivity and the availability of licenses for relaxing prayer rules in the Islamic legal tradition.

The umbrella of Islamic legal reform movements also covers voices of neotraditionalism (such as Wahhabism and Salafism). Despite the variety of neotraditionalism and its many mutations over the decades, neotraditionalists typically oppose the idea of altering Islamic principles for the sake of modernization. Neotraditionalists can also be distinguished from modernists by their refusal of the strong rationalism of some Muslim jurists who argue that all (or almost all) laws in Islam can be explained rationally. Interestingly, these neotraditionalist movements also argue against (what they consider irrational) forms of esotericism, such as Sufism, and have a tendency to bear strong animus toward Shiʿism.

For their opposition to rationalism and apparent intolerance for diversity, neotraditionalists frequently get quite a bit of bad press. One must bear in mind, however, their main contribution to Islamic legal reforms, that is, their questioning of the authority of the established Sunni schools of law (*madhhabs*), the Hanafi, Maliki, Shafi'i, and Hanbali. Neotraditionalists' call for independent reasoning and freedom from the established schools precedes the modernists' acceptance of the same principle.[11] Neotraditionalists have included erudite scholars who questioned legal doctrines from rituals to family laws, and from trade to crime and beyond—only based on traditionalist rather than rationalist principles.

Given its distinctive features and history, Shi'i law underwent a somewhat different reform path. Some scholars argue that reform in Shi'i jurisprudence does not seem to reflect either the quantity or intensity of reform in Sunni law. This is caused by the Shi'i immunity to penetration by external influences, owing to its esoteric qualities and, in the case of Iran, to the latter's relative isolation in the early modern era.[12] It may also be argued that the story of reform in Sunni Islamic law, which encompassed new trends in legal philosophical production, teaching, and legislation, has more texture than its Shi'i equivalent. This can be explained partly by the sheer size and geographic diversity of Sunni Muslim communities (roughly four times the size of Shi'i communities) among other factors. No one denies, however, that Shi'i jurisprudence has provided new responses to many external and internal stimuli for reform, including encounters with Sunni law in its premodern and modern varieties.

In its premodern history, Shi'i jurisprudence had already encompassed two juristic tendencies, one emphasizing rationalism (championed by the Uusulis) and the other traditionalism (the Akhbaris)—all due caveats acknowledged. By the end of the eighteenth century, the rationalists had the upper hand in Iran. Subsequently, most modern reforms in Shi'i law reflect the rationalist discourses with Western legal and political forces as well as a conversation with Sunni law. Novel ideas were introduced to Shi'i legal doctrines in politics, economics, and social life.

Anomalously, it is also probably true that the achievement of Shi'i reform, delayed and geographically more limited as it may have been, possessed a unique significance and magnitude and has the potential of influencing Sunni legal reforms in the future. The twentieth century witnessed not only one, but two major legal and political revolutions in Iran, which possessed measures of intensity unparalleled in Sunni countries (at least until recent changes in Turkey and Egypt among other places in the Sunni world, which seems to prepare for a new tipping point). Though affected by specific events, the constitutional revolution of 1905–1911 and what came to be known simply as the Islamic revolution of 1979 rightly represent a sophisticated culmination of these modern Shi'i reforms.

The intellectual legacy of these two revolutions is diverse and broad in scope. This legacy includes a well-developed idea of minimalist and constitutional government as a means to avoid tyranny [esp., Na'imi (1860–1936)], an emphasis on reconciling Shi'i and Sunni thought and on Islam's universalism, and attempts at showing that scientific discoveries are compatible with religious beliefs [esp., Bazargan (1907–1995)].

One of the most significant aspects of reform in Shi'i jurisprudence is the doctrine of *wilayat al-faqih* (authority of the jurist), introduced by Ayatullah Khomeni (1902–1989). This doctrine offers contemporary Shi'i jurists much room to offer answers to questions of politics traditionally relegated to the authority of the Imam, an authority in occultation to be revealed at the end of time, according to traditional Shi'i doctrine. Though not without its detractors, the authority this idea gave Shi'i temporal, religious authorities of the Iranian Republic has contributed much experimentation and ingenuity in devising new legal doctrines in modern Shi'i law and politics.

Ibadi jurisprudence, mostly produced in pockets in North Africa and Eastern Arabia, has undergone a process of reform proportionate with the limited size of its juristic production and following. Colonialism prominently occupied *Ibadi* jurists, such as the Algerian *Atafayyish* (1818–1914), who authored an encyclopedia of *Ibadi* jurisprudence titled *Sharh al-Nil.* In his legal writing, *Atafayyish* converses with many of the ideas propagated by his contemporary Sunni thinkers in Egypt and the Arabian Peninsula. Though he uses many rational arguments in his writings, *Atafayyish* like many of his contemporary reformers, focuses on text-based arguments from the Qur'an and the Prophet's Sunna. As he expresses his opposition to French colonialism, *Atafayyish* attempts to draw on the legacy of *Ibadi* jurisprudence to advance arguments for building unity among Muslims in North Africa.

These attempts at reforming the Shari'a changed much in the legal reasoning and production of law as discourses in every corner of the Muslim world. Governments also played a role, with appointments given to scholars to design *Shari'a*-compatible laws. The shift from simply producing "law" for consumption by both government and population undeniably changes the position of jurists and their law. This last point, as I indicated earlier, is behind the strength of Hallaq's argument of the demise of the Shari'a. I will come back to this point.

Chronology

The Syrian Ibn Taymiyya (1261–1328) is the premodern name most associated with modern reform in Islamic law, as his ideas, rejected by many of his seventh/fourteenth-century contemporaries, ignited the imagination of many moderns hundreds of years later. Though much more multifaceted than most of his modern followers make him out to be, there is no denying that Ibn Taymiyya's scholarship has introduced "emphases" of a unique flavor, which many modern reformers recycled and developed further. These include the emphasis on the original revelation (as contrasted to its interpretative tradition), the emphasis on "authenticity," defined as the connection with an earlier, uncorrupted age (the first few centuries of Islamic history), and the emphasis on the purity of the Islamic teachings coupled with suspicion of foreign influences. Ibn Taymiyya also championed "independence" in thinking, a quality claimed almost universally by reformers of different stripes. This is not to say that all modern reformers are followers of Ibn Taymiyya in either all his principles or specific issues; indeed, reformers' attitudes about Ibn Taymiyya cover a broad spectrum.

At any rate, when one attempts to delineate a chronology of modern reform in Islamic law, one must start much later than Ibn Taymiyya's times. Painting with a broad brush, I will provide the following temporal map for reform in Islamic law, encompassing four stages:

1. The dawn of reform 1700s–1760s
2. The age of populism and counter-populism 1760s–1850s
3. The age of experimentalism and multiple voices 1850s–1910s
4. The triumph of hybridism 1910s–present

The Dawn of Reform, 1700s–1760s

The birth of modern reform in Islamic law will remain debatable, given the multiplicity of perspectives used in describing and characterizing it. In the first half of the eighteenth century, one cannot miss the appearance of writings that show awareness of changes in the world, notably the rise of European power. One of the most significant figures of this stage was Shah Waliyyullah al-Dihlawi, a jurist and legal theorist who came from India, where British and Dutch power began to be felt by Southeast Asian Muslims. Dihlawi takes his nickname from the name of Delhi (Dihli), one of the Indian subcontinent's cities. In his writing, Dihlawi offers a new emphasis on two ideas, by themselves traceable to premodern Islamic law but appearing to be new as they are cast in novel forms in Dihlawi's writing.

The first idea is something of a summary of al-Qaffal al-Shashi's (d. 365/976) *Mahasin al-Shari'a*, with some twists. This is the idea that all laws in Islam, including those regulating rituals, are based on understandable and explicable rationales. The daily prayers and annual pilgrimage fulfill the individual's need for retreating and replenishing one's energy, building a connection with one's inner faculties, and advancing a sense of peace and balance. Almsgiving has a clear economic value and bolsters a community's sense of itself as an integrated whole. The prohibition of usury and other forms of unjust dealings is designed for the benefit of the community to live together without animus. Thus, to say that Islamic law simply provides tests for people's ability to obey God in order to deserve divine acceptance is a distortion of the nature of the Shari'a.

The second principle is that all laws are strongly tied to their context. This principle follows from the first but is clearly attested also in the language of the Qur'an and the Prophet's Sunna. According to this principle, jurists must attend to the context of any legal question before they offer their answer. This principle, long accepted by Muslim jurists, seemed to have lapsed into the backyard of juristic reasoning and appeared inoperative in many juristic debates. Dihlawi's call for an emphasis on the *irtifaqat*—matching laws with their context—was an attempt at reviving an old principle that was gradually forgotten and marginalized.

It is important to note that not all the religious figures of this period who may have felt imperial European pressures responded by a call to reform the law. Nabulsi (1641–1731) represents a group of religious leaders of his generation who witnessed new European influences and continued to emphasize personal "reform" and what was labeled "enlightenment" rather than legal thinking.[13] But we will continue to focus on the reform of the Shari'a as a system of norms under the influence of those external, *ready* norms given from outside of the Muslim world.

The Age of Populism and Counterpopulism, 1760s–1850s

Muhammad Ibn 'Ali al-Shawkani (d. 1250/1834) repeated an idea that reminds us of the Syrian Ibn Taymiyya (d. 728/1328): Islam is based on revelation by God to the Prophet Muhammad, and all interpretations of this revelation and the Prophet's tradition are secondary to the original revelations. All juristic traditions and technical juristic discourses were designed to serve these original sources and (more importantly) derive their authority from being interpretations of the original sources. This means that the interpretations must be discarded if they deviate from the path of the original sources. Muhammad Ibn 'Abd al-Wahhab, who journeyed from Northern Arabia to Syria and "discovered" Ibn Taymiyya, had made the same point. Ibn 'Abd al-Wahhab's followers employed these new ideas to reject the authority of the Ottomans, who emphasized the Hanafi legal tradition. Ibn 'Abd al-Wahhab's followers turned to military action when they conquered Mecca itself in 1803 and 1805, to be defeated later by an army sent by Muhammad Ali, the Pasha of Egypt. The Wahhabi revolt was seen by contemporary jurists, such as Ibn 'Abidin (1784–1836), as a revolt against all Muslim authorities, a replication of the Kharijites' revolution against both the authority of 'Ali and of his opponents in the seventh-century conflict over political authority. For Ibn 'Abidin, Ibn 'Abd al-Wahhab's followers are close to abandoning all Muslim communities and standing alone.

What emerged from these "back to the sources" movements was ultimately the seeds for a form of populism (the term being used here guardedly), attacking the elitism of the juristic academies, which emphasized jurists' unique capacity to understand legal sources and argument. The "back to the sources" call attempted to open the door for the average practicing Muslim a larger role in the theoretical basis of religiolegal practices they undertake. This call was faced with skepticism from jurists, such as Ibn 'Abidin (d. 1252/1836) in Syria and Bajuri (d. 1276/1860) in Egypt, among others. These jurists believed that the laity already enjoyed a sufficient measure of freedom in seeking religiolegal counsel and should not be led to believe that they should follow their own intuition or pick and chose haphazardly from the views of jurists based on their whims.

If the "back to the sources" movement produced a form of populism, albeit inadvertently, established jurisprudence continued to advance what may be called a form of antipopulism. These tendencies will continue to be witnessed in the next stages of the history of modern Islamic law.

The Age of Experimentalism and Multiple Reactions, 1850s–1910s

In this stage, rationalist responses to modern challenges grew louder and more sophisticated. Jamal al-Din al-Afghani's (d. 1314/1897) call for political and social reform, internalized and transformed by Muhammad 'Abdu (1265/1849–1323/1905), strongly affected reforms in Islamic law in this stage. Attacks on irrational following of popular religion and calls for adopting modern ways of life and reconciling them with Qur'anic teachings appear in much of 'Abdu's juristic reforms. Muhammad Ibn 'Ali al-Sanusi (d. 1275/1859) had already made similar points for a smaller audience in North Africa. Defenders of tradition, such as Muhammad al-'Abbasi al-Mahdi (1242/1827–1314/1897), continued to argue for the adequacy of the inherited juristic tradition, while mining it to produce novel arguments and occasionally modify standard legal doctrines to account for changes in the circumstances. 'Abdu's students went in different directions. Qasim Amin (1279/1863–1325/1908) further emphasized modernity and expressed suspicion of traditional arguments. Muhammad Rashid Reda (1281/1865–1353/1935) rejected extreme adherence to modern Western ideas of the successful society and insisted that Muslims needed to readopt traditional Muslim principles rather than abandon them. Reda essentially turned to a modified version of the "back to the sources" movement but employed a broader battery of arguments. In this stage, codification began in earnest in Ottoman jurists' *Majallat al-Ahkam al-'Adliyya* (a Herculean, comprehensive rearticulation of Hanafi law in a modern garb) and Muhammad Qadri Pasha's (1821–1888) *Murshid al-Hayran* (a modern rearticulation of family law). These efforts attempted to restate Islamic juristic doctrines in the form of legal codes, which changed some of its essential qualities, as has been established by many studies.

The Triumph of Hybridism, 1910s–Present

The legacy of the previous stages of development in legal thinking yielded different grades of adopting a call for change, but mostly bequeathed a measure of hybridism (mixing traditional Islamic and modern Western elements) in all thinking about Islamic law. Stronger measures of hybridism can be found in the juristic efforts of the late Sanhuri's (1895–1971) restructuring of premodern Islamic legal thinking to produce a version of it in conversation with modern Western legal systems. Early on, Sanhuri led efforts to write modern constitutions (in Sudan, Kuwait) and civil codes (in Egypt, Iraq, and Syria), which influenced constitutional and civil law thinking in the whole Arab world. Sanhuri also wrote legal commentaries in these laws and juristic treatises with pioneering analyses of basic concepts in Islamic law and comparisons with modern European laws. Sanhuri's method of abstracting from the language of Muslim jurists to provide equivalents for Western legal categories will become a prevalent method in modern Islamic legal research.

Religious scholars such as Mustafa al-Maraghi (d. 1364/1945) and Mahmud Shaltut (1310/1893–1382/1963), both of whom occupied the position of rector of al-Azhar in Egypt, have also participated in this stage of reform in Islamic law, through their writings and engagement in legislative activities. In the area of reforming the teaching and historical and conceptual study of Islamic law, Muhammad Abu Zahra (1315/1898–1371/1974), 'Ali al-Khafif (1308/1891–1375/1978), and 'Abd al-Wahhab Khallaf (1305/1888–1375/1956) have also played a role in establishing a new language for modern Islamic legal discourses, with a strong focus on modern questions and an assumed comparativist approach.

Philosophical approaches to the question of reform in law led to substantive changes in Islamic legal theory. Al-Tahir Ibn 'Ashur (d. 1393/1973) contributed to the discourse on the general aims of the law (*maqasid al-Shari'a*) by augmenting the idea expressed by Shatibi (d. 790/1388) in his book *al-Muwafaqat*. Ibn 'Ashur goes beyond the abstract aims of the law of protecting religion, life, reason, honor, lineage, and property to state more specific aims derived from specific basic laws in different areas of Islamic law. Ibn 'Ashur justifies his emphasis on the *maqasid* by an attempt to reduce unnecessary disagreement among jurists in the particulars of the law and argues that these *maqasid* should constitute a shared common legal sense among all jurists.[14]

But lesser measures of hybridism can be found in the views of adherents of neotraditionalism. Neotraditionalists accept the idea that the jurist must leave some questions of governance to political authorities who interpret the teachings of tradition for a special purpose (not that the authority of political leaders could not be questioned from time to time). This brings the influences of modern Western political and economic systems into the area of public life, which continue to be negotiated by neotraditionalists.

The Islamic revolution of 1979 is a significant development in this stage, just as the constitutional revolution of 1905 was the culmination of the previous stage in Shi'i Islam. The revolution of 1979 gave Shi'i Muslim jurists an opportunity to experiment with a new reality in Shi'i history, where administering the affairs of government became one of the tasks of jurisprudence. This produced much ingenuity in dealing with questions of how to administer the economy and adopt democratic ways of governance. Expanding on the principle of reason (*'aql*) as a source of law, following texts and consensus, Shi'i jurists advanced new solutions to many problems in family law, trade, and crime. Though benefiting from modern Sunni legal thinking, the Islamic revolution has forced Shi'i jurists to engage in new questions of law as a political system.

Questions Old and New

Reformers face questions that can be seen as old or new questions, depending on the perspective they employ. For example, the question of violating the integrity of the human body for legitimate reasons, such as administering organ transplants or performing autopsy on dead bodies, can be seen as an old or a new question. It can be seen as an old question to the extent that medieval doctors and jurists have already recognized and addressed the general issue of invasive intervention in the human body as a matter of balance between (a) the need to respect the human body (even of a dead person) and (b) the need for providing medical care and advancing medical education. But this question can be seen as a new question to the extent that organ transplants are a new medical achievement that introduced new ways of thinking about the human body itself. When donation of one's organ is part of the question, things get more complicated, as the question concerns one's ownership of her/his body and her/his heirs' capacity to make decisions regarding the body of a deceased person. Disagreement among modern jurists in issues like these reflect their conscious effort to identify what is old and what is new in the questions they address.[15]

Aside from questions raised by the advancement of science and medicine, the new questions of reform center on adopting modern systems of government, guaranteeing broader equality between men and women in financial and legal matters and in participation in public life. Again, many reformers believe that the Islamic legal tradition provides guidance about seemingly new questions. These reformers search for old generalities that capture the new questions. Others assert that new questions must be approached without any prejudice originating in tradition. Modernists have employed both types of argument to recommend the adoption of Western systems of government and finance. Many modernists who champion adopting modern democratic institutions argue that equality, the basic core of the principle of democracy, is an Islamic value heavily attested in religious texts and practice.[16] In this line of thinking, the argument for change is made from precedent. Many modernists also argue that a narrow definition of usury (*riba*) or the "excessively risky" (including an element of *gharar*) must be adopted and old definitions abandoned, since the new economic systems are hardly comparable to medieval ones. In this case, the claim that a new question is presented serves as a way to ignore or neutralize the influence of precedents, which leads to wide adoption of modern systems.[17]

Neotraditionalists who emphasize the comprehensiveness of revelation have leaned toward seeking guidance from the example of the Prophet and his companions. In their debates with modernists, neotraditionalists do not simply emphasize texts (as nonnegotiable foundations claimed to be shared by all Muslims) and reject "Islamic" modernization. Neotraditionalists enjoy a measure of sophistication in identifying the weakness in modernists' reasoning. For example, modernists' use of texts from the Qur'an and the Sunna to support their ideas in advancing modern concepts for women's equality with men is critiqued by neotraditionalists as opportunistic and self-serving, pointing to differences between premodern and modern societies in their expectations of women participation in public activities.

A Second Phase of the Debate

This long journey ended up shifting the debate on the *future* of the Shari'a into one about *what it is.* If you studied Islamic law at the start of the fifteenth hijri century (= end of the twentieth CE), you would find different "tracks" for its study even at the heart of Cairo, the Egyptian capital. There was (always) the way of the Azharis, who still, mysteriously, understood the arguments of al-'Adud al-Iji and his convoluted theology, for example, and read legal texts and applied them in their *fatwas* in creative ways. [A teacher of mine, 'Abd al-Jalil al-Qaranshawi, used to tell the story that Zaki Mubarak pasha (d. 1952), after earning more than one doctorate, tried to go back to study at al-Azhar to learn these difficult texts, and after ultimately failing, he confessed jokingly that "many intelligent people understand the language of the living; but only the Azharis can understand these long-dead fellows."] And there was Dar al-'Ulum, my school, which was founded in 1871/2 to counter al-Azhar's conservatism but became itself a hotbed of "conservative," religious thinking within the modern Cairo University. And there were the law schools, with their Shari'a departments and family law's inextricable connections with medieval Islamic legal reasoning and customs.

In these schools, master's and doctoral dissertations were produced at a high rate, by students from dozens of countries (only that privileged Egyptians such as myself did not have to pay the high tuition the foreigners paid, but these foreigners' academic contributions were substantial). These dissertations, it is true, have not all been published (many, we used to say, moved from the departments' "ceremony room" where they were publicly defended to the "cemetery of dissertations," also known as the library). But the medieval debate on *futur al-shari'a* continued in these dissertations' introductions and the debate could only get better and harder to engage in. Many of the authors of these dissertations moved on to continue the conversation in their writings after they finished their graduate work, and some of them had positions in the government where they implemented their ideas [an advisor of my master's thesis, e.g., went on to consult for the People's Council (the main legislative body) about Egyptian law's consistency with the Shari'a, and one of my colleagues, who came from Kuwait, left after his defense to become a judge in his country.] I was not as lucky (or maybe much luckier). I ended up becoming an academic at a research uniersity, but perhaps an impractical streak in my thinking is to be blamed.

This second phase of the debate seems more "muted" in certain ways (with no systematic positions and no standard or, *for a want of a better expression*, global arguments) but louder in the sense that the contentions involved more than theological and legal stances; the debate extended to political appointments and public discussions, a broad array of media for dissemination of views, and a sense of the bifurcation of the moral and legal space into two realms, one for *fatwa* and another for *adjudication*. This second phase of the debate will shift once again into a third phase, where the very presence of the Shari'a is disputed.

Lasting Impact?

Did the legal reform we have been discussing create a new legal science that effectively ended the relevance of the cumbersome *madhhab*-based legal science? If not, did either this reform or the social and political conditions that made it possible *completely discredit* the old legal science and its cultural and social echoes in Muslim societies? Without a positive answer to either of these questions, any lasting impact for this reform amounting to full transformation of the Shari'a, to the extent of announcing its demise as it has henceforth been known, could not be asserted.

From a fifteenth/twenty-first-century viewpoint, the legacy of reform in Islamic (Sunni, Shi'i, Ibadi) law seems to be a process of piecemeal change in Islamic legal discourses. It has been argued that only piecemeal juristic reform could have a lasting impact on any legal system.[18] The question remains, however, whether this change created a true alternative. Did the compartmentalization of the Shari'a coupled with a mix of abstract and low-level comparisons between *fiqh*/*usul al-fiqh* and European legal systems, tear the old system into pieces?

The discussion of the lasting impact of reform continues for the most part to be a bit quick and shallow. All observers note many reformers' emphasis on abstract principles as all-encompassing bases for legal thinking while giving little attention to specific premodern juristic discourses. Hence one notes the obsession with *maqasid* or abstract aims of the law, *masalih* or the benefits behind suggested laws, and perhaps in essence the *irtifaqat* or the insistence on matching laws with their context. *Maqasid* and *masalih* are old notions Muslim jurists have debated. While Shatibi (d. 790/1388) is often credited with the full exposition of how *maqasid* can be used as explanatory devices for legal doctrines, Ghazali (d. 505/1111) has spoken of *maqasid* and *masalih* in a fairly elaborate manner, and these notions can indeed be traced to earlier legal writings. In modern times, *maqasid* have been emphasized as a means to advance new legal doctrines (rather than explain existing ones). Thus, certain versions of the argument that certain transactions that may be suspect for their potential usurious nature are acceptable, since they are in line with the maqasid is possible only in a modern juristic discourse and might not be recognizable to a premodern jurist. The same can be said about general arguments based on *masalih* or the legitimate benefits expected from certain legal doctrines.

Many could also reasonably credit the literature on reforming Islamic law with confusions or novel usages of technical legal terms and a willingness to appropriate them without full comprehension of their significance. These include terms such as "*ijtihad*," which was destined to lose its technical denoting of the efforts of a trained jurist, either within a *madhhab* or independently. These also include more technical terminology being taken out of their context and explained anew. An example is using the term "*bara'a*" (meaning lack of legal value judgment) to indicate "innocence" of people by nature (in common modern usage, the Arabic word "bara'a" indicates innocence). Jamal al-Banna, for example, speaks of *bara'a* as an opposite of sin, while he attempts to point to the technical term, to which jurists refer in the legal principle *al-asl al-bara'a*. The principle normally indicates that acts do not receive legal characterization without evidence, and when it applies to one's *depository* of duties and liabilities (*dhimma*), it indicates that the *dhimma* is free of liabilities unless this liability is established by evidence.[19]

The war of terminology is symptomatic of a rift between those trained in the old ways and those who would like to break free out of these old ways. Those who use old terminology loosely sometimes consciously attempt to transcend it. The legacy of reform in Islamic law so far reflects the vastness of the task of reforming a labyrinthine structure of discursive, social, and political elements, referred to simply as the *Shari'a*. Some historians believe that successful reform only comes from trained jurists who can offer arguments that incorporate layers of the early tradition, in order to serve as a bridge between the old and new ways of thinking.[20] If those capable of being this bridge are decreasing over time, continuity may be unachievable, and many question marks force themselves on the debate.

Given the complexity of the matter, one must accept a nuanced reading of the nature and value of this reform and its potential lasting impact. Disagreement about how to read the history of Islamic law from the 1700s onward will probably continue among scholars for years to come. For our purposes, it bears much reflection, which will lead our discussion of the question of the fatigue of the Shari'a in the remainder of these chapters.

Accepting Second-Class Status

One could not deny that a result of this long process was that many traditionally trained jurists accepted their new status as second-class participants in public reasoning, out of realism or for having no other choice. It was not that they had a smaller audience; they simply had the poorer and less empowered audience. But they had an audience nonetheless. These jurists' own debating of the status of the Shari'a was affected more and more by a yearning to the foundation of this Shari'a. Shawkani deemphasized the *madhhab*, and Muti'i did not go as far, but both of them spoke of the centrality of knowledge of the Qur'an and Sunna. Let us note how this change in the jurists' position was covered by the strength of the emphasis on the foundation. I will now come back once more to Shawkani's discussion of the fatigue question.[21]

The question Shawkani sets out to ask is this: Is it possible for an age to be devoid of qualified jurists? This is the same familiar fatigue question of the medieval debate. The answer now reflects the richness of almost a thousand years of thinking about the issue: Some argued, he says, that it would never happen that an age be devoid of a conveyer of God's commands. *Ijtihad* is a collective duty to be fulfilled by the community as a whole, but what exactly is the duty? Is it having scholars of the caliber of Shafi'i and other founders of *madhhabs*, or is a jurist who may or may not be affiliated with one of these *madhahbs* sufficient? This leads Shawkani to a digression about cases in which *ijtihad* is a collective duty (*fard kifaya*) and cases where it is a personal immediate duty (*fard 'ayn*), which at least teaches us one aspect of the complexity of *ijtihad*: depending on the circumstance, different types and levels of *ijtihad* are required. It is obvious, in all cases, that this is a duty, and a divine imposition of a duty cannot amount to a request to do what is impossible. The prophecy of the persistence of the truth is cited (*la tazal*[u] *ta'ifat*[un] *min ummati zahirin*[a] *bi-l-haqq*), followed by the arguments of the other side (confused and confusing as these arguments usually are about the different levels of *ijtihad* involved in the discussion) with negations and assertions of the availability of *ijtihad* at this or that age. Shawkani believes that all those who claimed that there was no qualified jurist in their age lived at times where admitted masters of *Shari'a* knowledge lived. He then goes on to mention the names of some of these masters.

Shawkani also argues that the ease with which the foundations of *ijtihad* have become documented and preserved goes against the assumption of the end of *ijtihad*. Shawkani then concludes with a frustrated "there is no point in having the discussion." Developing this research is not of much use, he says, since this matter is more apparent than all apparent matters, and those chained by "imitation" cannot bind those to whom God opened the doors of knowledge, allowing them to escape imitating other men, and this is not the first and will not be the last of the imitators' invalid claims. Those who confine God's blessing to some of his creation or limit understating this *Shari'a* to the earlier generations have dared God and his *Shari'a*, which He has given to all whom he created. Finally, Shawkani equates a thesis of the fatigue of the Shari'a with the fatigue of God's revelation itself, an abrogation of the last of God's laws, which is impossible.

Shawkani's teacher, San'ani (d. 1182/1768), had started on a path of eclecticism in his jurisprudence, which paved the way for this unaffiliated, free adherence to the *Shari'a*. San'ani's *Rasa'il* shows a strong streak of direct reliance on the Sunna of the Prophet as the main basis for law, but these treatises also show much wavering on important issues and less-than-clear doctrines, compared to *madhhab* followers.[22] San'ani seems to study issues as he goes along, as opposed to approaching issues only after long reflections and consulting with teachers. Shawkani learned the lesson from San'ani's practice, it seems. He realized that learning from books was possible, after some basic initiation in the fields of *fiqh* and *usul* and other related fields.

Shawkani's argument about *ijtihad* remained suspect to many. At any rate, his arguments could hardly have ended the debate. At the same time Shawkani was practically dismissing the debate on the fatigue of the Shari'a as frivolous, his contemporary Hasan al-'Attar (d. 1250/1835) wrote in a supercommentary on Mahalli's commentary on Subki's statement in *Jam' al-Jawami'*: "It is possible for an age to be devoid of a *mujtahid*—this being held against the Hanabila." Ibn Daqiq al-'Id (d. 702/1302) interjected, so the text goes, by limiting the word "age" to times previous to the collapse of the foundations of the world, signified by things such as the rise of the sun from the West. Safiyy al-Din al-Hindi (d. 715/1315) explained that this disagreement was indeed two in one, addressing the absence of (i) founders of *madhhab*s or schools of law and of (ii) able followers of these founders. 'Attar notes that the *500 years before the end* that kept moving from Juwayni (d. 478/1085) to Zarkashi (d. 794/1392) have already elapsed (in his thirteenth/nineteenth century), and the *Shari'a* was still preserved (*al-shari'atu bi-hamdi* ^A^*llah*^i^ *mahfuza*) but after a millennium of Islamic history (*ba'da mujawazati* ^a^*l-alf*), so much contradiction can be found (*ishtadda* ^a^*l-tanaqud*) and in our age, which is the thirteenth century (nineteenth CE), he says, both the seekers and that which is sought have been weakened, by the accumulation of weighty events (*da'ufa al-talibu wa-l-matlub, bi-tarakumi 'aza'imi* ^a^*l-khutub*).[23]

History's Multiple Dialectics

I will conclude this long chapter with some reflections on the big historical picture of the Shari'a, with an acknowledgment of the difficulty of this exercise. The evolution of the Shari'a in its long journey leaves us with questions about whether any "causes" of this evolution may be identified, whether these were patterns of affinities between people, government, and scholars of the Shari'a in Islamic history that attended its developments and movement from one stage to another. Admittedly, raising these questions is much easier than answering them.

Is it the mere passage of time that creates *futur* of different grades? Or should one assume that a state of the fatigue of the Shari'a could happen only when something goes terribly bad (or if one assumes that Shari'a is simply an evil system, that it happens when something goes terribly well)? Should one assume that the very presence of a faithful Muslim population, aided and led by a government with a measure of respect for the Islamic tradition, sufficiently guarantees that this condition of *futur* does not exist, which entails an assumption that the occurrence of *futur* is an indication of an unusual condition within Muslim societies and polities? These questions cannot be answered without an idea of how history operates, a philosophy of history more or less.

The insistence on a strong causal relationship among these three elements (jurists; the presence of ideal government; and the presence of certain social customs) is governed by a condition that is perceived to obtain today, a condition in which the three debates (on the roles or sovereignty of jurists, government, and custom) may be revived as aspects of one and the same debate, forcing us to link them. While a minimum of governmental support for the practitioners of jurisprudence must be available for its survival, the evolution of Sunni jurisprudence challenges neat narratives that explain what may be perceived as its triumphs and failures in conjunction with governments' support for it. The relationship between jurisprudence and social standards, different in nature, suggests a different link. Some juristic explanations lose their relevance when social standards and collective sensibilities change. Yet, Sunni jurists have also demonstrated a strong ability to turn the shifts of social standards into opportunities for modifying the mode of negotiation between law and custom.

Less ambitious and problematic questions may be introduced. Should serious deficiency in educating good jurists itself be seen as symptomatic of other aspects of an overall *futur* in the status of the Shari'a in a Muslim society? In other words, regardless of the causes of the condition of *futur* in the narrow sense (lack of jurists), is it attended by more than its main symptom or basic constituent (the failure of generating jurists) or must it be attended by a larger picture, an atmosphere where the education of jurists is affected by social and political conditions that are themselves conducive to ignoring the education of jurists?

If we presume, against many temptations and intuitions, that the absence of ideal government and the fatigue of the Shari'a are not causally related, however softly, the historical coincidence of these debates and their constant reiteration and reformulation does not fall short of meriting investigation. Furthermore, the relationship between juristic explanations and social conditions merits another investigation, that of whether the change of custom in Muslim societies could be another attendant of the fatigue of the Shari'a and the end of its jurisprudence.

Dialectical relationships of mutual reinforcement are usually taken more seriously. One might take Juwayni's (d. 478/1085) discussion of the fatigue of the Shari'a as a sequel to the absence of good government to imply at least a form of soft causality between the latter and the fatigue of the Shari'a. On this reading, the absence of government, the latest stage in a series of failures starting from the absence of ideal government, which could in Juwayni's view be rectified only by reliance on the notables/scholars of the community, can be seen as a foundation for the fatigue of the Shari'a, whose scholars are the community's last resort, after the disintegration of the normal Muslim community. On an alternative reading, any occurrence of the absence of ideal government prior to the absence of qualified jurists would be seen as coincidental. The latter, the less presumptuous or burdened reading, opens up the door for an investigation of the older debates on the fatigue of the Shari'a. Is the end of the profession of "jurist" possible? And what are the duties of the Muslim populations at that time? I am unwilling to venture into answering these questions. I am certainly interested in the history of Sunni law and jurisprudence, which I see as more related to social than political history (though not unrelated to the latter). However, I resist the temptation to speculate about the future and even to generalize from what I know about the Muslim world today to form an assessment of the vividness of the Shari'a. My task is to provide a reading of debates and analyze and interrogate arguments and positions.

Four Eras of Islamic Legal History

I will venture only one assertion: Let us not exaggerate the role of government in the history of ideas (at least within Muslim societies). Islamic legal history is mostly something other than the history of governments' interaction with jurists. We have grown accustomed to the opposite of this assertion; so it might take time to undo its negative influence.

Whether the subject is literature, philosophy, art, or something else, Islamic history is divided into political ages—*Rightly Guided Caliphs, Umayyads, Abbasids*, and so on. Political shifts admittedly influence ideas. But this influence could be exaggerated. There is a mighty phenomenon that could serve as an organizing principle for Islamic history in the case of law, the *madhhab* or school of law, that is. If the fatigue question invites us to provide a sketch of Islamic legal history, we may then attempt the following division of Islamic legal history, to speak of its infancy and evolution until it reaches what may seem to some as its old age.

The first stage is the *sahaba/companions' era* (from 10/632 until before 100/720s). This stage provides the foundation of all subsequent knowledge of either the Qur'an or the Sunna, which are the basis of any version of the Shari'a. Yet, this is the hardest stage to study, owing mostly to its foundational nature, coupled with the scarcity of reports about it.

The second is the *first era of the* madhahib (100/720s–700s/1300s).

The third is the *second era of the* madhahib (700s/1300s–1250s/1830s). This stage was characterized by a revival of interest in the Sunna as a basis for law competing with the *madhhab*, summoning even Nawawi, the organizer of Shafi'i law, to report Shafi'i's view with a hesitation to fully adhere to it and including people such as Ibn Hajar al-'Asqalani (d. 852/1448), who rewrote Islamic law as a commentary on the *hadith*. This *hadith* movement may be reductively tied to the Mongol invasion or Ibn Taymiyya, and it may have sustained a soft causal affinity with these, but I think it is larger than either one of these two.

The fourth and current era is the *hybrid reasoning era*. In this stage, new forms of reasoning live side by side with old reasoning.

A fifth stage will begin, in my view, only when the obsession with comparison (with foreign laws) becomes a less significant feature in legal reasoning in Muslim societies, while a clear understanding of the social and political contexts is taken for granted. The main characteristic of this stage must thus be "immediate" proceeding to analyzing the questions without the "mediation" of European or American ideas and institutions. At the center of the tasks of the new jurisprudence is an analysis of how customs (broader than being popular, institutional, or governmental) have changed, and of how juristic thinking itself may have been *affected by* and must be *reconciled with* these new customs.

Chapter 8

Absent Good Government

Is government part of the Shari'a, or part of the faith itself, or is it only a practical need for all societies, Muslim societies included? If you take the Ash'ari view, establishing a government and what it should look like are questions of practical nature, not in any way foundational to the faith. The only justification for discussing government in theology manuals was to emphasize the importance of the matter of leadership in society, as "many heretics have held distorted views on it."[1] Many Muslims, especially Shi'is, will beg to differ. The idea that government is not an essential part of the faith should, however, not be taken to mean that government is an insignificant matter.[2] It is only that equating the health and compliance of government with the health of the Shari'a might not make much sense on mainstream medieval Sunni thinking. Many modern analyses of the health and frailty of the Shari'a, again, seem to have a different position. Without any turn toward Shi'ism, modern discussions of the end of the Shari'a embraced government as a major factor in understanding the role of the Shari'a in today's Muslim societies.

This position in a way is understandable when one of the goals of studying the Shari'a today is to test how far along the Shari'a is on its way toward extinction. Furthermore, and in any case, official laws are easier to study than unofficial, underground ones, if these could even be said to exist. It is easier to study the constitution, laws and regulations, and official policies of an identifiable political entity than to conduct any deep cultural analysis of Muslim societies to gauge how much sway the Shari'a holds in them. Moreover, law in the modern world is an inherently political institution (could this not be universal?). It simply makes sense to study the life of law in relation to the state in a context where law and state are partly interdependent. Many, hence, would be skeptical of the notion of a law functioning without a state. I am of course aware that studies of Islamic law go in different directions and cover aspects of the underground life of the Shari'a, but when the assessment of the vigor and strength of the Shari'a is considered, official laws tend to be emphasized.

My point is that there is something missing from an assessment of the health of the Shari'a that does not raise the basic question of the extent to which its underground life can be observed. As I said, there are difficulties facing the study of this underground life, let alone having to provide an overall assessment of its influence for the purpose of measuring its degree of fatigue. The way in which the underground life of the Shari'a may be assessed aside, the disentanglement of government and Shari'a, despite their historical alliances, half-alliances, and other postures each took vis-à-vis the other, received a theoretical treatment from a Sunni voice close to a millennium ago that ought to be remembered now. This treatment was born out of the realization that a mutual reinforcement between government (even the much weaker medieval government) and the Shari'a was not a prerequisite for the life of the Shari'a. This treatment and this voice was that of Abu-l-Ma'ali al-Juwayni (419/1028–478/1085), whom I already mentioned more than once.

The importance of Juwayni's work for my project stems from the fact that it captured an element of the discussion of the life of the Shari'a that has not been addressed by the debate I analyzed in chapters four–six. But his work gained added importance as it became clear to me over time that an essential element of normal politics is that most people do not, could not, and should not, participate in it (so-called democratic societies included), and it also seems to me that this realization is one of the basics of the knowledge and practice of politics. The fear of anarchy, and the attacks on anarchy by both politicians and political scientists is best understood as a consequence of this realization: that with too many participants in politics, it becomes something else. Telling the full truth (at the right time) and telling a lie or at least keeping correct and full information private (also at the right time) are an important part of good politics. The population could not participate in that. At least one *object* of political power in any case is *the population* the politician is meant to serve, for whom (the population) certain paths of behavior are recommended, which they may elect to disobey, as long as they are willing to face the consequences.

The Shari'a's disentanglement from government becomes more meaningful when we reflect on this quality in government. *The Shari'a* possesses almost the exact opposite quality when the issue of participation is considered: without the population's participation, the Shari'a could not have a full existence. Government could not coexist with any substantive participation from the population it rules, and the Shari'a could not exist without substantive participation from the population it rules. The intersections of Shari'a and government are not meant to be disputed here. This discussion concerns their disentanglement and contrasts.

As I was editing this chapter, revolutions at the heart of the Muslim world have created Juwaynian moments (a term that became established in conversations I had with many interlocutors since January and February 2011), where governments were overthrown without full replacements and without an immediate collapse of society or any realization of the exaggerated fear of self-destruction under an anarchy. The main point about the exaggeration of the role of government in mature societies has been vindicated. My interlocutors, including my graduate students, could see this point without need for an elaboration. I am, however, in need of an explanation for the reader who did not participate in the discussions we had about "resizing" government and questioning the contribution of the modern state to stability in the world and its prospects in the future.

The Egyptian revolution raises questions about a pattern, hitherto dominant in Muslim societies, where a small "powerful" minority exercises disproportionate influence on many facets of life in their societies. This minority, consisting not only of those in "government" but many who may or may not be connected to government but who seem to benefit from the virtual division of society into the few and the many—the financially secure, Western-bent, well-connected *few*, and the more religious but less financially secure, less Western-bent, less well-connected *many*. The influence of the "few" has been exaggerated repeatedly in the past, but it was certainly disproportionate. At this point, much doubt arises about the possibility of the continuity of this pattern.

Before I go any further, let me once again negate any recommendation of anarchy on my part. I also have no interest in adopting what some half-baked discussions recently imagined (based on scattered, secondary materials) about Muslim anarchists—the idea is that some Mu'tazilis such as Abu Bakr al-Asamm (d. 201/816) and some Kharijites could be seen as full-fledged Muslim anarchists. Anarchy and anarchists remain a difficult subject for Western history, and it is irresponsible and confusing to suggest analogies (as those who argue for Muslim anarchism did) between and among concepts whose delimitation requires much more work than is provided in these analyses.

Muslim anarchism aside, my point is "against" exaggerations of the role of government, rather than a claim that it plays no role whatsoever. Sunni jurists agree that, in normal circumstances, people need to be bossed over.[3]

Jahiz justified the need for government by the necessity of preventing "overreach" by the powerful. If there was no sovereign, he said, people would be in disarray, and the powerful would overreach, and injustice would take over the world.[4]

A famous line of poetry tells us in its first hemistich: People do not do well when they lack leaders (*la yasluhu al-nasu fawda la surata lahum*). Mawardi appropriately cites this line in his classic on government, the Ordinances or *al-Ahkam al-Sultaniyya*. There are general principles of politics from a Sunni juristic viewpoint—*al-siyasa al-shar'iyya*—which confirm a limited interest by these jurists' in government. Sunni juristic writings in this area (even by those who seemed to be politically savvy, who were close to the circles of political power) reflect their distance from the true subject of politics, its manipulation and rearrangement of positions. Juwayni's *Ghiyathi* does appear to be a strange loop. In it Juwayni takes interest in some of the details of political leadership and provides good justifications for its maneuvering. He also pushes the envelope; and he does seriously contemplate power vacuum—life without government.

The future may well be the theatre for applying this side of Juwayni's disentanglement of the Shari'a from government, which has significantly changed and become a basic element of the modern state. The recent global weakness of "government" as an institution may not be bad news for Shari'a norms. Revolutions in the Sunni world do not necessarily have to lead to establishing an old-style strong government that will create a new version of the Shari'a. A strong government may in fact weaken the Shari'a's already weak, underground life further. Also, a continuation of an underground life of the Shari'a does not have to mean a new thriving of the same *madhhab*-based Shari'a; only possibly a new mutation of the old Shari'a that is a couple of steps removed from its medieval version but more durable than any modern or reformed Shari'a-based state could offer.

This chapter will not address the possibilities of the future; it has the modest aim of addressing a basic juristic prejudice about the limitations of the importance of government in the survival of the Shari'a. A reading of Juwayni's classic on government, the *Ghiyathi*, anchors my discussion. Juwayni will not speak in any detail to a modern post-state world, but I will start with a translation of sections from his *Ghiyathi* as a prelude to a discussion of where government stands and should stand in the present and future of societies that take the Shari'a seriously. This will clarify why I cannot accept Hallaq's (still) government-centered analysis of the death of the Shari'a and its potential revival, despite much agreement with many of his premises.[5]

Juwayni's Classic on Government

Juwayni's *Ghiyathi* is an eleventh-century treatise addressing the two important hypotheticals: What should a community do in the case of the absence of ideal government, and what should the community do in the case of the absence or near absence of qualified jurists. Juwayni thus synthesized the two debates of the absence of ideal government and the fatigue of the Shari'a into one, where the fatigue of the Shari'a seems to be temporally subsequent to the absence of good government. For Juwayni, the absence of good government can be ameliorated by placing Muslim jurists in leadership positions in their communities, but if these were lacking, then we would be facing the question of the fatigue of Shari'a. Juwayni plainly states that the essential consideration in political leadership is competence and support for the population (*kifaya*), and that other conditions such as knowledge or piety are, while desirable, not indispensible. When the Shari'a experiences fatigue or begins to fade away, basic and essential precepts must be observed, as the details become increasingly inaccessible or inapplicable.

There are a couple of subtexts here. First, the foundation of government in Juwayni's thinking, which he believes should be thus understood by all who understand Islamic history and doctrines, is functional legitimacy, not legal or institutional legitimacy. Government is there to serve basic functions, and in the absence of all the ornaments available in the case of knowledgeable leaders, one has to go back to the basics and accept that government's efficacy in providing security, and basic services is more important than the embellishments of an awesome Caliphate. Second, the absence of qualified jurists in the presence of good government is unlikely. Not only does Juwayni address the absence of jurists as a condition of the aftermath of the failure of government, his detailed explanations of the failure at the top of society, while its foundations remain intact, show a strong prejudice against the possibility of a full and rapid transformation of society that starts from the top. In other words, a revolution and a change of government will not transform the society quickly; the other way around is more likely—a transformation in society leads to changing government more easily.

For Juwayni, if the Shari'a as a legal system with a philosophical and religious basis maintains different grades of support, by "government," "people," and "scholars," then it will continue to maintain different grades of presence, even when it loses some of its support. The Shari'a does not disappear when it is abandoned by the government but persists as authoritative for the people and the jurists. If the Shari'a is abandoned by the government but continues to enjoy deep support from "the elements" of society, (the second tier, third tier, fourth tier, etc. structures of society) on which "government" itself stands, then it survives on these levels. The same is true when it is abandoned by people but not by jurists, and when jurists cease to be available while the people simply rely on their memory of this Shari'a to the best of their ability. Even if the population includes strong elements of resistance to the Shari'a coupled with shortage in the scholars, propagators, and explicators of this Shari'a and its philosophy, the Shari'a might survive as discourse among the few and can regain strength at a later stage. The extinction of the law and of its philosophical basis is possible only when all its constituents are extinct—that is, its discourses, scholars, and the populations that consume it.

Juwayni's project is also an analysis of how communities could achieve the best order within and without a functioning government. His analysis is most distinguished by its exclusion of the prejudice that communities without perfectly functional government are doomed to the status of "anarchy" or (to use a term that gets tossed around frequently) becoming a "failed" community. Descending from the Caliphate directly to anarchy should not be an obvious possibility. Changes in the central government, whether in Damascus or in Baghdad, did not result in immediate change of government in all regional governments, and revolts against the central government took place from time to time (again none of this created anarchy, *pace* the apparent language of the talk of Muslim anarchism), which allowed for moments of reliance on notables, such as the 'Abd al-Hakam family in Egypt, to be entrusted with some of the functions of government while not being officially a government. The 'Abd al-Hakams were a family of prominent leaders and scholars, who took over the assets of large businesses during an interval of uncertainty about political leadership in Egypt. Later, the 'Abd al-Hakams were asked to release the assets they had kept upon the establishment of a new government. Even if their behavior was at times revolutionary and not supportive of the central Caliphal government, the 'Abd al-Hakams showed readiness to take on public responsibilities beyond the role of activists or rebels. This precedent serves as a foundation for the theory that prominent local leaders and scholars might replace the government in moments of crisis, which is one of the components of Juwayni's theory.

While emphasizing the organizational and supportive functions of government (embedded in terms such as *kifaya*, *najda*, and *shahama*) and considering its absence a cause for concern and action, Juwayni does not give up on a community simply because of the failure of its government. I will now offer a translation of sections from the *Ghiyathi*.

Absent Good Government

The *Ghiyathi* is divided into three sections. The first deals with the conditions of a normal government; the second with the absence of good government; and the third with the absence of qualified jurists.

What happens when society fails to find qualified leaders? Qualifications differ across time and place; so, the exact qualifications, although they would be relevant to certain aspects of this discussion, could be set aside for a moment to focus on the central question: What if we cannot have the government we would like to have? Some might say: let us do without government altogether. Others could say: let us have the best one available. One might accept the latter solution, yet ask further: What if none is available? What if no one is in charge? This is a bigger problem, and the solution we just accepted seems to take the form of rejecting the problem: We must have a government; living without a government is living in the state of nature, where all things go, where there is no safety, no justice, and so on. But what if we insist on the question: Can society live without government? Juwayni seems to think: yes. Juwayni is pretty emphatic on the importance of government. But he thinks that there are deeper structures for a community beneath its "high" governmental structure. These deeper structures, one might say interpretively, are the very basis for the "high" government.

But if we can live without a government, what is government for? Juwayni's answer is that government is necessary for certain functions. How could the Muslim populations in the Eastern Mediterranean have been defended against 200,000 Byzantine soldiers under Romanus IV in the year 463/1071 (when Juwayni was 43 years old)? This occurred only less than three decades ahead of the Crusades, and the decisive battle that ensued, known as Malazgird or Manzikert, which was won by the Saljuq leader Alp Arslan (420/1029–464/1072), is a case in point where government did indeed achieve basic goal of defending the population that would be otherwise unachievable.[6] The importance of this function of "the defense of the population" has affected Juwayni's *Ghiyathi* in several ways. But let us turn to the synoptic translation I promised.

A Synopsis from the *Ghiyathi*

The following are selections from the middle section of the *Ghiyathi*—the first and third of this section's three chapters. The middle section of this book addresses the absence of a sovereign (imam). This comprises three chapters. The first concerns lacunae in the qualifications of the sovereign, whether these lacunae be partial or total. The second concerns the ascension to the sovereign's position through mere power as opposed to contract. The third addresses the total absence of a sovereign either through power or appointment

Chapter I: On Lacunae in the Qualifications of the Sovereigns

We have already amply explained the conditions and qualifications, which the sovereign (imam) should possess. In this chapter we discuss the possibility that one of these qualifications is unrealized, and we begin with the least significant and ascend to those qualifications of greater impact, in order that (with God's aid and guidance) we fulfill the promise of the chapter. This requires us to begin with the condition of Qurashi "lineage" (*nasab*).

We have stated that being a descendant of the tribe of Quraysh is a consideration in the office of sovereign (imam). If we found no descendant of Quraysh to assume this office's responsibilities, but we found a person who fulfills the rest of the qualifications, we would appoint the one we find to be knowledgeable, competent, and to be of good character, and this person would be a sovereign with full jurisdiction over all peoples. Lineage, in fact, has been made a condition only as a way to honor the Messenger Muhammad's tree of descendants, since none of the objectives of the office of the sovereign hinges on being ascribed to any lineage. We also know with certainty that the sovereign is a supreme bond and a source of honor for people, and the goal behind appointing the sovereign is achieving order for the affairs of Muslims and Islam, and people should not be left without a bond, lest the treacherous waives of sedition's sea besiege them, ridden [as these waves may be] by excitable rebels.

For this high office we seek a man of Qurashi lineage to avoid people's descent into fatal ditches and getting lost among multiple paths and ways. The absence of a qualified ruler who also possesses this lineage does not prevent appointing a competent leader, whose orders should be followed, not unlike those of a descendant of Quraysh. This issue bears some reflection as follows: If we were to appoint a descendant of Quraysh who also possesses the rest of the qualifications of a sovereign and who had no contemporary peer and later found an alternative who is superior in the qualities of leadership, we would then depose the one with lineage, given the availability of the superior alternative. On the other hand, if we appointed a sovereign who did not fulfill the lineage condition because we could not find someone who fulfilled it and then found a qualified person who fulfilled this condition in addition to the rest of the conditions, we would not replace the current ruler with the person who fulfills the lineage condition, if we expected difficulties. But if this could be achieved smoothly, then it is up to the one who possesses the lineage among all conditions, since sovereignty is assigned to those who descend from the Prophet's tree, and the non-Qurashi in office is effectively a deputy to the Qurashi, and if we could give the office back to someone who combines lineage with all other qualifications, we would do that with no hesitation. This is analogous to the case of a judge who acts on behalf of someone in their absence, and when that person returns, she/her resumes her/his jurisdiction over their rights, and all delegation would end. This is our attempt to address the hypothesis of the lack of a sovereign who fulfills the condition of lineage.

We now turn to the lack of the capacity of independent legal reasoning (*ijtihad*). We have already stated that possessing this capacity is a condition in the office of the sovereign (imam). If we could not find someone who would be a leader in religious, legal matters but found an honorable man with the capacity to fulfill the sovereign's obligations and to ably handle grave matters with competence as we explained the concept of "competence" (*kifaya*) in an earlier section, then this person must be appointed with jurisdiction over all religious and worldly matters, and his orders must be obeyed, just as we would obey the orders of a perfect sovereign. The scholars must also take it upon themselves to advise him and explain to him all religious instructions (*ahkam al-shar' wa-l-'ilm*), including subtle ones, in all subjects—even though this sovereign's leadership derives from reason not religion. But if we could not find a knowledgeable candidate, then people may be bound to follow a competent leader who would then seek the advice of scholars. This is better than leaving people under no leadership, exposed to crises, attacks from enemies, and other perils.

If we failed to find a candidate who enjoyed competence and good character but found a competent candidate with an inclination to bawdiness and debauchery, and if his inclination to cross red lines and his unhinged character was such that he would be feared to transgress, then there is no justification for appointing such a person. The injustice of such a person, aided with power, would exceed any good that could come out of his competence, and under his leadership the tools that should be employed to defend Islam would be means of corruption and deviation from the guided paths, and this is contrary to the objectives of appointing sovereigns. And if we were to hypothesize a case in which a pressing need for a leader to address a religious obligation before the unbelievers attacked a corner of the lands of Islam, and we had no choice but to prepare an army and found only someone with a bad character [to lead] and it was hard for us to summon the soldiers without a leader with a disposition to lead, and we constantly failed to find a more pious alternative, then we would be forced, faced with a crisis that must be addressed nimbly, to appoint the person with inferior moral character, in order to mobilize the soldiers.

In the case of an impious person who drinks wine or does similar prohibited actions: if we found this person, despite his shortcomings and violations of good behavior, to be a leader of competence in defending good order, [that is], an order guided by religious principles, and he was competent, and we found no alternative, the stronger view for me is that we should appoint this person, while trying to offer him advice as much as possible, since leaving kingdoms without a leader has grave consequences as it causes disorder, not to mention neglecting the borders. If we appointed someone to fulfill the obligations of leadership, because he possessed competence and honorable character, and was already a leader in defense of the lands against those who enjoy power and would use it unadvisedly, then appointing such a person to a position of leadership is more likely to lead to improving matters in society and is better than leaving it without a leader. Indeed, we never equate the evil that could arise from this person's corruption with the disorder that could befall society, if it lacked leaders who had the power to direct its people and protect them against the rebels among them. Thus, the aforementioned must be appointed out of necessity in the conditions we described.

The reader who reflects on what we mentioned would understand that the objective behind stipulating the conditions of the sovereign, as we mentioned them, while we hope to fulfill them all, is ultimately the competence to lead independently. This is the foundation of government, but by itself, it cannot be sufficient when coupled with an ill character and deviation from the bond of piety, and it might even be a source of corruption, when joined with the readiness to abuse power. Knowledge comes [in importance] after competence and after good character, since knowledge is the best equipment and the strongest bond. With it, the leader can handle matters by applying the rules of Islam. Lineage, though considered when possible, does not fulfill an intelligible goal, but previous consensus is the basis of its consideration.

We could now address distinct hypotheticals, with God's aid. If asked, what is your view regarding a man who enjoys Qurashi lineage with neither knowledge nor competence, while a contemporary of this person is found, one who possesses knowledge, competence, and piety: Who is the one more worthy of leadership? We say we would never, in this case, put forward anyone other than the person with competence, piety, and knowledge, as the one with no competence would not even be considered here.

If asked, what if we found in one generation a knowledgeable man of Quraysh with no competence and a competent, honorable man who would ably handle the affairs of government: Who should we appoint? We say that if the man from Quraysh is not characterized by feeble reason, is teachable, and would be competent upon training and would subsequently be able to handle the affairs of government, then he is more worthy of it, but if he ascended to sovereignty, he must not make a decision on his own as if a dictator; rather, he must consult people of wisdom and reason, and only after that he should make his decisions. This would be applicable in the case of someone who possesses the intelligence required to reach a correct decision on his own after gaining experience in the world in both tranquil and troubled times. But if he was dimwitted and incapable of reflection and would not reach correct conclusions and would only decide based on an imitation of others, and if his imperfections and incapacity were made apparent and his "daring" and irrational decisions persisted, then this person could not be taken seriously as a candidate for leadership, and the competent and pious would be more worthy of leadership.

A competent leader who could support his people and who lacks knowledge of the religious law is similarly of higher value than a man of knowledge not coupled with the capacity to lead and support for the people. Ultimately, the most highly valued quality here is competence to lead, and the rest of the qualities are in a sense a "completion" or "perfection" for it. When we lack a competent leader, then we lack someone whose appointment brings about the effects of leadership, and in this case, we practically face the question of the absence of authority altogether, which we will address, God willing, in the third chapter of this section.

Chapter III

By now, we have completed the discussion of seizing power by someone who fulfills the conditions of leadership (*imama*) followed by the accession of a leader who enjoys the capacity to support and look after the population, and it is now time for me to address the hypothesis of the absence in a whole generation (*zaman*) of competent [people] who qualify for leadership and who enjoy decisiveness. The case of the hypothesis is a bit difficult to imagine, since it is unlikely that a whole generation would lack someone with political skills. We do not stipulate that the competent [leader] be "perfect" in his competence; rather, it is sufficient to have someone who possesses intelligence, carefulness, knowledge, right-mindedness, and the ability to handle serious matters. He also must be someone who would consult men of reason in perplexing matters and would resolve and nimbly move to take the right action. No generation is likely to lack someone who possesses these qualities, but it might help (in order to make the hypothesis more realistic) to presume a case where the one who enjoys competence and knowledge suffers oppression and injustice and is stricken by misfortune and dispossession. And as we said, leadership cannot be established without the support of power and accessible force. Similarly, competence without power has no impact in establishing the rules of Islam.

If a whole generation lacks a competent person who enjoys power, how could services be delivered in this case where the obstacles in its way are insurmountable? To this question the answer is: As for matters that people can administer on their own and where only the customs of propriety of living as one community demand seeking the advice of those in charge, such as organizing Friday prayers, deploying armies for jihad, imposing punishments for crimes against life and limbs, these affairs must be handled by the people on their own when they lack a qualified leader. If some groups of people who possess the appropriate competence and power took it upon themselves in this case to stop corrupt acts, this falls under the rubric of "support for the good and discouragement of evil" (*al-amr bi al-ma'rufwa al-nahy 'an al-munkar*), but individuals must be prevented from unsheathing their weapons, as long as there was someone with authority (*wazir*) who takes charge of the Muslim population. When such authority is lacking, then one must fend off calamities as much as possible, and the people must be discouraged from handling matters involving lives—all with the hope of achieving the best of available options.

In handling the affairs of politics, the government (*sultan*) is effective in ending vicious competition and creating the conditions of consent and concord, while allowing the population to handle capital crimes (*umur al-dima'*) and apply their weapons promotes types of unreason that cannot be denied by rational people. When people lack an authority to handle their affairs, an authority that can support them in their time of need, it would be impossible to order them to refrain from exerting some effort to avert bad conditions that might befall them, since, if they fail to act according to their own capacity, disasters would spread among the populations in every corner of the land. And when they are commanded to refrain from involvement in political matters while an authority (*sultan*) is in charge, the one in charge would fulfill their need in handling these matters in the right way. Scholars have said: when a generation lacks an authority, then the population (of each town) must summon men of reason among them for the position of leadership. The population must [then] follow the commands of these leaders and abstain from what the [leaders] banned. If the people failed to do that, they would experience indecisiveness in the face of grave matters and could indeed be confused in the face of crises.

If a group was charged with the duty of military expeditions while a leader is in power, and [the group] reached areas where one could fear their misjudgment, they must identify some of them as leaders to obey, since if they fail to do that, they are likely to fall in the traps of treacherous conditions and would never achieve any stability.

What must also be taken seriously are the *affairs* of provinces that are normally under the jurisdiction of provincial governors, *such as* marrying off unmarried females and managing the property of orphans. Some leading jurists think that marrying off unmarried females falls under the jurisdiction of government. Shafi'i (d. 204/820), may God be pleased with him, and other scholars argue that a free, adult female of sound judgment would be married off by a representative from her family if available; otherwise, the government is a representative of those with no representative. If she had no one to serve as such representative and the government was also lacking, we know that the practice of marriage could never be suspended (and whoever doubts this does not understand the wisdom of the law in Islam). Reaching the conclusion that marriages should be suspended is analogous to concluding that all lawful employment could cease to exist, as we will explain in the last section of this book. The impossibility of the suspension of marriage and of the ceasing of lawful employment is indisputable. One thus must go beyond this discussion in order to consider *how* as opposed to *whether* marriages should take place in this case.

In my view, if one could find a scholar with the required knowledge to establish and dissolve commitments, then this person must handle the affairs of marriage, which would in normal circumstances be handled by the government when in power. Reports conflicted as to Shafi'i's position on implementing the rulings of unofficial arbiters while a government is in charge, with one of the reports stating that Shafi'i held that the rulings of such arbiter, just like the orders of an official judge, must be implemented [which happens to be the apparent doctrine of Abu Hanifa (d. 150/767)].

This is an opinion based on analogical reasoning, and I elect neither to belabor this point nor explain its basis and ramifications. My objective is explaining what should be done when we are led to implementing the commands of jurists to maintain order, while applying a measure of caution. When a generation lacks a government, and it is indeed impossible to cease to issue valid marriages and the like, then the dicta of an arbiter, normally nonbinding for the people in the presence of regular government, are binding in the case of the absence of government. This is true if we find a scholar of reliable knowledge, but if a generation lacked such scholars, just as it lacked leaders who command obedience, then this is what I address in the third and last section of this book, which is the foremost objective of the book. We will later clarify our position in this matter, as we address different conditions and specific cases—and we will indeed articulate secrets for the Shari'a no one has hitherto fully contemplated, God willing.

All financial matters, which the sovereign handles in normal circumstances, are delegated to scholars at times when we lack a government and powerful rulers who are capable of supporting those in need of government's support and knowledge of how matters should be handled. All people of different types must defer to the counsel of their scholars and act according to their advice in all their affairs. When they do that, they will have taken the right course, and in this case, scholars become the leaders of the community. Should it prove difficult to bring multiple communities under the jurisdiction of one counsel, then every locality may be assigned a scholar of its own. Should there be multiple scholars in one region, the one who is most knowledgeable must be followed, and if they were all comparable in knowledge, which is rare, then their agreement while they belong to different schools and methodologies would be impossible; in such case, they all must agree to delegate one of them. Should there be conflict in that, and should this lead to fissure and quarrel, then one must apply some form of lot in order to stop all disputes.

A satisfactory statement can thus be articulated on the matter: Leaders who possess the qualifications needed for high office merely take the jurisdiction of applying the commands of God to people whether they were willing or not so that these commands fulfill their goal. Ideally, administering religious and worldly affairs would be through tying all responsibilities with one leader, if possible, and if this should prove difficult, then implementing God's commands must be delegated to notables in the countries.

One of the subtle points in this issue is that if a competent person [is found] who is capable of supporting those in need, someone who has not achieved the qualifications of knowledge in order to be able to judge matters independently but who has mustered supporters and seemed to be destined to become the leader, then this person becomes the leader, who is charged with all the duties of finance and defense among other responsibilities; nonetheless, he should not decide any matter without seeking the counsel of scholars.

If some object: Why would you not decide this issue by saying that the scholar of a given generation would be its leader who must be followed by the competent officer, as the latter submits to the judgment and knowledge of that scholar anyway [thus reversing what was just stated], I reply by saying that if the scholar was also competent and capable of handling grave matters, then, yes, the competent person with no comparable knowledge leading to independent judgment (*ijtihad*) must follow that scholar, if he found that scholar. However, if the scholar possessed neither an understanding of leadership nor the capacity to lead in grave circumstances, then the competent person would be the leader, provided he should consult in complicated matters. Since leadership is assigned to the competent, then financial matters are under his jurisdiction (in collecting, distributing, and otherwise administering resources), since the basis of government is men and their reliance is on resources. This leads to the third section of the book, which concerns the greatest of all issues—an issue whose benefit encompasses all people and the whole Earth—God grants us His guidance, through His own benevolence.

Law and State

When 'Ali 'Abd al-Raziq in 1925 got himself into trouble with the Egyptian King Ahmad Fu'ad and the British colonial government in Egypt with one act (by writing against the Caliphate), he may not have been as clear about the implications of what he was doing. In fact, no one could have fully understood the situation Abd al-Raziq's text (*al-Islam wa Usul al-Hukm*; Islam and the Foundations of Government) created at the time; much of it had to be understood in retrospect. I am thus not arguing with new evidence that 'Abd al-Raziq, who was an amateur in politics by consensus, did or did not know what the Egyptian King or the British occupation would think about the implications of his book. The point is that a religious thinker, open to foreign ideas or focused on his religious legacy, could not easily address the basic questions of government, what it is for, and what its possible replacements are. 'Abd al-Raziq could not have been aware of what the fluid and very significant moment in which he wrote his book entailed. It was only a year or so after the end of the Ottoman Caliphate, and as historians tell us, at least the Egyptian king was interested in becoming the new Caliph. However, it may have been too late for a Caliphate to come back. In any case, 'Abd al-Raziq argued the Caliphate was not only nonessential in Islam, it was bad on top of being gratuitous. He was both right and wrong.

He was right because the Caliphate literally means succession, and it is the succession of the Prophet, who did not (if you are a Sunni) regulate his succession. And he was wrong because the entrenched body of thinking about government within Sunni Islam could not simply be ignored in such an easy manner. Juwayni had the right tone—it is good but not irreplaceable, even smaller governments may be done without in certain circumstances.

At important junctures in Juwayni's *Ghiyathi*, the law can be detailed either without much reference to the state or with references to it that gives the government/*sultan* legal assignments after the laws have been decided. What, then, is the relationship between law and government in this paradigm, as applied to a modern context? First, remember that Islamic law consists of nonbinding opinions, which maintain an existence with or without the state (which encompasses people, land, and government), as well as binding rules. Second, given that the modern state does not attempt to regulate all actions, the Shari'a does occupy and fill in this vacuum, again without competition with the state. Even in the area where the Shari'a and the (modern) state compete, the Shari'a could still survive where state law enforcement fails to fully reign. Juwayni's assumption is that a state of bifurcation of society that separated people from government may cause the Shari'a to die politically (a narrower sense of the political here) while remaining an object of adherence among the population.

The state is neither God nor an essential manifestation of God, and a pious Muslim need not be state-pious. The modern experience may be responsible for the thinking that the state may be a replacement of God in certain ways. Piety is associated in the mind with divinity, but it is arguable that the modern state does command a type of piety from its citizens; the state indeed can be said to be an object of piety for many modern citizens. One thing that helps the state to replace God as an object of piety is its role in judging matters of religion. John Selden: "Question: Whether is the Church or is Scripture judge of religion? Answer: In truth, neither, but the State."[7] Gradually, some of human association with their humanity that was explained in religious terms involving God has passed to the state. Juwayni, who supposedly writes in a time prone to theocratic leanings (as so many Orientalists taught their followers), makes the state but a tool of justice, which could not on its own be the source of justice or even the source of a concept of justice.

Mainly based on the Sunni contractual theory of government, Islamic jurisprudence explains the legitimacy of government. This jurisprudence can also take this legitimacy back, in theory, through the laws of *baghy*, when a revolution is deemed successful, where a standing government would be replaced by rebels; hence the people who were on the side of *'adl* (justice and order) yesterday would be on the side of *baghy* (injustice, transgression) today. In some rare cases, the jurists could also declare a sitting government to be representative of *baghy*. From the perspective of jurists, the state is subordinate to legal frameworks. When the state appoints jurists as judges, thus exercising what seems to be an upper-hand position, it can only take that back when the jurist in question violates his own principles.

On the other hand, uncertainty, in practice, besieges all juristic attempts to take away legitimacy from a sitting government, and practical considerations force jurists to acknowledge the legitimacy of what was in its time the "illegitimate" ending of the jurisdiction of a qualified jurist/judge. This is not meant to be paradoxical; rather, it is a solution to the question of the interaction of legitimacy and power without ignoring either moral or practical considerations.

The state, in this scheme, could not be God in any metaphorical sense. Moreover, the absence of good government and state organization itself does not mean the absence of the Shari'a. The presence of good government contributes to the perfection of the Shari'a. But its absence is not a sufficient condition for its deterioration.

Faulty emphasis on the Caliphate as the only formidable political unit of Juwayni's time must be abandoned; there is overwhelming evidence that the Caliphate had been decentralized for many generations before Juwayni. Agents, such as the Tahirids, the Samanids, and the Tulunids, among others, have provided the real standards for the effective political units of the ninth, tenth, and eleventh centuries. Even Mawardi's (d. 450/1058) *al-Ahkam al-Sultaniyya*, though appearing to be a defense of the Caliphate as an ideal, does indeed institutionalize strong decentralized government. Descending from the Caliphate directly to the regional states, such as the ones we mentioned, once again, was not an obvious choice for a medieval Muslim society.

One question that must be addressed here is how to read Juwayni's emphasis on *the elements of the community/state* as the basic and most enduring "infrastructure" of a community, as opposed to the overall "governing" umbrella from the top, which tends to expand the size of communities by collating them into a larger community as well as defines the larger community's borders. One must again remember that Juwayni's analysis is not simply an anarchist's analysis, which condemns government as a gratuitous or even an entity that robs individuals of their legitimate freedom. Indeed, his analysis emphasizes the organizational and supportive function of government (imbedded in terms such as *kifaya, najda,* and *shahama*) and considers its absence a cause for concern and action. On the other hand, as we noted, Juwayni does not give up on a community simply for the failure of its government. This is one thing that separates his analysis from nation-based analysis and anarchist analyses at the same time.

Juwayni's scheme is not the opposite in every respect of what Hobbes taught a few centuries later. Hobbes's scholars teach that one of Hobbes' main contributions to political philosophy is his argument for political control to end the evil of the state of nature. The obvious Hobbesian prejudice is that the absence of government leads to the state of nature. This is what makes his perspective relevant to our consideration of Juwayni with his careful distinction among grades of social and political life not properly described as either "states" or "anarchies."

Juwayni brings down the subject of politics to the level of groups of individuals, rather than what we call states. In the centuries following Hobbes, and for several reasons, we may have gone too far in abandoning the individual. Out of the fear, rational or irrational, that an individual may not enjoy any reasonable measure of security without the support of the state, we may have gone in the direction of asking the individual to (almost) fully submit to the state. Juwayni's analysis places the emphasis back on the basic subject of life in a community, that is, the individual.

On the other hand, Hobbes's analysis falls in a contradiction by seeming to offer all his recommendations for the good of the individual, as if the survival and well-being of individuals is in itself a final goal. One must ask whether individuals possess any intrinsic good that justifies their preservation. Juwayni's analysis does not succumb to an assumption that individuals are simply a source of the good in society. Many individuals do stand against the valid interest of other individuals, especially in times of crises. This balanced view also deserves attention and further explanation. An individual is not, in herself or himself, a goal (with an apology to my friend Immanuel Kant), just as the state is not the goal. This is because both individuals and state are neutral tools, which could be the source of "good" and "bad" in the world.

At this point, one should not be surprised to face the skepticism of our modern believers in humanity and humans' full freedom to devise their own moral principles, accompanied by discomfort with any line of reasoning that subordinate individuals or people to some concept of good or bad. I ask these skeptics to consider the fact that this theory in itself does not provide any concept of good or bad and can be used to support values derived from the beliefs of the majority in society, from the beliefs of its wise minority, a hybrid of these, or something else altogether. The point here, one final time, is that neither individuals' sovereignty nor state sovereignty should in itself be the goal of a political community, as one could learn from Juwayni.

Skin-Deep Government

Modern Muslim societies live under governments that have controlled so much of individuals' life. The governments make the laws, affect people's livelihood, and to an extent control their "culture"—they have tools of social engineering unavailable to medieval governments. But the rule, rather than the exception, in governments in modern Muslim societies is that their control of the infrastructure of their societies has not been comprehensive. The elites surrounding and procreating governing bodies had much antipathy toward the Shari'a, and the few who had sympathy did not know how to satisfy their own sympathy, but overall, the Shari'a lived in a Juwaynian pattern. This in fact is not a totally new assertion. What I could add is to argue that if Juwayni's prose coincided with the foundation of the Shi'i revolution of 1979, as some argued, it does, even more profoundly, describe the state of the Shari'a in the Sunni world.

In its relationship to the role of government in the modern world, the fatigue debate was argued by reformers who wanted to replace or amalgamate Shari'a rules and modernize the courts and bureaucracies of the Muslim world. They succeeded, but they did not seem to be able to control an underground life for the Shari'a, which took political, theatrical manifestations from time to time. I am with Wael Hallaq that the current state of affairs bears very little resemblance to any moment in medieval Islamic history, where bifurcations of society involving governments and even Crusade and Mongol occupations have played a major role in unsettling the normalcy of Shari'a life. But I think that this should not be taken to deny the underground life of the Shari'a, which is the only reason there are still supporters for it who can publish to argue that it must be restored.

Hallaq and I may agree or disagree about the assessment of whether the Shari'a's different manifestations are available and whether these are sufficiently powerful. The territory is laden with much room for misunderstanding, overemphasis, generalization from limited experience, and so forth. I must, however, be clear that I reject the very engagement in the discourse of the death of the Shari'a. I recognize, in a way, that this discourse was inevitable; the age of ends (end of history, end of philosophy, end of education, etc.) in which we find ourselves had to claim the Shari'a at some point (only that this end in Hallaq's thinking preceded the other ends by half a century or so). The Shari'a as a legal science, as a language and a profession serving multiple professions, and as culture and sensibilities, as a political and social and organizational legacy, is too complex to be given a death certificate or authoritatively claimed to have reached a degree of unprecedented fragmentation. This is the point, not that I dispute every specific development that may be brought up in this discussion.

Discrepancy between Local Law and Global Laws

Modern Muslim populations found themselves answerable not only to European and American armies but also to new norms that overtook the whole world. These external norms or laws evolved, in due time, independently of any significant participation by the Muslim populations. Things got even more complicated. The result is multiple attempts at "retroactive" reconciliation, simultaneous with active reconciliation.

Today's governments in the Muslim world, headed by individuals and groups of different temperaments and orientation, have a difficult task. They cannot rule in today's world with any serious engagements with the (rich, medieval) experience that became disconnected from many of the norms governing today's life (with all the variety of modern life and all the diversity among peoples and norms acknowledged). But they can neither deny this Shari'a's importance nor easily trivialize it.

I do not want to overemphasize this point. The problem is not the lack of attempts in the Muslim world to respond to modern change; it is the lack of true transformation that penetrates into all levels of society. Outside pressure did not help (no matter how reluctant or partly indifferent), but I think the main responsibility lies in Muslim hands. Muslim societies' elites have not, it seems to me, taken their challenge seriously, and the population at large remains, surprisingly, unworried about the problem.

The future life of the Shari'a might not begin with political or legal institutions. Rather, it will probably start with surviving Shari'a-based customs and traditions. As I explained elsewhere, Ibn 'Abidin effectively argued that social standards of long duration and wide application that could be reconciled with the textual foundations of the Shari'a must be taken into account in any fatwa. Creative ideas will enlarge the scope of these customs and reconnect them to old Shari'a principles based on the same force that instituted these ideas. This will be the case whether the debate is on usury or men/women relations in the family and outside of it, or any other issue.

The idea of usury, for example, continues to be interpreted and reinterpreted by modern Muslim jurists, mostly with the goal of easing out what they deem unnecessary restrictions on trade stemming from attachment to old formulas and practices, which have had experienced changes over the centuries anyway. Creative ideas have come out of this challenge, but lack of economic independence in the Muslim world remains the main hurdle in the way of truly full solutions to the discrepancy. (Some say that modern Muslim jurists reinterpret usury in order to make Islamic law relevant! I wonder if these jurists' services were not in demand, how they could make themselves relevant by changing their law.)

In the area of family law, one cannot identify a central idea, such as usury, but a cluster of issues as the locus of the discrepancy between the Shari'a and today's West-dominated culture. These issues are roughly those of women's roles in the family and the conceptualization of childhood.

Modern society has yet to introduce a true alternative to the traditional family (which used to be the source of women's attachment to their houses and a small circle around it). But Muslim societies and jurists could not fully challenge this even broken model of modern life and discover a new system that works for Muslim societies. The extension of childhood, however, is an issue that goes beyond a juristic solution. A 16-year-old male or female in many societies today is certainly a new "animal," not to be analogized easily with the 16-year-old man or woman of old times. Life expectancy, if current trends persist, will also *factor in* in these discussions.

The complexity of these issues is not the only reason for current jurists' inability to understand them correctly and provide answers to questions that involve them. Jurists have devised answers to many complex questions before. But the jurists have to study the issues: they have to know what these modern questions involve.

The lesson to be taken from this discussion is that a death certificate could not be issued for the Shari'a with any degree of confidence by relying on the history of codification and the role of the modern state in serving as an anti-Shari'a agent. The life of the Shari'a thus far depended on more than one position by "government" and will take a while before succumbing even to the governments that are most antithetical to it.

Part IV

Beyond Modernity

Could the end of the Shari'a be discovered from outside of it, kind of part-outside, part-inside?

Chapter 9

Neglected Knowledge

The conditions created by the reform story I sketched in chapter seven continue to be debated. Hallaq's reading of the nature and results of this reform introduces the idea of the death of the Shari'a as a result of epistemic, social, and institutional discontinuity—attested in many aspects of Muslim life today. I have both partial approval of (and quarrel with) this thesis.

I hope not to give the impression that I am a believer that the Shari'a of medieval times is thriving. I had, in fact, entertained the idea of the death of the Shari'a about 20 years ago. The more I enjoyed reading legal texts with my mentors, the less willing I was to think of their possible application in today's world. (The entexted Shari'a was simply too good for the population around me.) The more secure I became about my knowledge of *fiqh* and *usul al-fiqh*, the less sure I became that their content could be related to my society, to the Egypt of the waning years of the twentieth century. I then decided, with all of my youthful might, that the Shari'a was "kind of dead" because it was too good for the people around me. I "acknowledged" that the Shari'a had died—killed, indeed, by those who claimed to be Muslim, not by colonial armies.

The years added reasons to this theory. The more history I read, the more assured I became of my conclusion—being particularly prone to the "constant transformation" idea, the idea that nothing stays the same, and even when we say (with a wise pretention) that, "as things change, they stay the same," we do not really mean the same *same*.

But I have subsequently come to question this "youthfulness" thesis, having started to see that this "condition" of believing that the Shari'a had died was nothing but a result of a perspective I bemoaned but was partly trapped into. It was a perspective mostly developed by those who *professed to think* that many of the teachings of Islam were "irrelevant" to the modern world. Whether they *believed* that or not, they repeated that assertion. Perhaps it comforted some of them; perhaps they thought that when this is said frequently enough, people will believe it. Some of the religious scholars whom I knew and who continued to guide questioners about how to live by the Shari'a expressed in their moments of frustration an agreement with the death-of-the-Shari'a thesis. But it is an interesting question then what their *fatwas* and peoples' application of these amounted to.

Out of habit, however, I continued to enjoy an exercise to which I became addicted over the years: Locate new ideas in the past (in the writings of major medieval Muslim jurists and historians); work on them and make them my own; and then think of their potential incompatibility with the present world, concluding that this medieval jurisprudence was indeed "lost knowledge," unavailable to this present world, and then move on. In the past three years, I *reconnected* with many medieval authors whose work I had partially known but never fully savored—including Juwayni, Mazari, Ibn Rushd, Nawawi, and Subki. Reading them with a measure of focus and intensity again revived the memory of my old death-of-the-Shari'a thesis. This time, I realized that the death-of-the-Shari'a was being debated for the Anglophone reader.

The conclusion I hold today and am willing to defend is that the death-of-the-Shari'a doctrine becomes weaker and weaker the more it is considered. The frustration experienced by Muslim jurists today could find equivalents in early centuries (true, with differences in the conditions, but the point is that the frustration of Shari'a jurists' is not evidence that the Shari'a died). The outsider's view of the issue is even less meaningful. In fact, the behavior of jurists, people, and even the governments in Muslim societies all show that the Shari'a is far from being dead. When a society is ready to give up on its tradition, there are strong signs for that. When this happens, it could not be contested. It would be too obvious to contest.

I have a good measure of respect for Hallaq's work, but I have much disagreement with his choice of language and his relaxed reliance on the neutral observer's privilege. I will certainly emphasize the disagreement here (and hope the respect is not doubted in any case). Hallaq's recent arguments and writings on the death of the Shari'a made me think of his 2001 work on the development of the *madhhab*s in "Authority, Continuity, and Change," but the later works went beyond the earlier work's convincing potential, a bit too far actually. That is, I think "Authority" has some good potential for making a death-of-the-*madhhab*s thesis tenable, but also not to the extent the author might think. As for the arguments that come from his reflections on areas "outside of the law," I think these are much less potent in making the case.[1]

The generation and loss of knowledge is complex. Shafi'i "founded" his school and passed away in the year 204/820. It took more than four centuries of accumulation of juristic production, extractions and extensions of Shafi'i's legal logic (the generation of *wujuh*, as the process was called), efforts to collect, collate, and systematize these views, not to forget the genius of Juwayni in his *Nihayat al-Matlab*—all until Rafi'i and Nawawi came in the seventh/fourteenth century to refine these and rewrite the *madhhab*. After Rafi'i and Nawawi, the *madhhab is* what these two agreed on, and given that Nawawi's work was more highly valued, it was decided that when these two disagreed, Nawawi was the standard. So much knowledge has been lost and so much generated in the process. But the Shafi'i *madhhab* grew rather than died. I might agree that the four *madhhab*s have been weakened in recent centuries to an unprecedented degree, but their death is not a death of the Shari'a, for complex reasons. Perhaps the Shari'a would have died if it *were* monopolized by a *madhhab* and then had to meet colonialism and more importantly the anti-Shari'a Muslim elites of the last two centuries. But the story was more complicated.

Aside from the considerations I have made thus far, I have, in the main, two arguments for rejecting the death-of-the-Shari'a discourse. First, this inquiry hinges too much on definitions; or to commit only a mild hyperbole: it is all a matter of definition—If I get to define the Shari'a tightly so as to allow my conclusion of its demise impossible to refute, I win. But what is the value of arguing in a circle in this manner? The Shari'a could be seen as an entity surrounded by "conditions" that support (rather than create) its vitality and energy—that is, these conditions are not fully decisive in making the Shari'a possible. One may argue that the partial availability of certain conditions can be seen as a source for the revival of the Shari'a (where revive, or reinfuse with life, means "recreate") or equally argue that its death is questionable, given the availability of the conditions that allow its continuity and support it. But we must note, in any case, that *the conditions* and *the Shari'a* should not be conflated.

The second argument benefits from reflecting on Juwayni's *Ghiyathi*. Juwayni could not convince his reader that there were clear limits that divided the different stages of weakness that befell the Shari'a, so as to demarcate its death point. Not even the fatigue, which was supposedly more narrowly defined, that is, tightly defined as the absence of jurists. Juwayni wavers when he imagines this condition, while he tries fairly hard. After Juwayni, no one seems to have succeeded in what Juwayni could not do.

I have a sense that argument will not solve this issue (argument indeed does not solve most issues.) But I am in disagreement; so, I still need to explain my stance. In my old (death-of-the-Shari'a) thesis, the weakest point was my sense that I comprehended the Shari'a. I thought I knew it, because I could identify a web of issues that relate and affect most questions of *fiqh* I came across. I could do it without any preparation; I must then know the whole system. I started to even dare to disagree with septuagenarians who had saved me from an embarrassing juristic illiteracy a few years earlier. I seriously thought I could understand certain things to a degree more satisfying than the degree to which they comprehended the issues. Interestingly, many of these old scholars would neither agree nor disagree with the death thesis (which was proposed many times in conversations that involved them). Aside from their moments of frustration, they came to think of this issue as unproductive. Maybe they thought what I think now; maybe they thought it was too hard to figure out.

The Shari'a, whose demise is under consideration, should be seen, based on Hallaq's argument, as an amalgamation of intellectual, social, and political legacy. As I stated in the previous chapter, government's support for the Shari'a can be seen as an element in the latter's thriving but with many caveats. The social element, encompassing the degree to which Muslim populations act on Islamic imperatives, is the hardest to study, but I am skeptical about any assertion that today's Muslim populations have gone beyond Shari'a-based practices in their lives. I question the argument that social customs in Muslim societies do not reproduce Islamic (i.e., Shari'a) values—in other words, I think that it is difficult to make a convincing argument that the degree to which Muslim societies are Shari'a-compatible in their social structure is insufficient.

One question that requires some attention is whether institutions that support "Islamic scholarship" have indeed ceased to exist. This question must be considered with caution, since one lesson we must learn from studying institutions of learning (especially modern institutions) is that they are capable of being transformed (and fairly fast) into something that fulfills the opposite of their intended goal (hence a nineteenth-century protestant college in Beirut could become a hotbed for anticolonial Arab nationalism in the twentieth, and Dar al-'Ulum of Cairo could become a formidable breeder of conservatism in the twentieth century, while it was founded in the nineteenth to counter al-Azhar's conservatism). In other words, it is not impossible that many of the modern schools that were founded to counter old legal and philosophical thinking would be instrumental in reviving and amalgamating the hitherto neglected knowledge of the medieval past.

It is not my intention to assert that the religious schools, such as al-Azhar in Egypt and al-Zaytuna in Tunis, do enjoy the relative independence religious colleges seem to have enjoyed in the past few centuries (although assuming that the Ottomans offered al-Azhar and its scholars a free reign to do as they please would be an exaggeration). I certainly think that the shrinking of the role of schools and the founding and dismantling of schools, such as *Madrasat al-Qada' al-Shar'i* in Egypt, and other political manipulations of like institutions changed the content and status of religious and old legal education over time. (Note, incidentally, that the decline of religious scholars is sometimes dated earlier than the nineteenth century, sometimes to the beginning of the eighteenth.)[2] The case can be helped by a retelling of certain aspects of nineteenth-century Ottoman history, whereby the disenchantment of those who enjoyed strong attachment to the ways of the past has become apparent (an Ottoman poet wrote in 1878: *The truth has become figurative, that which was once figurative become true; the foundations of old knowledge have collapsed*).[3] I remain unable, however, to see this change in the status of religious scholars, coupled with all possible lamentations of the lost-old-ways, as sufficient evidence of the end of the intellectual infrastructure of the Shari'a, just as I am skeptical about its social demise.

I partly agree that significant changes took place in the last two centuries and led to a new condition in the status of the Shari'a in the world. But the complexity of the evolution of the *madhhabs*, and their history during the Ottoman centuries, and the relationship among population, scholars, and government make me doubt that dating the death of the Shari'a to the end of the thirteenth/nineteenth century or the beginning of the fourteenth/twentieth century would be necessarily easier than dating it to the eleventh/seventeenth century, for example. It could have been the ignorant Turks as perhaps Subki would have it (not the Europeans) who at least tried (not always successfully) to change laws and customs and challenge established traditions and initiated new conditions (e.g., turning much land into state-owned land, when it was traditionally owned by people or left open for appropriation). I doubt that anybody would argue that the Ottoman centuries softened the Shari'a (whether because the Ottomans were bad Muslims, or because of an array of factors, not excluding mistakes they made) and "paved the way" for the final assault at the hand of European colonialism, which dealt the Shari'a the death blow. I also remain suspicious of the Arab secular approach to Ottoman history, which looked at it as *disaster history* that diminished great Arabic-speaking nations such as Egypt—an attack I heard from some of my professors. My point is that complex changes can be ascribed to the precolonial, just as it can be dated to the colonial era.

When we speak of lost knowledge, we must reflect repeatedly on what is meant by knowledge. There are two meanings of the word "knowledge" involved in this discussion. The first is a post-Foucaultian sense of knowledge as politically and socially manufactured. In this sense, access to knowledge is only possible if the historical mindset where "historical" knowledge applied and its attendant institutions could be said to survive. In other words, there are "conditions" for the possibility of this knowledge that must obtain for this knowledge to be said to exist, and when these conditions do not obtain, claims that this knowledge is available become unreasonable pretension.

The second sense is a medieval Islamic sense of knowledge as memory of tradition added to the capacity for readjustment to current conditions. Knowledge (*'ilm*) is certainly not simply information (*ma'lumat*). These are not unrelated, though; the first has multiple affinities with the latter. In one sense, the former is an outcome of the latter. I could tell you how to arrive at correct classifications of certain actions (prohibited, obligatory, etc.) if I possess the capacity and systematic thinking that allow me to determine these actions' desirability (or lack thereof) from a given viewpoint and consider the impact of circumstances on the actions in question. The political and social conditions are assigned a role in the classification of actions as obligatory, prohibited, and so on. But to assume that these political and social conditions create Shari'a norms would be a novel understanding of Islamic law (no, let's say the Shari'a).

One of the basic features of the Sunni (mostly Ash'ari) concept of divine guidance or the Shari'a is its insistence that human responsibility to live by divine norms is commensurate with available knowledge of these norms. Absent any decisive evaluation of what this availability means, one must search for full acknowledgment of the death of the Shari'a by all those who adhere to it. This is not an attempt to argue in a circle. The followers of Islam are the ones who will decide to appropriate the Shari'a of the past in their lives, as their parents and grandparents did. We cannot argue that they have no right to decide what the Shari'a is and then come back and decide *what it should have been like* and argue that it is dead.

That is, unless one insists that Ash'aris intended the end of the *madhhab* and its jurists as a de facto sign of the end of the Shari'a and follow their view as the final word on the matter. In a way, as I hinted, we could all agree on whether *death* has befallen the *Shari'a*, if one of us has the irrebuttable authority to impose on the discussion one sense of *death* and *Shari'a*. The same was done by the Hanbalis who attempted to establish the opposite view (that the Shari'a could never die) by theorizing about human life before all revelations, during access to revelation, and in the hypothetical fatigue stage, leaving us with no tools to judge, other than assessments and opposite assessments that could not easily be anchored or adjudicated.

The theology of our imprisonment in the present might come back with what sounds like a potent argument. According to this theology, it is obvious that knowledge in our world today (post-Foucault) is one thing, and since I have not been living on an island, I have been influenced by

Foucault's sense of knowledge and history. Look at the definition of knowledge given earlier as *memory adjusted to the present*, so the argument against my stance goes: does not this sound like a repetition of something Foucault said? I have no energy for arguments like these; they are simply irrefutable; so, let me pursue my argument for now.

Insisting on knowledge of divine norms as "memory adjusted to the present" does, at least, deny political considerations an inflated value in our assessment of knowledge. This is an important issue, as the Shari'a has been seen from the outside as *a problem* (for politicians and Western-educated elites), but *it had to be judged from the outside and the outside only.* The extent to which the Shari'a suffered from political and social pressure in the past is neutralized only to the extent that this does not affect the thesis of its incompatibility with sociopolitical realities today. Then this incompatibility is seen as an inevitable killer today, while the Shari'a's past life is only assessed with ambivalence or a degree of contradiction. This is why we must insist that the Shari'a as knowledge should be conceived as *knowledge adjusted to, rather than negated by, circumstances.* The degree to which this knowledge could be seen as lost must then come from its consumers rather than observers. (Once again, the point is not that political and social conditions do not affect knowledge; only that their role in creating knowledge or making it possible could be exaggerated.)

If we pretend that the Shari'a could be comprehended through practice, that is, through participating in issuing Shari'a norms for everyday life (issuing *fatwas*, that is), the point is fairly obvious. Neither Hallaq nor I have the right to decide this matter as a simple matter of intellectual history. How could someone who is not only a non-*mujtahid* but a non-practicing jurist, such as myself, enter into a debate about whether *ijtihad* is or is not extinct and whether this itself is an appropriate measure for assessing the vigor of the Shari'a and its frailty? Entering into this debate was a privilege only practicing jurists enjoyed in the past. One must at least pretend (from practice, not concepts) to understand what *ijtihad* involves. That is, one must wrack his brain to answer a practicing Muslim about what to do in a real-life situation, and one must do that for a sufficient number of years and with a degree of frequency to develop a sense of where the conditions of real life affect the possibility of certain *fatwas*. But if all this is lacking, could a prima facie reasonable assessment of the vitality of the Shari'a be done? The ghost of Shawkani (asking who appoints a *mujtahid*?) insists that this cannot be done. Who can tell those who think of themselves as *mujtahid*s that they are not, especially without carrying the burden of *ijtihad* at all?

This argument does not presuppose that practicing jurists could agree easily on who was or was not a *mujtahid*, as it must have become apparent from previous chapters. Disagreement in assigning the status of *mujtahid* to an individual scholar was certainly possible in medieval times, but the judgment here is made within parameters that could be debated in reference to personal knowledge and experience. Different is judging those who claim to be *mujtahid*s today not to be *mujtahid*s without claiming that to oneself. The idea that *ijtihad* can be identified and debated by all—-*mujtahid*s and non-*mujtahid* alike—is different from denying someone the status of being a *mujtahid*, as Sakhawi, for example, did with Suyuti, while sharing one understanding of what *ijtihad* roughly meant and having participated in the same scholarly discussions that produce *mujtahids*.

Some of our contemporaries believe themselves to possess the rank of *ijtihad*. If they are simply deluded (if this is not an incautious inference from the assertion that we would be living in denial, if we could not recognize the demise of the Shari'a), then a heavy burden of theorizing the unevenness of scholarly production over centuries is required—a task beyond any individual scholar. If there are living *mujtahid*s but the Shari'a is nevertheless dead, then this death of the Shari'a is a unique type of death—one that must perhaps be reconsidered anew.

The debate could not continue based on terms that have been decided for *mujtahid*s and participants in *Shari'a knowledge* in advance. We must attempt then to invite these *mujtahid*s and participants in *Shari'a knowledge* to influence the discussion about the death of the Shari'a, by allowing them to at least complicate our picture of what *ijtihad* and *Shari'a knowledge* represent. This will invite many epistemological inquiries about the nature of knowledge, its affinities with disagreement, ignorance, and validity, among other terms.

Knowledge and Disagreement

How could a death-of-the-Shari'a—its scholars and institutions, and its intersections with people and governments—be correct but remain incapable of explaining much of what is going on in today's world of support for the Shari'a by scholars, governments, and populations? How is the Shari'a judged to be both accessible and inaccessible, dead and alive? Is this simply a question of perspective?

An Ash'ari participant in law and theology has to understand a distinction between possessing *correct* knowledge and possessing *agreed-upon or transferable* knowledge. I might believe that I have knowledge of the correct doctrine in a given issue but still think that my knowledge will not be a matter of consensus. On this basis, an Ash'ari might believe that those who disagree with him are wrong, but he still can't necessarily convince them of his view. This perspective is immune to critique from outside of it, but all the details and generalities of this view are open for discussion by insiders who adhere to Ash'ari foundations and postulates. That is, this is not simply a system of (unjustified) personal beliefs; you could enter and engage those who work within the system and convince them to change their views. There is just no way you will do it from the outside.

The insider/outsider division, already touched on in chapter three, could be easily misunderstood and deserves a note of clarification. It is also a particularly touchy topic among scholars of Islamic studies in the Euro-American world. But when the sensitivity is set aside, people seem to be largely in agreement that every outsider is an insider of something else. When one feels excluded by being seen as an outsider of a certain view or paradigm, one must remember that being an insider allows one to understand something from practice and not be able to share it with anyone who was not exposed to similar experiences. In any case, denying that there is such a thing as outside or inside because borders are mobile or similar arguments does not past muster.

The basic insight Ash'aris argue could be seen from different angles. Suppose one bases his view on something universal (universal mathematics, universal experience, etc.), one is still bound to run into disagreement with others. But the epistemological value of this disagreement in itself is trivial. It should not bother us, and we should and do continue to think what we think (and think we are correct), or believe what we believe, if using this word does not confuse some scholars (I have a hunch it will). However, when our arguments are cracked, we should ask whether these were bad arguments for good doctrines or whether the doctrines themselves were bad. Knowledge could hence change, but it does not simply change because others disagree with us. There has to be a reason independent of this disagreement. People's disagreement does not mean that our knowledge is not knowledge at all, or that all knowledge is perspectival. Our *knowledge* could be knowledge, properly speaking, and it is potentially transferrable in principle to others, but its actual transfer depends on factors we do not control. Change in our knowledge should hence bear the high burden of showing an error in what we deemed knowledge in the past.

As I said, opponents may help one change his position, through new arguments that compel one to reconsider this old position. But there is something else one does with opponents: argue with them without any change in the positions. This arguing is about winning, not acquiring knowledge. When an argument with an opponent leads to change of one's view, this is caused by internal reflection and might entail reconsidering more than one view or doctrine. This internal reflection (rather the outsider's argument) is what leads to the modification of one's position. This is not an attempt to trivialize the opponent's role. It is only that it is impossible that the opponent will do the job of rearranging and reconsidering other views in light of a possible shift in one's view on a given subject. Your consistency is your job.

The extent of possible "knowledge" is always larger than "shareable" knowledge. The disagreement on the validity of "*istihsan*" in the Sunni juristic tradition illustrates this point. Hanafi jurists realized that the reasons for going against what seems to be the more easily articulated argument (*qiyas jaliyy*) may not always be easily articulated; Shafi'i, in an emotionally charged reaction, said "those who base their views on *istihsan*, make their own law (*man istahsan sharra'*)." Shafi'i certainly had a point; jurists could not simply say, this is the way it is, and I can't tell you why. But, to my mind, anyone who says that all juristic knowledge must be easily explained and shared with others, jurists and nonjurists, could not be a jurist. The term we employ in expressing the faculty needed for performing juristic functions is called "*fiqh*" (lit. understanding). The faculty of *fiqh* is based on a quasi-aesthetic capacity than mere abundant information. This capacity is recognized to various degrees by nonjurists and jurists, but there are always moments where the jurist's conclusion precedes an articulable explanation, and in some cases the conclusion continues to lack a full explanation, as far as the outsider is concerned.

A *mujtahid* does not consider the fact of limited adherence to the Shari'a a barrier to practicing ijtihad. Ignorance may be abundant and even dominant. People may believe that there is no God or that prophecies are mental illnesses, and this does not affect the continuity of *ijtihad* and making it available to its seekers. True, when no one in the world believes in God and the prophecy of Muhammad, then the Shari'a could not be said to exist in people's opinions. The presence of knowledge of the Shari'a, however, does not follow abundance or favorable social and political conditions. Partial political and social attacks on Shari'a norms affect people's understanding and application of these norms, but unless these attacks are left to function for a long time so as to create full discontinuity between the old and the new eras, it would be an exaggeration to say that Shari'a norms have become inaccessible or unintelligible. There is a tipping point after which human affairs could not be governed by *ijtihad*. Before that point, "knowledge" of the Shari'a remains possible.

This view remains an easy target for the accusation of religious obscurantism or a confusion of belief with knowledge or, in Weber's scheme of the tensions between religiosity and "the world," knowledge becomes a means to justify failure to make sense of the world as it is.[4]

Be that as it may, the discussion, once again, is beset by more than one understanding of knowledge. Participants in Sunni jurisprudence, at least of the Ash'ari variety, "live" in a world where authority sort of wraps them inside itself. An individual could make a claim to being a *mujtahid* and others' acknowledgment may be delayed but later attained. How could one reconcile a death-of-the-Shari'a with the genuine confidence of a contemporary jurist that he attained the status of *ijtihad*, coupled with a large following for this jurist, also joined by institutional and even governmental support for these "unofficial" views?

Valid Positions

What is the standard by which one could test the following proposition: "Racism" against Muslims in the American society is healthy? Is it reasonable for someone to say that, having lived in the United States for decades and encountered racism frequently, racism against Muslims should be judged to be healthy? This sounds fairly reasonable, but it clearly does not establish that the majority of Americans has racist attitudes or would be racist against Muslims. But, again, why should it matter whether the majority is racist, or how they would act with other Muslims, whether with mild or stark or no observable measure of racism at all? Racism is healthy for those who experience it, and it won't matter what the books or social scientists think.

Defending this measure of disjunction could be a recommendation of solipsism. My point, though, is that there are different degrees and meaning of "validity" in the expression "valid positions." The case of the health or frailty of racism and the health or fatigue of the Shari'a are disanalogous in obvious ways, but they are also analogous. If our standard of what is true is its very presence, regardless of whether this presence reflects a universal condition, our judgment of many positions as valid or invalid will change with changes in our "personal experience."

There are other things that could change one's sense of what is correct or valid. For example, a change in the circumstances attending the question as it was understood might allow a reconsideration of either the initial question to make sense in a new context or a reconsideration of the answer to the same question in light of certain consequences. Given the fluidity of circumstances, one could change his view. But does this mean that there is no such a thing as knowing? If disagreement with others does not negate knowledge, could disagreement with oneself do that? Consider the idea of "deferring to the opponent."

Deferring to the Opponent

Malik Ibn Anas (d. 179/795) is credited with the doctrine or principle of "deferring to the opponent." The term Maliki jurists use is *ra'y al-khilaf*, which literally means taking the disagreement (of an opponent) into account. In practice, this means adopting a position with which the same person had previously disagreed. In other words, it amounts to adopting aspects of a view one had rejected before. On the face of it, this doctrine is problematic. What does it mean for me to enter into a debate and win it, only to come back and say that my opponent, whom I refuted, was sufficiently right that I am willing to adopt his view in a future application of the question we once answered differently? This seems to be a contradiction.

Interpreting and defending this doctrine was a major task for Maliki jurists, and Wansharisi (d. 914/1508) reported that many have offered different explanations and defenses of the doctrine.[5] A student from Granada asked Ibn 'Arafa (d. 700/1301) in Tunis about what the principle of "deferring to the opponent" meant, and Shatibi (d. 790/1388) mailed his contemporaries in Fez and Tunis to ask them what they understood by the principle. Some said that *ra'y al-khilaf* meant deferring to the arguments of an opponent until these arguments have been rejected—that is, it did not mean real deference to the opponent, only willingness to understand any argument until one either adopts it (thus, it becomes his own) or rejects it (hence, deference to it happens at the stage of reflecting on the question at hand, but it does not survive that reflection). Some explained the doctrine of *ra'y al-khilaf* by saying that it meant accepting the opponent's view only in certain circumstances, after the question that caused the disagreement with the opponent has changed so much that it became a different question. For example, a Maliki jurist would deem invalid a marriage that includes inequitable conditions, which deprive a woman of her dowry, but when this marriage takes place and the same jurist is asked 25 years later whether the wife in this marriage could inherit her deceased husband (based on the bad marriage), the jurist must allow the inheritance, given the fact that the marriage took place anyway and that denying the wife inheritance in this case would be unfair, even if the marriage itself was unfair when it took place.

Malikis who defended the principle still acknowledged that it represented a challenge. They said that when one realizes there are two paths to a town, one must choose one of them and cannot walk in both of them at the same time. Thus, the doctrine could not have meant continuous suspension of judgment while traveling in multiple paths at the same time.

This debate provides many insights. First, one must be truly neutral when considering evidence, that is, until this evidence is judged. And one must, on the one hand, not pretend to be sure when one is not—one could not say that this is good or bad evidence without truly holding that things could not be otherwise. On the other hand, one cannot continue to hesitate about one's own view forever.

The second insight is that one must distinguish questions that seem to be the same but are in fact different. It is not inconsistent to discourage people from entering into bad contracts then accept some consequences for these contracts after they have taken place. The underlying principle is that law's role in society is not only *regulative* of actions before they occur; it is also *ameliorative* of the bad consequences of actions that already occurred. Malikis, by the way, are not alone in their willingness to judge the same act differently based on "its stage," If someone unsuccessfully searches for water to fulfill her ablution and decided to pray with dry ablution instead, she may only interrupt her prayer if water became available while she was at the beginning of the prayer. When water is available toward the end of her prayer, she is not expected to interrupt the prayer, nor will she be asked to redo it. This point is made by a legal maxim stating that juristic ruling changes based on the stage of an action [distinguishing an act's early stages (*al-hukm fi al-ibtida'*) from its later stages (*al-hukm fi al-intiha'*)].

The important point is that the strategy of differing to the opponent is made out of epistemological concerns rather than pragmatic ones. It is not that Maliki jurists simply need to search for relevance to their jurisprudence; they assume it is relevant. They are observing a fact of epistemological nature: Full knowledge of who was correct in the initial question (of whether marriage without dowry could be deemed valid) persists until there is direct knowledge that an implication of the opponent's view should be adopted. This allows a partial adoption of this opponent's view to solve the practical question. Otherwise, this adoption would not be possible.

Despite its apparent limitation to Maliki legal thinking, this doctrine also offers general insights about the debate of what the Shari'a is and is not. The availability and knowledge of divine norms as interpreted by jurists both (a) require some adherence from the Muslim populations (and internalizing the values embedded in the *fatwas* of these jurists) and (b) stand at a distance from social behavior—it assumes a variety of roles toward social life: preventative, regulative, and corrective or ameliorative.

Ash'ari doctrines do not give social norms on their own much power in the absence of jurists. Popular consensus is either part of (binding) juristic consensus or not, and either way could not be relied on after the end of jurists. Zarkashi (d. 794/1392) writes[6]:

> Popular consensus, after the absence of jurists, bears no value, since we either do not consider them when assessing whether consensus took place,

> in which case we could not assume the possibility of the question, since it is impossible for an age to be devoid of those who convey the truth (!) And if we consider their views in whether a consensus exists, then we do not accept that their consensus is a legally binding consensus.

In this brief and convoluted statement, Zarkashi (while confusing Ash'ari and Hanbali doctrine on the fatigue question) insists that popular consensus does not replace juristic consensus. His statement, however, captures the limited credence given to social customs by jurists. This issue could be studied further, but it will take us away from the core of the discussion. Suffice it to say that social life is both necessary and incapable of controlling juristic production. Social life in Muslim societies will remain for many the preserve of Shari'a norms, but because social life could not be fully trusted as a reflection of divine norms, reconciliation of customs and law must continue.

Knowledge and Ignorance

Human knowledge of the world is limited, but this should neither serve as a discouragement from seeking more knowledge, nor as a source of desperation from knowledge altogether. Knowledge in the Muslim intellectual traditions, in my understanding, is characterized by a "moderate" position toward the limitations of humanity and the human capacity to learn about the world. It is characterized by a sense of deference to the past, deference to God who established the natural world, repulsion at the thought of human control over other humans' affairs (hence suspicious of the notion of maximizing resources).

To my knowledge, there is nothing in the Islamic traditions that parallels modern naturalist concepts of knowledge with their assertion that the basic structure of knowledge of the world, including humans, has been completed by successive scientific revolutions and one only needs to fill in the missing details. The "Islamic" picture is also distinct from post-modern negations of the possibility of knowledge, knowledge of nature and of populations, given the limitations and possible value of all "valid" positions taken vis-à-vis the phenomena under investigation. The concept of knowledge that contrasts with both of these modern and postmodern positions is not fully foreign to some commonsense understanding of "knowledge" in our life today, but it is distinct from commonly defended understanding of knowledge in important ways. In this "Islamic" concept, divine revelation should not be ignored, for example. This concept of knowledge will also allow basic epistemological stances that could not be conceded by today's understanding of knowledge.

The medieval fatigue debate ended up, on one side (the Ash'ari), with a sense of resignation to God's control of human destiny, to the way things seem to be and might become, but not with a sense of despair. On another side (the Mu'tazili), reliance on "reason" created a different stance. In either case, human knowledge remains limited. Knowledge indeed is nothing but the best available position, which is in fact surrounded by measures of *absence of knowledge*, measures of ignorance. For practical purposes at least, *'ilm* and *zann* may ultimately be one and the same thing.

For the purposes of ethical and legal inquiry, a jurist might decide to "ignore" some available information as irrelevant to the question, and there is room for disagreement among jurists there. For example, being the husband of a pregnant woman is sufficient for a presumption of being the father of a child birthed by this woman during the marriage. When a jurist/judge is called upon to inquire whether this presumption is correct in a given case (e.g., where the man denies he is the father or accuses his wife of having had sex with another man), assuming our evidence is not conclusive (say, before DNA analysis was available), a jurist might simply ask the man to engage in the long procedure of *li'an*, allowing him to terminate the marriage but prohibiting him from ever remarrying this same women in the future. This would be done in the presence of tools, presumably inferior to DNA analysis, that might give us a probability of the child's fatherhood but does not have any claim to being conclusive. The new tools' claim to conclusiveness certainly affect many jurists' decision as to whether they must be used or ignored. When there is no decisive knowledge of who the father is, the presumption of fatherhood for the husband coupled with the freedom to end the marriage is all that is available to the man. DNA analysis' higher claim to conclusiveness presents a new condition, but the modern jurist may decide to either (a) employ this available knowledge and limit the *li'an* option to cases where DNA analysis could not be used or (b) insist on the old position, to avoid subjecting social relations to the influences of changing scientific research, which would be a reliance on a position that does not benefit from what is available and considered knowledge today.

In most cases, however, the highest ceiling of human understanding is what matters in moral/legal issues, and positions against it bear the burden of argument to establish its reasonableness. The best *biology* or *physics* of today is what a jurist needs to employ, unless one believes that research in biology and physics has deteriorated and that the natural philosophy of five hundred years ago, for example, described natural phenomena better. The same is true of any factual research in criminal cases. If one could not *use* the highest available "science" in a given legal matter, then one is not qualified to answer that question. Knowledge can then change, but what we are required to go by is the same: the best that is available in a given time and place.

The Shari'a and the Laws of Nature

Human knowledge is the best available *human ignorance*, the closest to an ideal truth, and the Shari'a will have, based on multiple considerations, to reconcile itself to the conditions of human knowledge at a given age. One way it addresses this "knowledge" is by neutralizing it, as I just explained, if social and moral considerations make this knowledge "unusable." But this is pretty much the exception. Most of the time, the Shari'a not only will use current knowledge, it will have to readjust itself to it.

It would probably be offensive to the scientists of our time to suggest any analogy between the Shari'a and what they consider their superior, empirical, well-established knowledge of the world, which they find not to be simply their perspective but rather the way things are. But since the question at hand is not how to engage or evaluate their science in any way but to consider the relationship of a system of legal and moral norms to this science, no offence should be taken. My question is about how specialists in devising Shari'a norms are affected by the notion of science that dominates their day.

Jurists such as Qarafi (d. 684/ 1285) provide an insight. Qarafi demonstrated his interest in basic science, going beyond what a jurist needs, to answer questions of physics, optics, and optical and terrestrial illusions in his book *al-Istibsar*. This interest in the nature of light and the angles from which the horizon and its elements are observed has an impact on rituals, since many of these rituals are tied to the worshipper's sense of the time of the ritual, the direction that should be taken in a prayer, among other aspects where some understanding of time and place is either required or would influence the worshipper's behavior once acquired.

This point also has other connections. Ahmad Dallal's Yale Terry Lectures titled *Islam, Science, and the Challenges of History* asserted (as George Saliba repeatedly demonstrated) how inquiries of Islamic jurisprudence maintained a strong link to many scientific inquiries, including determining the division of the day and night (to determine prayer times), determining the exact direction toward Mecca (to specify how an individual, starting from any angle on the uneven surface of the Earth, could face the correct direction for the prayers), the division of the lunar year (to account for time-specific duties such as fasting and pilgrimage), to say nothing of a transformation of mathematics, as algebra came to most capably solve inheritance questions (all shares in an inheritance question are fractions that must add up to 1 exactly), among other examples.

To understand the nature of the constant change in the relationship between the Shari'a and dominant "science," some research also needs to go in the direction of examining socioscientific conditions and their connection with sociolegal research. Steven Shapin's work, emphasizing the relationship between scientific knowledge and what counts as truth in a given age must be exploited to understand how a relationship between the Shari'a and science could change over time. Without contradicting this mostly historical and factual exercise, the idea that jurisprudence and science are naturally compatible or not must be discarded for a complex view that takes into account the impact of an immanent frame where explanations are contained within the world of experience (Charles Taylor's *A Secular Age*).

There is another level of intersection between Shari'a knowledge and common or established knowledge. In this intersection, a religious philosopher is needed to reflect on how basic beliefs may be affected by one's understanding of the world. This is a task Ibn Rushd happily took in his *Tahafut al-Tahafut* (Incoherence of the Incoherence), a response to Ghazali's attack on philosophers. Ibn Rushd's *Tahafut* is sometimes seen as an attempt to reconcile religion and philosophy (including scientific knowledge and principles of pure reason) and mistakenly so, as Jabiri argues.[7] There may in fact be no such a thing as reconciling religion and science. They are either compatible or not (in someone's view). Just as attacks on religion as incompatible with science do not regularly convince believers in religion to abandon them and seek the truth in science, so-called reconciliations of religion and science do not stop unbelieving scientists' irritation with religion. Many in modern North America draw the radical conclusion that this is because everything is a matter of perspective.

Ibn Rushd saw matters a bit differently. There is no such a thing as (correct) knowledge that could be contradicted, he believed. In *Fasl al-Maqal*, Ibn Rushd insisted on a simple formula to say true religion and correct knowledge will always be compatible: If a foundational doctrine in the Shari'a contradicts what is claimed to be scientific or philosophical knowledge, the latter is invalid; and if a proven doctrine of science or principle of pure reason contradicts an interpretation of the Shari'a, the latter is invalid. There is no case where basic doctrines of revelation and experience or valid systematic reflection clash. Ibn Rushd's *Tahafut* is an exercise in determining where bad interpretations of the Shari'a and bad "science" crowd and confuse the picture. Ibn Rushd here is hence a self-appointed arbiter who will decide what should be eliminated from religion and from "science" so as to preserve their harmony. He is often seen to take the side of philosophy/science all the time, but this is a bit simple. Consider the following.

1. Philosophy/science is right about the fact of the lack of evidence of generation *ex nihilo*, and those who claim that revelation contradicted that are wrong.
2. Revelation is correctly understood to assert God's knowledge of all detailed events, and those who think philosophers contradicted that are wrong; philosophers only denied that God knows new events through a new knowledge emanating from the happening of these events in the world.
3. Revelation is correctly understood to assert postbody/extra-body life, but we do not need a simple notion of resurrection in the same bodies, and those who believe philosophers said anything against that are wrong (philosophers may have said nothing about that at all).
4. Philosophy, via an *a priori* principle here, is right about causality being inherent in the laws of nature, rather than dependent on God's intervention in every case, and those who think believing in God contradicts that engage in sophistry. When prophets learn what is hidden they are simply allowed to learn more about nature than others, rather than allowed to change nature itself. Hence miracles happen to prophets because they know more about natural laws (a flying man, e.g., will have used a law of nature that is unknown to his contemporaries, rather than broken the laws of nature at the time).

Ibn Rushd, however, does not provide a law to distinguish good from bad "science." And there is no way to claim that a ready law to distinguish good from bad understanding of the Shari'a is available. The Shari'a manifests itself in human understanding, which even in its most careful form is dependent on correct information. The only way one could assume any stability in this relationship between religion and science is to assume the highest level of critique and reflection, so that what is proposed for consideration is only established science, and where only the basics of revelation that could not be altered are taken into account as religion.

Ibn Rushd's view will take us away from the mundane world of the Shari'a's practical task of regulating everyday human actions. But it raises a large question about the future of the Shari'a, which will constantly engage in a Rushdi or Averroeian project, where the distance between laws governing human behavior and the laws of nature is kept, but a measure of harmony and turf-determination is achieved.

Hurdles to Overcome before Considering the Shari'a as Lost Knowledge

One of the arguments leveled by Hallaq to defend his thesis that the Shari'a had died about a century ago is that certain juristic forms of reasoning and research are now unavailable to those who claim to carry the mantle of Sunni jurisprudence. The examples given by Hallaq, as I indicated earlier, raise a larger problem, that of the constant discontinuity in juristic activities, performed by Nawawi (d. 676/1277), Subki (d. 771/1369), Haytami (d. 974/1566), or others. All these and some of their Shafi'i successors exercised *ijtihad* in the sense of providing answers to real-life questions, and they did disagree on many questions of *usul* and *furu'*. We must remember, as we hinted earlier, that *ijtihad* is an art (a *malaka*) rather than a body of information. This is a double-edged sword for the argument on the life of the Shari'a as knowledge or arguments, since this knowledge will be assessed differently by different participants and even more differently by observers from outside.

If we split the question of the fate of the Shari'a into several questions, this discussion would end up becoming several discussions of how the different juristic activities of different generations of Shafi'i jurists and their practice of everyday *ijtihad* was both governed by and generative of social norms. That is, since the life of the Shari'a is not simply the availability of ideas but also the (at least partial) popular adherence to these ideas, then any research that attempts at gauging the vigor of the Shari'a will have to show the availability of practice corresponding to the *fatwas* issued by different *mujtahids* (noting the degree to which the Shari'a of old times has already been preserved by and cemented in the customs of Muslim populations). This will make the matter much more complicated, but this procedure is necessary before any assertion of the death of the Shari'a as a system of law, morality, and social customs.

The argument that discontinuity in certain juristic activities indicates the end of jurisprudence does not work, especially when juristic activities are not fully accounted for by empirical radars, as much of the Shari'a production today is found "underground"—unsupervised by government activities and officials. The task of assessing the existence of *ijtihad* activities of this type by isolated academics, scholars of the history of Islamic law, is harder than it appears. This is especially the case when the academic exercise is governed by scholarship in "history" (as isolated and distinguished from any participation in or internalizing of *ijtihad*).

The discussion of "lost arguments and forms of reasoning" invokes multiple types of reflection. If one knows what is being described as "lost," then it is not lost, and if one does not know what it is exactly, then one cannot be sure that it exists or does not exist. The only thing we can speak of is something like "what is hard to access" (a claim that should be verified with examples, again harder than it seems). Neglected knowledge thus remains more elusive than is assumed.

* * *

Knowledge is neither "fully" universal nor simply subjective. No one should believe that they possess any knowledge of something, unless one thinks that this "knowledge" applies universally. But this recognition of the universality of the purported "knowledge" is according to this person. Poor Weber probably did not fully imagine that his berating of those who "rejected the world" shared an important quality with his objects of critique. They were both "understandings" of what is universally true. If you keep looking for what is truly universal, what all people agree on, you will get something trivial or abstract. If this remains your standard, you will have no knowledge. And if you think it is all subjective and perspectival, what should I say, you are just "tired." Knowledge will maintain its subjective nature but will be sharable. Knowledge of the Shari'a will not be different. Foucault's contingencies will not resolve this matter (with all due respect, and appreciation for Foucault and his powerful intellect).

Chapter 10

Constant Interpretation

The language of this recent discussion of the status of the Shari'a in today's world was influenced by the times that made the discussion itself possible. One of the factors that condition the current debate is that it takes for granted *an assumption* that should and will *itself* likely be debated anew. Many scholars of Islam are increasingly more comfortable speaking of "interpretation" as the essence of law in Islam. This language may as well describe contentions and debates about other systems of law and legal theory (I am thinking of the Anglo-American legal systems, dealing with H. L. A. Hart's *Concept of Law* and Donald Dworkin's *Matter of Principle* and *Law's Empire*).[1] True, the extent to which "interpretation" is seen as the central and most significant fact of American law's evolution varies, and the meaning and value of interpretations of the law also vary. For example, while acknowledging the existence of good and bad interpretations, Dworkin's belief in the integrity of the American legal system leads him to argue that, over all, the evolution of the system has been through reasonable interpretations of its foundation. Justice Scalia (in his Tanner Lectures, published under the title "*A Matter of Interpretation*"),[2] hardly in agreement with many of Dworkin's basic stances in reading and participating in American jurisprudence, heaps scorn on this attitude of "constant interpretation" as a legitimate exercise for the judges participating in the American legal system in order to argue for continuity based on text. From opposed viewpoints, both Dworkin and Scalia had to succumb to a condition of a certain type of thinking about law that colors the participants' sense of what law is or is not. This also happens to be the same world in which the debate on the Shari'a's survival or demise takes place. It is the world in which the Shari'a may have undergone constant interpretation to a point of fatigue.

My point is not that American judges, lawyers, and jurists would agree about the degree to which law is interpretation; it is that they admit or are forced to admit the reference to interpretation as a question of what the law is or has become, and Islamic law scholars have to apply this same language to their debates. Well, there is a sense in which the main activities in developing and applying Islamic law can be called *interpretation*, even according to medieval Sunni jurists, but using this language without qualifications faces difficulties. Islamic law, the rulings and opinions given by authoritative jurists, which are reflected at least to an extent by social and public customs, comes out of a process of reflection about the Prophet's revelations and example. The process also involves reflection about the conditions of living people who seek to regulate their lives by these revelations and instructions. This, in a very important sense, is not simply interpretation. It is a very specific kind of interpretation, if one insists on thrusting the word, and as those who know about the clashes of *hadith* and *fiqh* scholars have learned, it is burdened with a very specific legacy that could be "revised" only incrementally and only according to an "internal" juristic logic. Medieval Sunni jurists use the term *ijtihad*, which means exertion or effort, but they do not just include in it any exertion or any effort that aims to uncover moral and legal norms. The term *ijtihad* has over the centuries accumulated so much texture that it does not simply mean exerting effort any more.

As I argued in chapter nine, the old sense in which the Shari'a is *knowledge of tradition adjusted to the present* does not obey the modern usage of the term *knowledge as a product of context*; nor would it recognize modern assessments of the loss of knowledge based on the latter concept. It is obvious that when we have to use English terms when we talk about this issue, we will use terms such as *epistemic shift*. Of this I am as guilty as the next participant in any of these debates. And this, without a question, is part of the condition of the debate and the condition of the world surrounding the Shari'a, whose fatigue is under investigation. But it is something to overcome rather than reinforce.

There are adherents of the death of the Shari'a who share very little with Hallaq's analysis or may opportunistically use it but could not really get into its details with any authority or deep understanding. These adherents eclectically and in an undisciplined manner would draw on what may be referred to as the postmodern condition, where words such as interpretation (in the same family, politics, perspective) are overused and thrust into most debates.

The essence of "interpretations" remains a mix of context (political, social, etc.), ideas and beliefs, temperaments (of jurists, judges, and other participants), and factors of this order. No one could deny the availability of these factors in Islamic legal history—in the history of the Shari'a. In a sense, a claim that new conditions allow us a new assessment of the viability of the Shari'a attempts to establish distinctions between the present moment and every moment of the past to accentuate and leave no doubt about the proposed shift. Take, for example, jurists' independence of government and political pressure, which the evidence of history allows us to see and assess differently. The Shari'a, ideally, is an exercise of the jurists with only a degree of tolerance for, and limited incorporation of, government regulations and has thus always been independent of government to a great degree. Thus, when the health and frailty of this Shari'a is assessed, the role of government in supporting the Shari'a judicially and "academically" in the past should not be inflated. Consider this description in light of the suggested limitations of the value of a jurists/government alliance:

> The multiplicity of doctrinal narrative resulted in the development of a technical terminology whose purpose was to distinguish between types of legal opinion. The evolution of this terminology was symptomatic of the staggering variety of opinion that resulted from a fundamental structural and epistemological feature in Islamic law, a feature that emerged early on and was to determine the later course of legal development. Its root cause was perhaps the absence of a central legislative agency—a role that could have been served by the state or the office of the caliphate but was not. The power to determine what the law was had lain instead, from the very beginning, in the hands of the legal specialists, the proto-*fuqaha'*, and later the *fuqaha'* themselves. It was these men who undertook the task of elaborating on the legal significance of the revealed texts, and it was they who finally established a legal epistemology that depended in its entirety on the premise of an individualistic interpretation of the law. This feature was to win for Islamic law, in modern scholarship, the epithet "jurist's law." The ultimate manifestation of this individual hermeneutical activity was the doctrine of *kull mujtahid musib*, that is, that each and every *mujtahid* is correct.[3]

There are ideas here lying in wait for abuse by the death-of-the-Shari'a camp. The potential of abuse is obvious: *Both previously and today, the Shari'a is itself a body of interpretations, and since the conditions that allowed Muslim jurists a measure of independence have changed, the old Shari'a must be dead.* Some of Hallaq's language is reconciled with this idea, and his stance, with all its admirable complexity, could allow for similar views that I cannot accept.

There seems to be an *authoritative* vagueness overtaking this discussion, where many participants critique positions but do not have ones of their own. Each search must have a target (*li-kull^{i} talab^{in} matlub*), Juwayni asserted, and if one does not seek a position, she/he is not participating in the search. The ability to offer critique without the willingness to present an alternative benefits from the overall disenchantment with systems and with research that attempts to uncover systems and systematic thinking. This condition is exacerbated in our specific field by scholarship about Islam that consists of information about "some" issues here and there with no concern for a big "Shari'a" picture or any big picture for that matter, and no serious consideration of the implications of the presented arguments and conclusions for practicing Shari'a jurists. The participants in studying Islamic law who now contribute to an assessment of its current status have been influenced in their education by "other" fields and other systems that offer ready conclusions.. The task of thinking about the Shari'a as a whole could not be achieved from a stance uninterested in it as a system. Yet, this is what much current scholarship concerned with the Shari'a today sets out to do..

Fatigue of Different Types

Concern with the big picture invites questions of its own. For example, the loss of correct understanding of God's relationship to the world must be seen as part of the loss of the Shari'a. This aspect of "the fatigue of the Shari'a," which was less of a concern to legal theorists who discussed the absence of qualified jurists, appears in other debates. Ibn Rushd (d. 595/1198) mentions an example of this loss in his debates with Ash'ari theologians and philosophers. He speaks of the failure of Ash'aris to commit to the standard path to knowing God, which the Qur'an shows to be by focusing on His signs in the world. Ibn Rushd argues that Ash'aris worked too hard to emphasize God's lack of need for natural laws and hence made a joke of the world God created, which was supposed to indicate the Divine Creator through the world's near-perfect status rather than its incoherence and need of God's preservation to ameliorate its inherent inconsistencies. This, he says, is an instance of distortion (*taghyir*) that befell the Shari'a.[4]

In the specific area of the loss of knowledgeable conveyers of God's moral and legal norms, however, the loss is a loss of specific training rather than loss of simple insight. Many generations before Ibn Rushd, Juwayni had in the *Ghiyathi* hinted that his age may be seen as one of scarcity of qualified jurists, and as we noted in chapter four, Ibn Rushd also made a similar statement. Other medieval jurists who debated the absence of qualified jurists were able to *anticipate* the weakness in people's interest in their jurisprudence and the changes in the times that attend that loss of interest. Some, such as Majd al-Din Ibn Taymiyya (d. 651/1254) in his

Talqih al-Afham, are credited (by Ibn Abi Zur'a 826/1422) with explicitly identifying the immediate cause of the fatigue as loss-of-interest as opposed to any lack of the availability of the sources.

Aside from lack of interest in the traditional legal sciences, *futur* may consist in the failure of *muftis*, educated in the Islamic tradition and partly informed about the modern world, to provide convincing Shari'a-based answers to modern questions. Even in almsgiving or *zakah*, which was mostly based on the idea that real wealth is associated with basic resources such as land, crops, and livestock in a world where "value" was generated and destroyed according to different laws, jurists may fail to adjust the logic of Shari'a discourse to modern conditions. This failure can also be seen in issues such as usury and family structure. The new fatigue is, interestingly, also understandable in terms of the partial support for the Shari'a by Muslim governments, populations, and scholars. The survival of the Shari'a thus stems from the same elements that force its functioning in a state of fatigue.

There are different ways one may explore the fatigue that consists in the failure of juristic explanations to make sense within a given generation. Consider the language used in the following example. In a debate between a Maliki and a Hanafi jurist about the marriage *wali* (male representative of the bride) imagined by Mazari (d. 536/1141), an argument (going back and forth) includes an assertion that the prospective bride is in need of a representative by the law (*shar'*) as well as custom:

> you (Hanafis) would then say that the prospective bride (*mar'ah*) is in need of a male representative (*wali*) by law (*shar'an*), and we (Malikis) then say "she is in need of that out of respect for custom and propriety (*'adatan wa 'urfan*)," as we know that the woman, even the one who does not have a conservative garb in public (*mutabarrija*) often projects coyness and shame to be in the position of someone who is contracting for the utility of her body (*an ta'qid 'ala farjiha*) and negotiating for a compensation for access to sexual intercourse with her . . .[5]

The analysis may hearken back to the Muslim populations' desire to keep a Muslim female's sense of respect for herself tied to her being part of a family. The medieval juristic schemes might change; they might be modified in a limited way; or they may be reconfigured creatively. To my mind, without some of that, *ijtihad* will not have been preserved. This is one reason I think that changing the existing juristic structures in a limited way would be a sign of the Shari'a's vitality rather than demise.

If all that is needed is a combination of minds to solve "Shari'a" problems correctly, you may not require an extension of what has been already accepted: that "councils" of scholars (such as the several versions of *majma' al-fiqh* that could be found today) accept the idea that *ijtihad* may indeed be compartmentalized. Each member will have a specialty within the different aspects and tools of theoretical and practical legal reasoning. Ideally there should still be encyclopedic scholars. Sam'ani had good reasons to reject the idea that the collective duty of *ijtihad* will have been fulfilled if there were scholars of *usul* and others of *furu'*, as he believed that only those who combine the two could be true *mujtahids*.[6] But it is increasingly unrealistic in this generation at least to insist that encyclopedic scholars be the norm.

The Search for a Trap

The inquiry into the health or frailty of the Shari'a at a given moment can be a major trap. How much should one know about the Muslim world, with all its languages and cultures, legal and political institutions, and even private and social life in its cities, villages, and so on, before being willing to give the vitality of the Shari'a a grade? An even bigger trap lies in wait in an attempt to speak of the future.

Two important issues must be tackled if we were to agree that one must say something "descriptive" about the state of the Shari'a today. The first is determining what questions are being asked as these are deemed important and which ones are marginalized or ignored. This amounts to clarifying the criteria based on which one exercises this "power to describe or characterize" today's Shari'a. The second is to continue to do one's best to clarify the terminology; yes, just as our medieval predecessors have, we will likely struggle and most likely fail to do a perfect job, but we should try to do something about the terminology.

I suggest separating the large issue of the life and death of the Shari'a into several issues. In each case, different criteria can be introduced to test or assess the vitality of the Shari'a, and these may also be compared to the old criteria known in the medieval and early modern fatigue debates. With this I hope to avoid any excitement to show whether the Shari'a has died or that it will never die. The issues must be separated, and the result is likely to be neither a simple "yes" nor a simple "no."

This should also be taken as an indirect rejection of studies that attempt to provide a modern commentary on the old debate by simply weighing the arguments given in the medieval sources (grading the arguments) based on whatever belief or foundation the author finds compelling. A recent article, published only one year before Hallaq's "Can the Shari'a be Restored," in the Umm al-Qura University Journal levels what Hallaq would likely judge (correctly) an indefensible argument that *ijtihad* was alive and well, without any work beyond a rehashing of the old arguments.[7] Although it might be useful for educational purposes (although warnings must be issued about curt and confused citations and misunderstandings in this article), this discussion is far from relevant to a serious consideration of the issue of the fatigue of the Shari'a meriting interest. I hope my discussion did not give the impression that I recommend studies of this nature or support their narrow perspective.

Still, a bigger trap than all the traps resulting from terminology or overgeneralization is the trap of the search for a "neutral" position in these charged subjects. Let each position expressed from a certain viewpoint not pretend to encompass all viewpoints. This pretension has not served us well so far and is unlikely to do better in the future.

Conclusion

One may believe (with the Mu'tazila) that the human intellect is capable, independently of divine revelation, of arriving at norms by which individuals may live and for which they may expect divine reward and punishment. Alternatively, one may argue (with the Ash'ariyya) that the human intellect's job is to receive the divine revelation and it is incapable, independently, of arriving at binding norms, at least not ones with which God's reward and punishment is concerned. Or, one may hold (with the Hanabila) that human reason should only be minimally involved in devising rules on behalf of God but that access to the basic truth in the last revelation of the Prophet Muhammad will be with us until the end of time. Or, finally, if a follower of Ibn Rushd is allowed to come to the debate, she/he would come to say that any conflict between "correct" arguments from reason or "true" divine revelation exists only in the imagination of the feeble-minded. Reason and revelation are two paths toward the same target.

As you read the arguments described here in their original sources, you will note that the disagreement (at some junctures) is caused by those disagreeing ultimately answering slightly different questions. I came thus to find reconcilable insights in the opposed views, believing, for example, that an assertion of (the unaided) reason's authority (from a Mu'tazili, such as Abu al-Hysayn al-Basri) in the absence of all access to revelation could be reconciled with an Ash'ari application of uncertain-but-probable "benefits" (*manafi'*) from this reason's memory of a partly forgotten revelation, and an minimalistic (text-bare) Shari'a may (with some difficulty) be reconciled with both of these. True, all parties would disagree once we raise theoretical questions such as the source of religious obligation in any of these cases, but let this disagreement be what it is.

As they differ in theory or in practice and some of the time in both, these different recipes for how to reach desirable norms have the same thing in mind—the Shari'a given to humans by God. And on all these accounts, living by the Shari'a would be the best life. These positions partly influence, though don't fully guarantee, an answer to whether this

Shari'a will experience fatigue. One may, again, believe (with some of the Mu'tazila and Hanabila this time) that it is not going to happen. One may believe (with some of the Mu'tazila and some of the Ash'ariyya) that if it were to happen, we have nothing but our unaided human reason to resort to. One may believe with Juwayni (d. 478/1085) that our faint memory of the fully functioning Shari'a should be the basis for the way forward.

What would the follower of these ideas do in a postmodern, partly post-secular, partly postreligious world, that is also getting ready to be a post-state world, where "markets," "media and public conversations" are part of the mix? Is this the world of the fatigue of the Shari'a, perhaps alternatively defined as a world where the impact of what qualified jurists think is not easily identifiable (rather than a world with no qualified jurists)? This may be it, and it may be that the basic answers still work: a combination of the memory of the old Shari'a and personal and communal applications of Shari'a norms is all the Shari'a will stand on until the end.

* * *

In the preceding chapters, I have not attempted to provide a historical narrative of the debates on the fate of the Shari'a. In any case, I have been a few steps removed from the Rankean aspiration to write a history that would limit itself to representing things the way they really were (*wie es eigentlich gewesen*). I certainly did not labor to avoid thinking of the present and the future as I thought of history, nor did I attempt to avoid judging the past. I think of past discussions on the fatigue of the Shari'a as "present" and relevant to today's world, and as I hinted repeatedly, I came to believe in the strategy of splitting the question of where the Shari'a stands today into several questions in order to make the discussion meaningful, which came to me only through reflecting on these discussions of the "past."

If this is a modern commentary on an old debate, did I have anything new to say? I assume "yes." The most important assertion I make here is that it is very hard for those who would like to participate in an assessment of how "alive" the Shari'a is today to not have any sense of entitlement to participate in it. Being a qualified jurist by any "medieval" standards is not intended here, and even being a good Muslim may or may not be a prerequisite. What matters is that the participant possesses a sense that he could seriously suggest solutions to Shari'a problems. (And I do not mean the types of solution that assume that the Shari'a is a problem.)

Those who feel entitled to contribute to specific debates as insiders may not be jurists in the traditional sense (think of Tariq al-Bishri) and may argue that adopting aspects of democracy, for example, in the sense in which it manifested itself in modern Islamic history in Muslim societies (under the pressure of colonialism and postcolonial, colonial-like systems), and considering it part of Muslims' Shari'a today is justifiable. It will not likely matter that some will argue that the Islamic legal tradition has not been democratic in this sense. If the new participants think that democracy must be incorporated, this will likely prevail.

* * *

The medieval Islamic legal tradition functioned on the assumption that revelation provided basic guidance that humanity desperately needed. Muslim jurists disagreed as to what humans had been expected to do before this revelation. As I said, some championed the idea that reason, unaided by revelation, either can capture the essence of revelatory guidance or reach otherwise binding conclusions humans must make as their point of departure. Others insisted that humans, before revelation, simply had no responsibility to follow any standard, in the absence of standards. After the revelation is forgotten, humanity falls back into the same condition they experienced before the revelation. Between these two stages, revelation-based law functions with a maximum standard of "probability" (as *fiqh* is simply a *zann*-based system of doctrines). Despair before and after the law is thus implicitly rejected, just as complacent certainty is rejected during the lifetime of revelation-based law.

* * *

On the current status of the Shari'a, I argue that one must suggest strategies for understanding the broad question more effectively, propose ways to split the large question into several questions in order to get closer to a reasonable answer to it, and connect the question to other inquiries without which our question remains vague. But this study also has other implications, as it recovers the nuances of how the Shari'a, one of the systems accused of being unable to adjust to the modern world, can be seen from the inside, rather than from an outside, which allots it only a role of complying with dominant worldviews. I am unsympathetic to the very steep paradigms dominant in philosophical, sociocultural, and political arenas, which assigns the Shari'a this defensive role. These include the issues of coexistence between incommensurable systems and reforming those less adjusted to modern worldviews.

Through philosophical debates (I am thinking of the works of Tim Scanlon and John Rawls), we learn that coexistence and tolerance are difficult tasks. There are many premises that make this limited claim defensible, but its undertone is hardly innocuous. Since it is ultimately better for humanity to adjust itself to the best available philosophy or worldview instead of working from diametrically opposed or "incommensurable" ones, systems that are unable to adjust themselves to the latest and the best will require to be tolerated, which requires major effort.

This presumptuous, hegemonic understanding of the world and its assumptions about how to address its complexity has led to many distortions of our view of the world and its components. It made many people think of coexistence as a lofty goal, which requires so much effort. Does coexistence really require that much effort, compared to, say, avoiding it? Even exerting influence and a degree of dominance on the world leaves (should leave) much space for what is counter-, what is opposite, to survive, indeed to flourish. We are sometimes told that it was the wars of premodern times that led moderns to think of competition as a natural human quality. This is another debate I will not set out to have, since it changes my subject and defeats my posture of asserting that modern perspectives may be suspended or critiqued from viewpoints unwilling to begin from modernity's assumptions, even when it concedes its strong impact.

* * *

When the Shari'a becomes history, we will all think of it the way we think of history. We will disagree about what it was like. Perhaps we will consider speaking of it as a source of entertainment [as the poetry-line goes, without history, much staying-up at night (*samar*)[1] would not be possible]. Perhaps we will discuss "when did it really become history"? There is a type of disagreement that is appropriate only for history, speaking of history's shifts, "what history is for" and how it relates to the present, and whether knowing it is possible, to what extent is knowledge of the past possible? These are the questions that will be raised "after the law."

Continuity and change will always be debated, because neither absolute stability nor full discontinuity truly occurs in the evolution of human cultures. In asserting the legitimacy of a new culture and a new set of conventions, similarities are ignored, whether deliberately or inadvertently, between what is called the "new" and the "old." Asserting that a new human is created with the coming of a certain age could be an exaggeration. (On or about December 1910, human character changed!) For example, when moderns assert that the old habits of relating myth as if it was reality disappeared with scientific thinking, they are falling in an exaggeration. The point here is not that the continuity of attachment to myths among modern people is caused by their failure to adhere to the high standards of science; it is that science itself will bear the marks of the same humans whose ancestors produced what moderns call, with shame and disgust, myths.

Again, only when the Shari'a is history will we begin to think of it as history. Ibn Daqiq al-'Id (d. 702/1302) may end up being right, and in this case, there will not be sufficient "human history" after the Shari'a to reflect on it as history. But he may end up being wrong, and in this case there will be sufficient time to reflect on the Shari'a as history. It is hard to guess what this will look like, a feeling we have with as much intensity as Juwayni did. We do not know what the future looks like; we can only imagine it.

* * *

Let me end this conclusion on a lighter note. We learned from the pseudo-William of Tripoli in the 1270s that Islam was designed to expire some time in the thirteenth Christian century, that is, very soon after the author wrote his prophecy. Prophecies from the Muslim side about what will expire and when can also be found. 'Abd al-Wahhab al-Sha'rani (d. 973/1565) and others predicted that, of all *madhhab*s, the Hanafi *madhhab* would be the latest to wither away, just as it was the first to be documented. This was not a rational calculation; it was the result of *kashf*—essentially a revelation of a type to be received by friends of God of ranks lower than prophets (since Muhammad is the last of these): "It was disclosed (*inkashafa*) to some of those known for inspiration, such as Imam Sha'rani and others, that the *madhhab* of Abu Hanifa is the last of all to die, just as it was the first to be documented."[2]

There was certainly no reason to assume in Sha'rani's time that all schools of law should meet their end at the same time. We know that during their time of vitality, these schools did not flourish at an equal rate or to the same degree. Why, then, should these *madhhab*s experience fatigue at the same time? In addition, Hanafi law received the largest spread of all schools of law, Sunni or Shi'i. But this prophecy offers us more when taken seriously as a prophecy. For now, I hope my work will not be employed by those who like to issue prophecies.

Notes

Introduction

1. Suyuti's claim of being *mujtahid* faced strong criticism from Sakhawi, among others. In his biography of Suyuti in *al-Daw' al-Lami'*, Sakhawi mocks Suyuti's hastening to understand his rejection of the presence of a *mujtahid* in the narrow sense of school-founder as indicating a rejection of the presence of all qualified jurists in the broad sense, including school followers and propagators. See also Suyuti (ed. E. M. Sartain), *al-Tahadduth Bi-Nimati-Allah* (Cairo: al-Matba'a al-'Arabiyya al-Haditha, 1972; Cambridge: Cambridge University Press, 1975), 203–214. Suyuti claims to be a *mujtahid* in law, language, and *hadith* and diffuses claims that *ijtihad* in language and *hadith* is a novel concept. He also engages in a discussion of whether being an authority in *hadith* is required in being an authority in law.

1 Truth and Fatigue

1. Ibn Rashiq al-Qayrawani (d. 463/1074) (ed. Nabawi Sha'lan), *al-'Umda fi Sina'at al-Shi'r wa Naqdih* (Cairo: Maktabat al-Khanji, 2000), vol. 1, p. 186.

2 Open Questions

1. Saskia Sassen, *Territory, Authority, Rights from Medieval to Global Assemblages* (Princeton NJ: Princeton University Press, 2006), 6.
2. Kevin Reinhart addressed aspects of this issue in his *Before Revelation: The Boundaries of Muslim Moral Thought (Albany,* NY: State University of New York Press, 1995), focusing on an evolution within the debate in its early centuries.
3. Al-Juwayni (d. 478/1085) (ed. 'Abd al-'Azim al-Dib), *Ghiyath al-Umam fi Iltyath al-Zulam* (Doha, Qatar: Ministry of Religious Affairs, 1981), pp. 854–5.

4. Al-Jassas (d. 370/980) (ed. M. Tamir), *al-Fusul fi al-Usul* (Beirut: Dar al-Kutub al-'Ilmiyya, 2000), vol. 1, pp. 493–501.
5. Ibid., p. 497.
6. Ibid., p. 499.
7. Fu'ad Sayyid, *Fadl al-I'tizal wa Tabaqat al-Mutazila by Balkhi (d. 319); Qadi 'Abd al-Jabbar (d. 415); Jashmi (d. 494)* (Tunis: al-Dar al-Tunisiyya li al-Nashr, 1974), p. 43.
8. Al-Zarkashi (d. 794/1392) (ed. A. al-'Ani), *al-Bahr al-Muhit fi Usul al-Fiqh* (Kuwait: Ministry of Endowments, 1992), vol. 1, p. 165.
9. Ibid., p. 164.
10. Al-Juwayni (d. 478/1085) (ed. 'Abd al-'Azim al-Dib), *al-Burhan fi Usul al-Fiqh* (Mansura, Egypt: Dar al-Wafa, 1997), article # 1520.
11. Abu al-Husayn al-Basri (d. 436/1044) (ed. M. Hamidullah), *Al-Mutamad fi Usul al-Fiqh* (Damascus: al-Ma'had al-Ilmi al-Faransi, 1964), vol. 1, 401–406.
12. Muhammad Zahid al-Kawthari, *Ihqaq al-Haqq bi Ibtal al-Batil fi Mughith al-Khalq* (Cairo: al-Azhariyya li al-Turath: Cairo), 22.
13. Ibid., 23–24.
14. Juwayni (d. 486/1058) (ed. A. al-Dib), *al-Burhan fi Usul al-Fiqh* (Doha: Qatar, 1983), vol. 2, articles 1528–1529.
15. The Prophet Muhammad is reported to have foreseen a time *when two people would struggle to solve an inheritance question without any authority to guide them to the correct answer.* In his *al-Bahr al-Muhit*, Zarkashi (d. 794/1392) takes note of this tradition after reporting that the proper view is that this law (*Shari'a*), not unlike previous laws, could suffer extinction. Ghazali (d. 505/1111) reported a consensus among previous jurists that pre-Islamic laws of the prophets before Muhammad had already experienced that extinction.
16. This history is complicated by an additional wrinkle: The precolonial emergence of *nations* or something like nations in parts of the Muslim world, especially in Egypt and Iran, starting from the fourteenth and fifteenth centuries in Egypt and the sixteenth and seventeenth in Iran. [Incidentally, those most uncomfortable with applying the word "nation" to premodern history will happily refer to the Abbasid Empire and even early Islamic imperialism or even *Jihadic* imperialism. I could see some of Charles Taylor's points—in *Dilemmas and Connections: Selected Essays* (Cambridge, MA: Harvard University Press, 2011), 81–107; chapter 5: Nationalism and Modernity—about nationalism's connection with dignity indeed its transformation of the conditions of dignity, and I have no interest in debating any of the obvious points here.] Despite its geographic specificity, the premodern idea of a Muslim *nation* played a major role in shaping responses to modern questions on the role of the caliphate and the Shari'a. The 'Abbasid Caliphate collapsed in 656/1258, but long before that it was taken over (in its capital) by the Buwayds and the Saljuqs, and after 'Abbasid agents in Iran and Egypt (Tahirids, Samanids, Tulunids, etc.), among other areas, have at times ruled independently of the 'Abbasid government. While Eurocentric and modernity-centered political science assures us that *nations* in the Muslim world was a reaction to colonialism,

at least our confidence about the apparent force of this assertion would be shaken after a close reading of the histories of *Maqrizi* (d. 845/1442), *Ibn Hajar* (d. 852/1448), *Ibn Taghribirdi* (d. 874/1470), *Sakhawi* (d. 902/1497), *Suyuti* (d. 911/1505), and *Ibn Iyas* (d. 928/1522), which help uncover conspicuous premodern origins for the idea of an Egyptian nation. In these works, rehashing an old argument for Egypt's uniqueness that could be found in Ibn Abd al-Hakam's (d. 257/871) *Futuh Misr wa al-Maghrib* (Conquests of Egypt and North Africa) and Ibn Zulaq's (d. 385/996) *Fada'il Misr* (On the Merits of Egypt) is transformed into a clear identification of Egypt as a *nation* consisting of a land and a population, while "government" remains a transient aspect of this nation. Comparisons between Cairo and Baghdad in the ninth and fifteenth centuries to highlight Cairo's capacity to be an independent center for a Muslim culture and even surpass the Baghdad or the whole of Iraq in the ninth/fifteenth century are symptomatic of this precolonial sense of an Egyptian nation [Ibn Taghribirdi (d. 874/1470), *al-Nujum al-Zahira fi Akhbar Muluk Misr wa-l-Qahira* (Beirut: Dar al-Kutub al-'Ilmiyya, 1996), vol. 1, p. 59]. Cairo is also a new center for the Muslim world, given its role in maintaining the Two Sacred Precincts (*al-haramayn al-sharifayn*) (*ibid*, vol. 1, p. 4). Ibn Taghribirdi's teacher Maqrizi (d. 845/1442) had justified writing a history of the geography of Cairo (*al-Khitat*) based on the fact that Egypt was the place where he was born and grew up among his peers, and where his people gathered, and is the *mawtin* (arena, origin) of this people, those of a close affinity and those of a farther one (*masqat ra'si wa mal'ab atrabi wa majma' nasi... wa matwin khassati wa 'ammati*). Al-Maqrizi (d. 845/1442), *al-Mawa'iz wa-l-I'tibar bi-Dhikr al-Khitat wa-l-Athar* (Cairo: Maktabat al-Thaqafah al-Diniyya, 1987), vol. 1, p. 2. The Egyptian "country" consists of a people and a land, both of which are included in Maqrizi's aforementioned text. The land, however, is often indicated in clearer terms. The term *al-Diyar al-Misriyya* "the houses of Egypt or better: its abode," is what signifies the land, which contrasts with Syrian houses, *al-Diyar al-Shamiyya*, for example. Thus, Sakhawi tells us that his teacher, Ibn Hajar, traveled to the Shami abode, Syria, leaving the Egyptian abode, in order to complete his studies. Sakhawi (d. 902/1497) (ed. Ibrahim 'Abd al-Majid), *al-Jawahir wa-l-Durar fi Tarjamat Shaykh al-Islam Ibn Hajar* (Beirut: Dar Ibn Hazm, 1999), vol. 1, p. 156. Despite the sometimes elaborate descriptions of governmental formalities in many late Mamluk histories, the role of government in constituting a nation is less clear. [Consider, e.g., the procedures of crowning the general deputy of the Sultan (*na'ib al-saltana*) in Muhammad 'Abd al-Ghani al-Ashqar, *Na'ib al-Saltana al-Mamlukiyya fi Misr min 648/923 ila 1250/1517* (Cairo: al-Hay'a al-'Amma li-l-Kitab, 1999), pp. 105–108—originally an MA thesis from the Faculty of Arts in 'Ayn Shams University, Egypt.] The fact that members of the government were of foreign origin did not matter; they could be seen as both "Turk" and Egyptian. Ultimately, the nation absorbed even its rulers, rather than the other way round. Egypt's economic autonomy and definability, which went much deeper in history than Islam itself, once it became independent of other centers such as Damascus and Baghdad, enabled it to claim a form of "national" independence. This premodern idea of nation contributed to the stabilization of a de facto acknowledgment of the limitation of the meaning of the Shari'a to a geographic/national meaning. By reviving the old title of the caliphate, the Ottoman unification of the Sunni world interrupted further growth of this precolonial national sensibility. The rise of Europe, however, initiated new concepts of nations, and widened its application in the Muslim world.

17. Khaled Abou El Fadl, *Rebellion and Violence in Islamic Law* (Cambridge: Cambridge University Press, 2001).
18. Ahmad Atif Ahmad, *Islam, Modernity, Violence and Everyday Life* (New York: Palgrave Macmillan, 2009), 53.
19. Ibn 'Abidin (d. 1252/1836), *Radd al-Muhtar 'ala al-Durr al-Mukhtar* (Beirut: Dar Ihya al-Turath al-'Arabi, 1980), vol. 3, p. 257.

3 *IJTIHAD* THEORY

1. Sakhawi (d. 902/1497), *al-Jawahirwa al-Durar fi tarjamat Shaykh al-Islam Ibn Hajar* (Beirut: Dar IbnHazm, 1999), 55–85; see especially 78, 82–83, for the impact of context on how the terms were understood.
2. Muhammad Bakhit al-Muti'i (d. 1935), *IrshadAhl al-Milla fi Ithbat al-Ahilla* (Cairo: Matba'at Kusdistan, 1911), 363–380. This section on Ibn Kamal Pasha was also reedited separately by Hasan S. Suwaydan as *Risala fi Bayan al-Kutuballatiyu'awwal 'alayhawa Bayan Tabaqat al-Madhhab al-Hanafiwa-l-Radd 'alaIbn Kamal Pasha* (Damascus: Dar al-Qadiri, 2008).
3. *IrshadAhl al-Milla*, 316; *Risala fi Bayan al-Kutub*, 40.
4. Miskawayh (d. 421/1028), ed. A Amin and A. Saqr, al-Hawamil wa al-Shawamil (Cairo: Dar al-Ta'lif wa al-Tarjamah wa al-Nashr, 1951), 330.
5. Ibn 'Abidin (d. 1252/1836), *Majmu'at Rasa'il Ibn 'Abidin: 7 Shifa' al-'Alilwa Ball al-Ghalil fi Hukm al-Wasiyya bi-l-Khatmatwa-l-Tahalil* (Beirut: Dar Ihya' al-Turath al-'Arabi, n.d.), 1/163, where Ibn 'Abidin argued that charging for worship ought to be prohibited. San'ani (d. 1182/1768) argued pretty much the opposite position in *Tuhfat al-Ikhwan fi Hill ma Yu'khadh 'ala al-Wajibat min al-Ujraka-Imamat al-Salah wa-l-Adhan*. San'ani (ed. Khalid 'Uthman al-Masri), *al-Rasa'il al-Fiqhiyya* (Cairo: Dar al-Faruq al-Haditha, 2004), 261–269.
6. I concluded that many jurists, theologians, and legal theorists have struggled with the conceptualization of an individual's *ridda* or exit from Islam, even though they may have accepted applying the death penalty in some cases as a political punishment. One could consider Ibn Hajar al-Haytami's *al-Sawa'iq al-Muhriqa*, for instance, as he discussed the case involving Subki's (d. 771/1369) decision to execute a man who abused Abu Bakr and 'Umar verbally. This is an interesting discussion; Haytami said Subki's ruling does not conform with Shafi'i principles but might work with Maliki principles, while

in fact many Malikis do not think it works with their principles either. At any rate, the fact remained that a sense that even recurrent doubt might attack a Muslim and does not establish this person's overall belief, since he/she is not beset by these doubts all the time. Ibn Amir Hajj even says that this is the norm (*aktharahl al-millakadhalik*). Ibn Amir Hajj (d. 879/1474), *al-Taqrirwa al-TahbirSharh al-Tahrir li-Ibn al-Humam* (d. 861/1456) (Cairo, 1316/1898), vol. 3, p. 318.

7. Muhammad Bakhit al-Muti'i (d. 1935), *IrshadAhl al-Milla fi Ithbat al-Ahilla* (Cairo: Matba'at Kusdistan, 1911), 308–309. Muti'i gives examples of this technical language afterward. He continues: "such as what Muhammad [Ibn al-Hasan 189/805] said in the *Ziyadat*: '*a man bequeaths to another a share equal to that of one of his sons, excepting a third of the remainder of the third of the inheritance [assigned to wills] after either distributing the shares or after the will is fulfilled (or said excepting the third of the remainder of the third [assigned to the wills] and did not add an explanation) and this person died afterwards, leaving three sons*, then the subject of inheritance [what inheritors divide among themselves] is the sum of the inheritance added to one ninth [of the same] minus a share and a third, and similar countless statements." This section on Ibn Kamal Pasha was also reedited separately by Hasan S. Suwaydan as *Risala fi Bayan al-Kutuballatiyu'awwal 'alayhawa Bayan Tabaqat al-Madhhab al-Hanafiwa-l-Radd 'alaIbn Kamal Pasha* (Damascus: Dar al-Qadiri, 2008), 33–34.
8. Muhammad Ibn 'Ali al-Shawkani (d. 1250/1834), *Irshad al-Fuhulilalhqaqa al-Haqq min 'ilm al-Usul* (Riyadh: Dar al-Fadila, 2000), pp. 1035–1042.
9. Al-Zarkashi (d. 794/1392) (ed. A. al-'Ani), *al-Bahr al-Muhit fi Usul al-Fiqh* (Kuwait: Ministry of Endowments, 1992),, vol. 6, pp. 201–202.
10. Ibid., p. 202.
11. Ibid., p. 205.
12. Abu al-Husayn al-Basri (d. 436/1044) (ed. M. Hamidullah), *al-Mutamad fi Usul al-Fiqh* (Damascus: al-Ma'had al-'Arabi, 1964), vol. 2, pp. 949–952, 956–957; Suyuti (ed. E. M. Sartain), *al-Tahadduth bi-Ni'mati-Allah* (Cairo: al-Matba'a al-'Arabiyya al-Haditha, 1972; Cambridge: Cambridge University Press, 1975), 208–209.
13. Abu al 'Abbas Ibn al-Qass (d. 335/946) (ed. M. al-Zabibi), *Nusrat al-Qawlayn* (Beirut: Dar al-Biruni, 2009), 61–64.
14. Ibid., p. 147.

4 SUPPOSE WE FORGOT THE LAW

1. Abu al-Husayn al-Khayyat (d. 299/912) (ed. H. S. Neiburg), *al-Intisar wa-l-Radd 'ala al-Rawandi al-Mulhid* (Beirut: al-Dar al-'Arabiyya li-l-Kitab, 1993), reprint of the 1925 Cairo edition, pp. 162–163. This view of 'Allaf is included in Shahrastani (d. 547/1153), *al-Milal wa-l-Nihal* (Cairo: Bulaq,

1263/1847), p. 28, as the last of ten points specific to his system, but the adjective "infallible" (*ma'sumin*) is added to the description of those who convey God's message as part of 'Allaf's view. In a digression during his discussion of Mutawakkil's support of what he referred to as the path of the Prophet's Sunna, Mas'udi (d. 344/956) included in his *Muruj al-Dhahab* (Beirut: Dar al-Qalam, 1989), vol. 4, pp. 100–101 (events of the year 232; Mutawakkil's reign) a story quoted from Abu 'Isa al-Warraq's *Majalis* about a debate between Hisham Ibn al-Hakam (d. 179/795), a representative of the Shi'i view of the need for an imam, and the Mu'tazili 'Amr Ibn 'Ubayd (d. 144/761), where the need for an imam is likened to the need in the body for an intellect, without which all senses are ultimately useless. The story finds its way to many sources afterward.

2. Al-Shahrastani (d. 547/1153), *al-Milal wa-l-Nihal*, p. 27.
3. 'Amr Ibn Bahr al-Jahiz (ed. A. Harun), *Majmu' Rasa'il al-Jahiz* (Cairo: al-Khanji, 1964) (*Faslu ma bayna al-'Adawati wa-l-Hasad*) vol. 1, p. 338.
4. Ibid. (*Hujaj al-Nubuwa*), vol. 3, p. 231.
5. Ibid., p. 227.
6. Juwayni (d. 486/1058) (ed. A. al-Dib), *al-Burhan fi Usul al-Fiqh* (Doha: Qatar, 1983), vol. 2, pp. 879–881.
7. 'Abd al-Jabbar al-Hamadhani (d. 415/1025) (ed. M. Qasim), *al-Mughni fi Abwab al-'Adl wa-l-Tawhid* (Cairo: Wazarat al-Thaqafa, 1960s), vol. 20a, p. 19.
8. Ibid., p. 22.
9. Abu al-Husayn al-Basri (d. 436/1044) (ed. M. Hamidullah), *al-Mutamad fi Usul al-Fiqh* (Arab Institute: Damascus, 1964), vol. 1, p. 11.
10. Ibid., vol. 2, p. 524.
11. Ibid., p. 510.
12. Ibid., pp. 719–720.
13. There is a disagreement about what Abu al-Hasan al-Ash'ari's view exactly was in this matter, with much controversy about what *ma la yutaq* meant. See, e.g., Abu 'Abd Allah al-Mazari (d. 536/1141), *Idah al-Mahsul min Burhan al-Usul* (Beirut: Dar al-Gharb al-Islami, 2001), pp. 63–70.
14. Al-Tahir Ibn 'Ashur (d. 1393/1973), *al-Tawdih wa-l-Tashih li Mushkilat Kitab al-Tanqih* (a Commentary on Qarafi's *Tanqih al-Fusul*) (Tunis: Matba'at al-Nahda, 1341/1922), vol. 1, p. 110.
15. *Ziyadat Sharh al-Usul*—published under the title *A Basran Mutazilites Theology: Abu 'Ali Muhammad b. Khallad's Usul and its Reception* (Leiden: Brill, 2011), edited by Adang, Madelug, and Schmidtke, pp. 284–285.
16. Al-Hakim al-Jashmi al-Bayhaqi (d. 494/1001) (A. Wajih), *Tahkim al-'Uqul fi Tashih al-Usul* (San'a: Mu'assasat al-Imam Zayd al-Thaqafiyya, 2008). For Jashmi, the pillars of knowledge are four: reason ('uqul), Kitab and Sunna, and consensus. See, e.g., p. 22 and after.
17. Al-Zarkashi (d. 794/1392) (ed. A. al-'Ani), *al-Bahr al-Muhit fi Usul al-Fiqh* (Kuwait City: Ministry of Endowments, 1992), vol. 1, p. 151.
18. Zamakhshari (d. 538/1144), *al-Minhaj fi Usul al-Din* in Sabine Schmidke, *A Mutazili Creed of az-Zamahshari* (Abhandlungen für die Kunde des Morgenlandes, Bd. 51, 4), pp. 68–72; esp. p. 70.

19. 'Abd al-Azim al-Dib's (d. 1431/2010) introduction to his edition of Juwayni's (d. 478/1085) *Nihayat al-Matlab fi Dirayat al-Madhhab* (Beirut: Dar al-Minhaj, 2007), p. 247.
20. Ibn Rushd (d. 595/1198) (ed. M. A. Jabiri), *al-Kashf 'an Manahij al-Adilla fi 'Aqa'id al-Milla* (Beirut: Markaz Dirasat al-Wahda al-Arabiyya, 1998), pp. 175–176; articles 243–246.
21. Ibn Rushd (d. 595/1198) (ed. J. al-'Alawi), *al-Daruri fi Usul al-Fiqh* (Dar al-Gharb al-Islami: Beirut, 1994), pp. 144–146.
22. Ibn Rushd (ed. 'Ivry, Mahdy), *Talkhis Kitab al-Nafs* (the Middle Commentary) (Cairo, 1994), p. 125.

5 The End of Jurisprudence

1. Shatibi (d. 790/1388) argues in the *Muwafaqat* against the idea of the end of access to God's guidance (as we will explain in detail).While acknowledging in theory that a layperson may not be required to follow any specific law if the scholars are not available to him (ed. M. A. Diraz; vol. 4, p. 291), he argues in effect that a universal inaccessibility of this knowledge is not imaginable.
2. In *Before Revelation: The Boundaries of Muslim Moral Thought.*
3. Al-Sharif al-Jurjani (d. 816/1413), *Sharh al-Jurjani 'ala al-Mawaqif* (Cairo: Matba'at al-Sa'ada, 1325/1907), vol. 1, p. 17.
4. Of course, it is unfair to Mu'tazili theologians to say that they expected humans' and God's acts to be equivalent in every respect. If one reads Zamakhshari's (d. 536/1144) brief treatment of the questions of the reasonableness of the presence of pain (*al-alam*) in the world (in his brief *Minhaj*), one realizes a clear contrast between God and humans, who could not be allowed to inflict pain on others, given the limitation of their knowledge of the full picture of the world and their ability to control it in the long term. Zamakhshari (d. 538/1144), *al-Minhaj fi Usul al-Din* in Sabine Schmidke, *A Mutazili Creed of az-Zamakhshari* (Abhandlungen für die Kunde des Morgenlandes, Volume 51, # 4), pp. 68–72; note 70.
5. See John Selden (ed. S. W. Singer), *The Table Talk of John Selden* (London: John Russell Smith, 1856), p. 84; Richard Tuck, *Natural Rights Theories: Their Origin and Development* (Cambridge: Cambridge University Press, 1981) (text on p. 92); and *Philosophy and Government 1572–1651* (Cambridge: Cambridge University Press, 1993) (text on p. 217) for important comments on his concept of the law of nature; for a slightly different version of this text, see David Wootton (ed.), *Divine Right and Democracy: An Anthology of Political Writings in Stuart England* (Indianapolis: Hackett Publishing, 2003), p. 450.
6. Ibn Hlulu (d. 1493), *al-Diya' al-Lami' Sharh Jam' al-Jawami'* (Ryadh: Maktabat al-Rushd, 1994), vol. 1, p. 150.
7. Mansur Ibn Muhammad al-Sam'ani (d. 489/1094) (ed. Hafiz Hakami), *Qawati al-Adilla fi Usul al-Fiqh* (Riyadh: Maktabat al-Tawba, 1998), vol. 1, pp. 3–4.

8. Social custom as a source of law. See chapter 4 in *Islam, Modernity, Violence, and Everyday Life* (London: Palgrave, 2009).
9. Hobbes asked: What happens if the same planks of the old ship, which were replaced gradually, were gathered and made into another ship? Which one of these would be the original ship? Half a millennium earlier, Juwayni (in the Ghiyathi) had raised the question of what happens were the absence of correct Shari'a jurisprudence leads to developing an alternative (custom-based) Shari'a and then later Shari'a jurisprudence is recovered through new scholars. Which version should be followed in this case?
10. Al-Juwayni (d. 478/1085) (ed. 'Abd al-'Azim al-Dib), *al-Burhan fi Usul al-Fiqh* (Mansura, Egypt: Dar al-Wafa, 1997), article # 1523.
11. Al-Tahir Ibn 'Ashur, *al-Tawdih wa-l-Tashih li Mushkilat Kitab al-Tanqih* (a commentary on Qarafi's *Tanqih al-Fusul*) (Matba'at al-Nahda, Tunis, 1341/1922), vol. 1, pp. 105–106.
12. *Hashiyat al-Bannani 'ala Sharh al-Jalal al-Mahalli 'ala Jam' al-Jawami'* (Dar al-Fikr: Beirut, 1982), vol. 2, p. 398.
13. Ibn Amir Hajj (d. 879/1474), *al-Taqrir wa al-Tahbir Sharh al-Tahrir li-Ibn al-Humam* (d. 861/1456) (Cairo, 1316/1898), vol. 3, p. 340.
14. *Sharh al-Jurjani 'ala al-Mawaqif*, vol. 1, p. 39.

6 *IJTIHAD* FOR ALL

1. Ibn Taymiyya (d. 728/1324), *Majmu' al-Fatawa* (Medina, Saudi Arabia, Majma' al-Malik Fahd: 1425/2004), vol. 13, pp. 27–65. Ibn Taymiyya's effort relies on previous attempts to account for the earliest heresies, such as 'Abd al-Jabbar's and Shahrastani's in the opening pages of his *Milal*, who themselves rely on earlier accounts such as Ibn Qutayba's and Ka'bi's. Fu'ad Sayyid, *Fadl al-I'tizal wa Tabaqat al-Mu'tazila by Balkhi 319; Qadi 'Abd al-Jabbarl 415; Jashmi 494* (Tunis: al-Dar al-Tunusiyya li-l-Nashr, 1974), pp. 142–162.
2. Ibn Taymiyya (d. 728/1324), *Majmu' al-Fatawa*, vol. 13, p. 36. Fu'ad Sayyid's introduction to *Fadl al-I'tizal wa Tabaqat al-Mutazila* includes a reconciliation among the three possible genealogies of *I'tizal*, based on the accounts of Ibn Qutayba, Nawbakhti, Ka'bi/Balkhi, Mas'udi, among others. Fu'ad Sayyid, *Fadl al-I'tizal*, pp. 12–25.
3. Ibn Taymiyya (d. 728/1324) (ed. M. al-Dawish), *Bughyat al-Murtad fi al-Radd 'ala al-Mutafalsifa wa al-Qaramita wa al-Batiniyya min Ahl al-Ilhad* (Medina: Maktabat al-'Ulum wa al-Hikam, 2001). In this book, Ibn Taymiyya addressed heresies emanating from accepting a tradition establishing "reason" as God's first creature, which is the basis of all of His rulings and actions. In this book Ibn Taymiyya establishes that Mu'tazilis are closer to those on the correct path than philosophers, despite the similarities in the basis of their deviation.

4. Al-Tahir Ibn 'Ashur, *al-Tawdih wa al-Tashih li Mushkilat Kitab al-Tanqih* (a commentary on Qarafi's *Tanqih al-Fusul*) (Tunis: Matba'at al-Nahda, 1341/1922), vol. 1, p. 107.
5. Abu Ya'la al-Farra' (d. 458/1066) (ed. A. Mubaraki), *al-'Udda fi Usul al-Fiqh* (Riyadh: n.p., 1990), vol. 4, p. 1250. This edition is based on a doctoral dissertation that was defended in 1977 at Umm al-Qura University in Mecca, and the publisher of this five-volume edition of the work is not indicated in my copy.
6. Kalwadhani (d. 510/1116) (ed. M. A. Ibrahim), *al-Tamhid fi Usul al-Fiqh* (Mecca: Umm al-Qura University Press, 1985), vol. 4, pp. 405–406.
7. Ibid., p. 406.
8. Ibid., pp. 406–408.
9. Abu Ya'la al-Farra' (d. 458/1066), *al-'Udda fi Usul al-Fiqh*, vol. 4, p. 1250
10. Kalwadhani (d. 510/1116), *al-Tamhid fi Usul al-Fiqh*, vol. 4, p. 272.
11. Ibid., p. 396.
12. Ibid., pp. 396–397.
13. Ibid., p. 397.
14. Ibid., p. 398.
15. Ibn Taymiyya, *Bughyat al-Murtad*, pp. 171–531.
16. Ibid., p. 283.
17. Ibid., pp. 335–336.
18. Abu Ya'la al-Farra' (d. 458/1066), *al-Udda*, vol. 4, pp. 1238–1250.
19. Ibn al-Najjar (ed. M. Zuhayli), *Sharh al-Kawkab al-Munir* (Damascus: Dar al-Fikr, 1987), vol. 3, pp. 90–92.

7 A New Picture

1. Muhammad al-Muwilhi, *Hadith 'Isa Ibn hisham aw Fatrah min al-Zaman* (Cairo: al-Maktabah al-Azhariyya, 1330/1911), pp. 41–46.
2. *Ahmad 'Urabi al-Misri* (Cairo: AUC Press, 1982), p. 27. This short volume includes an Arabic edition of 'Urabi's court defense and an English translation and introduction.
3. In *Mafhum al-'Aql* (Beirut: al-Markaz al-Thaqafi al-'Arabi, 1996), for example.
4. Shah Waliyyulah al-Dihlawi (d. 1176/1762) (ed. M. al-Khatib), *'Iqd al-Jid fi Ahkam al-Ijtihad wa al-Taqlid* (Cairo: al-Matba 'a al-Salafiyya, 1385/1965).
5. I am thinking of the works of Quentin Skinner and Richard Tuck on early modern Europe.
6. Hans J. Hillerbrand (editor-in-chief), *The Oxford Encyclopedia of the Reformation* (Oxford: Oxford University Press, 1996), pp. ix–xiv.
7. Alan Watson, *Law Making in the Later Roman Republic* (Oxford: Oxford University Press, 1974), pp. 96–101; Charles Donahue Jr., "Reform, Renewal, Religion, and Social Discipline: Reflections of a Medievalist," in Peri Bearman,

Wolfhart Heinrichs, and Bernard Weiss, *The Law Applied: Contextualizing the Islamic Sharí'a* (London: IB Tauris, 2008), pp. 1–22.

8. Muhammad 'Imara, *Islamiyyat al-Sanhuri Pasha* (Mansura, Egypt: Dar al-Wafa', 2006), vol. 1, pp. 275–290.
9. Muhammad Ahmad Darniqa, *al-Shaykh Muhammad Ibn 'Abd al-Wahhab Ra'id al-Da'wa al-Salafiyya fi al-'Asr al-Hadith* (Beirut: al-Dar al-'Arabiyya lil-Mawsu'at, 2008), pp. 103–139.
10. Muhammad 'Abduh, *al-A'mal al-Kamila* (Collected Works) (Cairo: al-Mu'assa al-'Arabiyya lil-Dirasat wal-Nashr, 1972), vol. 2, pp. 53–59; Mahmud Shaltut (d. 1383/1963), *al-Fatawa* (Cairo: Dar al-Qalam, 1963), pp. 191–193.
11. Bernard Haykel, *Revival and Reform in Islam: The Legacy of Muhammad al-Shawkani* (Cambridge: Cambridge University Press, 2003), pp. 76–108.
12. A. Merad, Hamid Algar, N. Berkes, and Aziz Ahmad, "Islah," In P. Bearman, Th. Bianquis, C.E. Bosworth, E. van Donzel, and W. P. Heinrichs, eds., *Encyclopaedia of Islam* (Leiden: Brill, 2008).
13. Samer Akkach, *'Abd al-Ghani al-Nabulsi: Islam and the Enlightenment* (Oxford: One World, 2007), p. 104.
14. Muhammad al-Tahir Ibn 'Ashur, *Maqasid al-Shari'a al-Islamiyya* (Cairo: Dar al-Salam, 2005), p. 3.
15. M. B. Hooker, *Indonesian Islam: Social Change through Contemporary Fatawa* (Honololou: Allen & Unwin, and University of Hawaii Press, 2003), pp. 178–190.
16. 'Abbas Mahmud al-'Aqqad (d. 1964), *al- Dimuqratiyya fi al-Islam* (Cairo, 1952); Khaled Abou El Fadl, *Islam and the Challenge of Democracy* (Cambridge, MA: MIT Press, 2004).
17. Shaykh al-Azhar Muhammad Sayyid Tantawi (in office 1996–2009), who employed this argument in his effort to support modern banking, cited many authorities, such as 'Abd al-Wahhab Khallaf and Muhammad Abu Zahra, among others.
18. Alan Watson, *Law Making in the Later Roman Republic* (Oxford: Oxford University Press, 1974), pp. 96–98.
19. Jamal al-Banna, *Nahw Fiqh Jadid* (= Toward a New Jurisprudence "in 3 volumes") (Cairo: Dar al-Fikr al-Islami, 1995), vol. 1, p. 12.
20. Watson, *Law Making in the Later Roman Republic*, p. 102.
21. *Irshad al-Fuhul*, pp. 1035–1043.
22. San'ani (d. 1182/1768) (ed. A. Masri), *Majm'uat al-Rasail al-Fiqhiyya* (Cairo: Dar al-Faruq, 2004).
23. *Hashiyat al-'Attar 'ala Sharh al-Mahalli 'ala Jam' al Jawami'* (Beirut: Dar al-Kutub al-'Ilmiyya, 1980), vol. 2, p. 438.

8 Absent Good Government

1. Al-Sharif al-Jurjani (d. 816/1413), *Sharh al-Jurjani 'ala al-Mawaqif* (Cairo: Matba'at al-Sa'ada, 1325/1907), vol. 1, pp. 21–22.

2. As I explain later, Juwayni emphasizes that government is necessary for supporting the population against foreign enemies, pointing to thedecisive battle, known as Malazgird or Manzikert, which was won by the Saljuq leader Alp Arslan (419/1029–463/1072), as a case in point where government did indeed achieve basic goals for the population that would be otherwise unachievable. 'Ali Ibn Muhammad Ibn al-Athir (d. 631/1233), *Tarikh al-Kamil* (Cairo: al-Matba'a al-'Amira, 1874), vol. 10, p. 22—events of the year 463 AH (=1071 CE). Ibn Qadi Shuhba's prosopography shows that the passing of time changes the functions of jurists and reacts to forms of the fatigue of the Shari'a or its transformation over time. See my review of "Authority, Conflict, and the Transmission of Diversity in Medieval Islamic Law," by R. Kevin Jaques in *Journal of Islamic Studies* (Ed. Farhan Ahmad Nizami, Oxford Center for Islamic Studies), published by Oxford University Press, vol. 18, no. 2, May 2007, pp. 246–248.
3. For example, Al-Qaffal al-Shashi (d. 365/974), *Mahasin al-Shari'a* (Dar al-Faruq al-Haditha: Cairo, 2008), p. 561, for a dramatic description of society without government.
4. Jahiz (ed. A. Harun), *MajmuRasa'il al-Jahiz* (Cairo: Maktabat al-Khanji, 1964) (Fi al-Nisa') vol. 3, p. 150.
5. My point is far from making (what would have been) a false claim that Hallaq cares only about government in his analysis. I found, indeed, much to admire and learn from in his insistence to depict the complexity of his issue. See *Shari'a: Theory, Practice, Transformations* (Cambridge: Cambridge University Press, 2009); note "Reprecussions: Concluding Notes," pp. 543–550. But I only have partial approval for sentences such as these: "The foregoing characterization of the Shari'a and its fiqh, partial as it may be, bespeaks a complex reality that has largely disappeared. Over the past two centuries or so, the Shari'a has been transformed from a worldly institution and culture to a textuality that not only represents the subtracted differential between the pre-modern organic structure and its entexted version, but also engages the very characteristic of being entexted in a politics that the pre-modern counterpart did not know" (see pp. 546–547). (The excessive fascination with texts, by the way, is certainly precolonial, as Hallaq knows.)
6. 'Ali Ibn Muhammad Ibn al-Athir (d. 631/1233), *Tarikh al-Kamil* (Cairo: al-Matba'a al-'Amira, 1874), vol. 10, p. 22—events of the year 463 AH (=1071 CE); Juwayni, *Ghiyath al-Umam*.
7. John Selden (ed. S. W. Singer), *The Table Talk of John Selden* (London: John Russell Smith, 1856), p. 142.

9 NEGLECTED KNOWLEDGE

1. Almost simultaneously with "Can the Shari'a be Restored?" came Hallaq's "Juristic Authority vs. State Power: The Legal Crises of Modern Islam," in the *Journal of Law and Religion*, vol. 19, no. 2 (2003–2004), pp. 243–258.

The latter article cites the former in a footnote, but it includes stronger hints that the thrust of Hallaq's confidence about the death of the Shari'a started with his sense that the jurists have lost their battle with government, which I concede, but I ultimately see things to be more complicated as I argue here.

2. Şükrü Hanioğlu, *A Brief History of the Late Ottoman Empire* (Princeton, NJ: Princeton University Press, 2008), p. 25. Other theses and ideas in this book contradict the assumption that the nineteenth century was the start of the trend of decline in religious education and in the independence of religious scholars.
3. Ibid., p. 139.
4. Max Weber (eds. Hans Gerth and C. Wright Wills), *Essays in Sociology* (Oxford: Oxford University Press, 1946), p. 328.
5. Al-Wansharisi (d. 1508), *al-Mi'yar al-Mu'ribwa-l-Jami' al-Mughrib 'an Fatawa Ahl Ifriqiyya wa-l-Andalus wa-l-Maghrib* (Rabat, Morocco: Wazarat al-Awqafwa-l-Shu'un al-Islamiyya, 1981), vol. 6, pp. 368–381.
6. Badr al-Din al-Zarkashi (d. 794/1392) (ed. Abd al-Sattar Abu Ghudda), *al-Bahr al-Muhit* (Kuwait: Ministry of Religious Affairs, 1992), vol. 4, p. 165.
7. M. A. al-Jabiri's edition titled *Tahafut al-Tahafut: Intisar*[an] *li al-Ruh al-'IlmiyyawaTa'sis*[an] *li-Akhlaqiyyat al-Hiwar* (Beirut: MarkazDisarasat al-Wahdah al-'Arabiyya, 1998).

10 Constant Interpretation

1. H. L. Hart, *The Concept of Law* (Oxford: Oxford University Press, 1997); Ronald Dworkin, *A Matter of Princple* (Cambridge, Mass.: Harvard University Press, 1985); Ronald Dworkin, *Law's Empire* (Cambridge, Mass.: Harvard University Press, 1986).
2. Antonin Scalia (ed. Amy Gutmann), *A Matter of Interpretation* (Princeton, NJ: Princeton University Press, 1998).
3. Wael Hallaq, "Can the Sharia be Restored?" in Y. Haddad and B. Stowasser, *Islamic Law and the Challenge of Modernity* (Walnut Creek, California: Altamera Press, 2004), p. 27.
4. Ibn Rushd, *al-Kashf 'an Manahij al-Adilla fi 'Aqa'id al-Milla* (Markaz Disarasat al-Wahdah al-'Arabiyya: Beirut, 1998), article 224, p. 171.
5. Mazari (d. 536/1141) (ed. A. Talibi), *Idah al-Mahsul min Burhan al-Usul* (Dar al-Gharb al-Islami: Beirut, 2000), p. 377.
6. Abu al-Muzaffar al-Sam'ani (d. 489/1094) (ed. Hafiz Hakami), *Qawati' al-Adilla fi Usul al-Fiqh* (Riyadh: Maktabat al-Tawba, 1998), vol. 1, p. 25.
7. Mukhtar Baba Adu, Fasl Khuluww al-Zaman min al-Mujtahid bayna al-Mani' wa-l-Mujiz, *Majallat Jami'at Umm al-Qura li-l-Shari'a wa-l-Lugha al-'Arabiyya wa Adabiha*, vol. 17, issue 35, 1425/2003, pp. 51–103.

CONCLUSION

1. This line tends to appear in the introductions to histories and biographies. See, e.g., Safadi's (d. 764/1363) *al-Wafi bi al-Wafayat*:

   لولا أحاديث أبقاها أوايلنا | من الندى والردى لم يعرف السمر

   For more on the uses of history, see Ahmad al-Nasiri al-Salawi (d. 1314/1897) *al-Istiqasa li-Akhbar Duwal al-Maghrib al-Aqsa* (al-Dar al-Bayda: Manshurat Wazarat al-Thaqafa, 2001–2005), vol. 1, p. 4.
2. Muhammad Ibn al-Hasan al-Shaybani (d. 189/804) (ed. M. Qadiri), *Kitab al-Hujja 'alaAhl al-Madina* (Beirut: 'Alam al-Kutub: 1981), vol. 1, p. 10.

Bibliography

Primary

Ibn 'Abidin (d. 1252/1836), *Radd al-Muhtar 'ala al-Durr al-Mukhtar* (Beirut: Dar Ihya al-Turath al-'Arabi, 1980).

———, *Majmu'at Rasa'il Ibn 'Abidin*: 7 *Shifa' al-'Alil wa Ball al-Ghalil fi Hukm al-Wasiyya bi-l-Khatmatwa-l-Tahalil* (Beirut: Dar Ihya' al-Turath al-'Arabi, n.d.).

Ibn Amir Hajj (d. 879/1474), *al-Taqrirwa al-TahbirSharh al-Tahrir li-Ibn al-Humam* (d. 861/1456) (Cairo, 1316/1898).

Ibn'Ashur, al-Tahir (d. 1393/1973), *al-Tawdihwa al-Tashih li MushkilatKitab al-Tanqih* (a Commentary on Qarafi's*Tanqih al-Fusul*) (Tunis: Matba'at al-Nahda, 1341/1922).

———, *Maqasid al-Shari'a al-Islamiyya* (Cairo: Dar al-Salam, 2005).

Ibn al-Athir, 'Ali Ibn Muhammad (d. 631/1233), *Tarikh al-Kamil* (Cairo: al-Matba'a al-'Amira, 1874).

Al-'Attar, Hasan (d. 1250/1835), *Hashiyat al-'Attar 'ala Sharh al-Mahalli 'ala Jam' al Jawami'* (Beirut: Dar al-Kutub al-'Ilmiyya, 1980).

Al-Basri, Abu al-Husayn (d. 436/1044) (ed. M. Hamidullah), *Al-Mutamad fi Usul al-Fiqh* (Damascus: al-Ma'had al-'Arabi, 1964).

Al-Daraqutni (d. 385/995), *Akhbar 'AmrIbn 'Ubayd* (manuscript).

Al-Dihlawi, Shah Waliyyulah (d. 1176/1762) (ed. M. al-Khatib),*'Iqd al-Jid fi Ahkam al-Ijtihad wa al-Taqlid* (Cairo: al-Matba'a al-Salafiyya, 1385/1965).

Al-Jashmi/Jishumi al-Bayhaqi, al-Hakim (d. 494/1001) (A. Wajih), *Tahkim al-'Uqul fi Tashih al-Usul* (San'a: Mu'assasat al-Imam Zayd al-Thaqafiyya, 2008).

'Abd al-Jabbar al-Hamadhani (d. 415/1025) (ed. M. Qasim), *al-Mughni fi Abwab al-'Adlwa-l-Tawhid* (Cairo: Wazarat al-Thaqafa, 1960s).

Al-Jahiz, 'Amr Ibn Bahr (d. 255/866) (ed. A. Harun), *Majmu' Rasa'il al-Jahiz* (Cairo: al-Khanji, 1964).

Al-Jassas, Abu Bakr (d. 370/980) (ed. M. Tamir), *al-Fusul fi al-Usul* (Beirut: Dar al-Kutub al-'Ilmiyya, 2000).

Al-Juwayni, Abu al-Ma'ali (d. 478/1085) (ed. 'Abd al-'Azim al-Dib), *al-Burhan fi Usul al-Fiqh* (Mansura, Egypt: Dar al-Wafa, 1997).

——— (ed. 'Abd al-'Azim al-Dib), *Ghiyath al-Umam fi Iltiyath al-Zulam* (Doha, Qatar: 1981).

Al-Juwayni, Abu al-Ma'ali (d. 478/1085) (ed. 'Abd al-'Azim al-Dib), *Nihayat al-Matlab fi Dirayat al-Madhhab* (Beirut: Dar al-Minhaj, 2007).

Ibn Hlulu (d. 1493), *al-Diya' al-Lami' Sharh Jam' al-Jawami'* (Riyadh: Maktabat al-Rushd, 1994).

Al-Kalwadhani, Abu al-Khattab (d. 510/1116) (ed. M. A. Ibrahim), *al-Tamhid fi Usul al-Fiqh* (Mecca: Umm al-Qura University Press, 1985).

Al-Kawthari, Muhammad Zahid (d. 1371/1951), *Ihqaq al-Haqq bi Ibtal al-Batil fi Mughith al-Khalq* (Cairo: al-Azhariyya li al-Turath, n.d.).

Al-Khayyat, Abu al-Husayn (d. 299/911) (ed. H. S. Neiburg), *al-Intisar wa-l-Radd 'ala al-Rawandi al-Mulhid* (Beirut: al-Dar al-'Arabiyya li-l-Kitab, 1993), reprint of the 1925 Cairo edition.

Al-Mas'udi (d. 344/956), included in his *Muruj al-Dhahab* (Beirut: Dar al-Qalam, 1989)

Al-Maqrizi (d. 845/1442), *al-Mawa'izwa-l-I'tibar bi-Dhikr al-Khitatwa-l-Athar* (Cairo: Maktabat al-Thaqafah al-Diniyya, 1987).

Al-Mazari, Abu 'Abdillah (d. 536/1141) (ed. A. Talibi), *Idah al-Mahsul min Burhan al-Usul* (Dar al-Gharb al-Islami: Beirut, 2000).

Al-Nasafi, Abu al-Mu'in (d. 510/1116) (ed. Claude Salama), *Tabsirat al-Adilla fi Usul al-Din 'alaTariqat al-Imam Abi Mansur al-Maturidi* (Damascus: al-Ma'had al-Ilmi al-Faransi li al-Dirasat al-Arabiyya, 1990).

Al-Muti'I, Muhammad Bakhit (d. 1935), *IrshadAhl al-Milla fi Ithbat al-Ahilla*(Cairo: Matba'atKusdistan, 1911); sections of it (ed. Hasan S. Suwaydan) as *Risala fi Bayan al-Kutuballatiyu'awwal 'alayhawa Bayan Tabaqat al-Madhhab al-Hanafiwa-l-Radd 'alaIbn Kamal Pasha* (Damascus: Dar al-Qadiri, 2008).

Ibn al-Najjar (ed. M. Zuhayli), *Sharh al-Kawkab al-Munir* (Damascus: Dar al-Fikr, 1987).

Ibn al-Qass, Abu al-'Abbas (d. 335/946) (ed. M. al-Zabibi), *Nusrat al-Qawlayn* (Beirut: Dar al-Biruni, 2009).

Al-Qayrawani, Ibn Rashiq (d. 463/1074) (ed. Nabawi Sha'lan), *al-'Umda fi Sina'atal-Shi'rwaNaqdih* (Cairo: Maktabat al-Khanji, 2000).

Ibn Rushd (d. 595/1198) (ed. J. al-'Alawi), *al-Daruri fi Usul al-Fiqh* (Dar al-Gharb al-Islami: Beirut, 1994).

——— (ed. M. A. Jabiri), *al-Kashf 'anManahij al-Adilla fi 'Aqa'id al-Milla*(Beirut: Markaz Dirasat al-Wahda al-Arabiyya, 1998).

——— (ed. M. A. Jabiri), *Tahafut al-Tahafut: Intisar^{an} li al-Ruh al-'IlmiyyawaTa'sis^{an} li-Akhlaqiyyat al-Hiwar* (Beirut: Markaz Disarasat al-Wahdah al-'Arabiyya, 1998).

——— (ed. 'Ivry, Mahdy), *TalkhisKitab al-Nafs* (the Middle Commentary) (Cairo: Majma' al-Lugha al-'Arabiyya, 1994).

Al-Sakhawi (d. 902/1497) (ed. Ibrahim 'Abd al-Majid), *al-Jawahirwa-l-Durar fi TarjamatShaykh al-Islam IbnHajar* (Beirut: Dar IbnHazm, 1999).

Al-Sam'ani, Mansur Ibn Muhammad (d. 489/1094) (ed. Hafiz Hakami), *Qawati al-Adilla fi Usul al-Fiqh* (Riyadh: Maktabat al-Tawba, 1998).

Al-San'ani, Ibn al-Amir (ed. Khalid 'Uthman al-Masri), *al-Rasa'il al-Fiqhiyya* (Cairo: Dar al-Faruq al-Haditha, 2004).

Sayyid, Fu'ad (d. 1387/1967), *Fadl al-I'tizal wa Tabaqat al-Mutazila by Balkhi (d. 319); Qadi 'Abd al-Jabbar (d. 415); Jashmi (d. 494)* (Tunis: al-Dar al-Tunisiyya li al-Nashr, 1974).

Al-Shahrastani (d. 547/1153), *al-Milalwa-l-Nihal* (Cairo: Bulaq, 1263/1847).

Al-Shashi, al-Qaffal (d. 365/974), *Mahasin al-Shari'a* (Dar al-Faruq al-Haditha: Cairo, 2008).

Al-Shatibi, Abu Ishaq (d. 790/1388) (ed. M. A. Diraz), *al-Muwafaqat fi Usul al-Shari'a.*

Al-Shawkani, Muhammad Ibn 'Ali (d. 1250/1834) (ed. S. al-Athari), *Irshad al-FuhulilaIhqaqa al-Haqq min 'ilm al-Usul* (Riyadh: Dar al-Fadila, 2000).

Al-Shaybani, Muhammad Ibn al-Hasan (d. 189/804) (ed. M. Qadiri), *Kitab al-Hujja 'alaAhl al-Madina* (Beirut: 'Alam al-Kutub, 1981).

Al-Sutyuti, Jalal al-Din (d. 911/1505) (ed. E. M. Sartain), *al-Tahadduth Bi-Nimat'-Allah* (Cairo: al-Matba'a al-'Arabiyya al-Haditha, 1972; Cambridge: Cambridge University Press, 1975).

Ibn Taghribirdi (d. 874/1470), *al-Nujum al-Zahira fi AkhbarMulukMisrwa-l-Qahira* (Beirut: Dar al-Kutub al-'Ilmiyya, 1996).

Ibn Taymiyya (d. 728/1324), *Majmu' al-Fatawa* (Medina, Saudi Arabia, Majma' al-Malik Fahd: 1425/2004); also (ed. 'Abd al-Rahman al-Najdi and Muhammad al-Najdi), *Majmu' al-Fatawa* (Cairo: Dar al-Rahma, 1961–1967).

——— (ed. M. al-Dawish), *Bughyat al-Murtad fi al-Radd 'ala al-Mutafalsifawa al-Qaramitawa al-Batiniyya min Ahl al-Ilhad* (Medina: Maktabat al-'Ulumwa al-Hikam, 2001).

Al-Wansharisi (d. 914/1508), *al-Mi'yar al-Mu'ribwa-l-Jami' al-Mughrib 'an Fatawa Ahl Ifriqiyya wa-l-Andalus wa-l-Maghrib* (Rabat, Morocco: Wazarat al-Awqaf-wa-l-Shu'un al-Islamiyya, 1981).

Abu Ya'la al-Farra' (d. 458/1066) (ed. A. Mubaraki), *al-'Udda fi Usul al-Fiqh* (Riyadh: n.p., 1990)—based on a doctoral dissertation that was defended in 1977 at Umm al-Qura University in Mecca.

Yahya Ibn al-Husayn Ibn Harun al-Buthani (d. 423/1033) (eds. C. Adang, W. Madelug, and S. Schmidtke), *A Basran Mutazilites Theology: Abu 'Ali Muhammad b. Khallad's Usul and its Reception* (Leiden: Brill, 2011).

Al-Zamakhshari (d. 538/1144), *al-Minhaj fi Usul al-Din* in Sabine Schmidke, *A Mutazili Creed of az-Zamahshari* (Abhandlungenfür die Kunde des Morgenlandes, Bd. 51, 4)

Al-Zarkashi (d. 794/1392) (ed. 'Abd al-Sattar Abu Ghudda), *al-Bahr al-Muhit fi Usul al-Fiqh* (Kuwait: Ministry of Religious Affairs, 1992).

Secondary

'Abdu, Muhammad (d. 1323/1905), *al-A'mal al-Kamila* (Collected Works) (Cairo: al-Mu'assa al-'Arabiyya li al-Dirasatwa al-Nashr, 1972).

Abou El Fadl, Khaled, *Islam and the Challenge of Democracy* (MIT Press: Cambridge, MA, 2004).

Abou El Fadl, Khaled, *Rebellion and Violence in Islamic Law* (Cambridge: Cambridge University Press, 2001).

Adu, Mukhtar Baba, Fasl Khuluww al-Zaman min al-Mujtahidbayna al-Mani' wa-l-Mujiz, *MajallatJami'at Umm al-Qura li-l-Shari'awa-l-Lugha al-'ArabiyyawaAdabiha*, vol. 17, issue 35, 1425/2003, pp. 51–103.

Al-'Arawi, 'Abdullah, *Mafhum al-'Aql*, for example (Beirut: al-Markaz al-Thaqafi al-'Arabi, 1996).

Akkach, Samer, *'Abd al-Ghani al-Nabulsi: Islam and the Enlightenment* (Oxford: One World, 2007).

Al-'Aqqad, 'Abbas Mahmud (d. 1383/1964), *al-Dimuqratiyya fi al-Islam* (Cairo, 1952).

Al-Ashqar, Muhammad 'Abd al-Ghani, *Na'ib al-Saltana al-Mamlukiyya fi Misr min 648/923 ila 1250/1517* (Cairo: al-Hay'a al-'Amma li-l-Kitab, 1999).

Al-Banna, Jamal, *NahwFiqhJadid* (=Toward a New Jurisprudence "in 3 volumes") (Cairo: Dar al-Fikr al-Islami, 1995).

Darniqa, Muhammad Ahmad, *al-Shaykh Muhammad Ibn 'Abd al-WahhabRa'id al-Da'wa al-Salafiyya fi al-'Asr al-Hadith* (Beirut: al-Dar al-'Arabiyya li al-Mawsu'at, 2008).

Donahue, Charles Jr., "Reform, Renewal, Religion, and Social Discipline: Reflections of a Medievalist," in Peri Bearman, Wolfhart Heinrichs, and Bernard Weiss, *The Law Applied: Contextualizing the Islamic Shari'a* (London: IB Tauris, 2008).

Hallaq, Wael, "Can the Shari'a be Restored," lead article in Y. Haddad and B. Stowasser (eds.), *Islamic Law and the Challenges of Modernity* (Walnut Creek, CA: Alta Mira Press, 2004).

———, "Juristic Authority vs. State Power: The Legal Crises of Modern Islam," *Journal of Law and Religion*, vol. 19, no. 2 (2003–2004), pp. 243–258.

———, *Shari'a: Theory, Practice, Transformations* (Cambridge: Cambridge University Press, 2009).

Hanioğlu, Şükrü, *A Brief History of the Late Ottoman Empire* (Princeton, NJ: Princeton University Press, 2008).

Hillerbrand, Hans J. (editor-in-chief), *The Oxford Encyclopedia of the Reformation* (Oxford: Oxford University Press, 1996).

Hooker, M. B., *Indonesian Islam: Social Change through Contemporary Fatawa* (Honolulu: Allen & Unwin, and University of Hawaii Press, 2003).

Haykel, Bernard, *Revival and Reform in Islam: the Legacy of Muhammad al-Shawkani* (Cambridge: Cambridge University Press, 2003).

'Imara, Muhammad, *Islamiyyat al-Sanhuri Pasha* (Mansura, Egypt: Dar al-Wafa', 2006).

A. Merad, Hamid Algar, N. Berkes, and Aziz Ahmad, "Islah," in P. Bearman, Th. Bianquis, C.E. Bosworth, E. van Donzel and W.P. Heinrichs (eds.), *Encyclopaedia of Islam*. (Brill, 2008).

Al-Muwilhi, Muhammad (d. 1348/1930), *Hadith 'Isa Ibnhisham aw Fatrah min al-Zaman* (Cairo: al-Maktabah al-Azhariyya, 1330/1911).

Al-Salawi, Ahmad al-Nasiri (d. 1314/1897), *al-Istiqasa li-AkhbarDuwal al-Maghrib al-Aqsa* (al-Dar al-Bayda: ManshuratWazarat al-Thaqafa, 2001–2005).

Sassen, Saskia, *Territory, Authority, Rights from Medieval to Global Assemblages* (Princeton NJ: Princeton University Press, 2006).
Shaltut, Mahmud (d. 1383/1963), *al-Fatawa* (Cairo: Dar al-Qalam, 1963).
Charles Taylor, *Dilemmas and Connections: Selected Essays* (Cambridge, MA: Harvard University Press, 2011).
'Urabi, Ahmad (d. 1328/1911), *Ahmad 'Urabi al-Misri* (Cairo: AUC Press, 1982). This volume also includes a translation by Trevor Gassick titled "The Defense Statement of Ahmad 'Urabi the Egyptian."
Watson, Alan, *Law Making in the Later Roman Republic* (Oxford University Press, 1974).
Weber, Max (eds. Hans Gerth and C. Wright Wills), *Essays in Sociology* (Oxford: Oxford University Press, 1946).

Index

www.ingramcontent.com/pod-product-compliance
Lightning Source LLC
Chambersburg PA
CBHW071642030826
49219CB00005B/318
9780230340367